UNEASY
PATRIOTS

UNEASY PATRIOTS

Western Canadians in Confederation

DAVID KILGOUR

LONE
PINE

The Publisher:
Lone Pine Publishing
414, 10357-109 Street
Edmonton, Alberta
T5J 1N3

Canadian Cataloguing in Publication Data
Kilgour, David, 1941-
  Uneasy patriots
ISBN 0-919433-53-7

  1. Regionalism - Canada, Western. 2. Federal-
provincial relations - Canada, Western.* 3. Canada,
Western - Economic conditions. 4. Multiculturalism
- Canada, Western.* 5. Canada, Western - Biography.
FC3209.A4K55 1988   971.2'03   C88-091562-5
F1060.K55 1988

Cover photo: Brenda Bastell
Cover design: Yuet C. Chan
Editorial: Jim Ogilvy, Mary Walters Riskin
Printing: Jasper Printing Group Ltd., Edmonton, Alberta

Publisher's Acknowledgement
The publisher gratefully acknowledges the assistance of
the Federal Department of Communications, Alberta
Culture, the Canada Council, and the Alberta Foundation
for the Literary Arts in the production of this book.

*For Laura, a Western Canadian
by birth and conviction.*

Acknowledgements

As the writing of *Uneasy Patriots* took much precious time from my wife, Laura, and our children over the past seven or eight months, I thank them all. On many evenings as I worked at the kitchen table, I might as well have been absent. Laura's advice on the various chapters was always useful.

I must also acknowledge my parents, both of whom long believed in the West's potential and accomplishments. My late father's confidence in the good judgement of the Canadian people as a whole never lagged throughout his life.

Special thanks must also go to Grant Kennedy, founder and president of Lone Pine Publishing, for the invitation to undertake this book, my first. His personal support and that of editors James Ogilvy and Mary Walters Riskin, have been at all times helpful. Thanks also to my friend David Levy and to Robin Bovey for useful advice on the editing front.

The House of Commons Speaker, John Fraser, when approached on the basis that I wanted to write a book about Western Canada within Confederation saw it as a legitimate function for a Western MP. He also proposed the solution to a conflict-of-interest sensitivity: all proceeds from the sale of the book will be paid by the publisher to the Receiver General of Canada.

Among the other persons who made the book possible was Danuta Rybicka-Tardif, a researcher-editor extraordinaire, who not only located and organized countless articles and other sources, but kept me on a time schedule when the spirit flagged. Canada itself is the beneficiary of Poland's deteriorating economic and political situation during 1981 and subsequent declaration of martial law, because these events caused her to come to Ottawa in 1982 to live. Also Lise Saulnier, who typed and re-typed so many drafts of the entire book, never once upending her word-processor to protest the latest avalanche of changes.

For reading and commenting on drafts of the particular sections on which they are authorities: Claudette Cyr (Alienation); Chuck Day of Grant MacEwan Community College (Grant MacEwan); Maxwell Foran (Grant MacEwan); Hon. Eugene Forsey (Meech Lake); Professor Roger Gibbins of the University of Calgary (Alienation); David Levy (Introduction, Whither Reform); Hon. Grant MacEwan

(Frederick Haultain); Christine Mander, author (Emily Murphy); Don McLean (Louis Riel); Professor Edward McWhinney Q.C., of Simon Fraser University (Meech Lake); Peter Meekison, Vice-President of the University of Alberta (Constitution of 1982); Professor Ahmed Mohiddin (Alienation and My West); Dr. Bruce Nesbitt (Alienation); Professor Brian Scarfe of the University of Alberta (Western Economy); Hon. G.F.G. Stanley (Louis Riel); Ann Sunahara, author and lawyer (Peoples and Japanese Canadians); Dennis Vincent (Bilingualism in the West).

For correcting factual errors in sketches in the original "My West" chapter, (much of which was later cut for reasons of space): David Bai and Wendy Danson; John and Eleanor Cross of Nanton, Alberta; Robert and Margaret Engel; Procter Girard; Peter St. John and Barbara Huck; Ian and Rae Jessiman of Victoria; Dr. J.M. Kilgour of Winnipeg; Kalman and Judith Kovacs; Ken and Joanne Manning of Calgary; Edgar McAllister of Summerland, B.C.; Patrick and Hilary Oswald; David and Joy Thompson of Onoway, Alberta; Fred and Yetta Turner of Yellowknife, N.W.T; Bud and Bev Wong.

For providing much useful material and assistance: Bruce Amos and staff, National Parks, Environment Canada; Louis 'Smokey' Bruyère and the staff of the Native Council of Canada; Barry Cooper, University of Calgary; George Erasmus, President, Assembly of First Nations; Kim Greenback, Alberta Energy/Forestry, Lands and Wildlife; Dr. R. Kimmett, Director and J.S. McLaurin, of Water Resources Branch Inland Waters Directorate, Environment Canada; Edward Manning and staff, Land Division, Land Use Policy and Research Branch, Environment Canada; Robert Newstead, Canadian Forestry Service, Edmonton; Edward Stanek, University of Saskatchewan Law Library; staff of the Library of Parliament; Charles Tarnocai, Land Resource Research Institute, Agriculture Canada; Susan Wolff, Canadian Parks Service, Western Region, Calgary; Canadian Forestry Service, Pacific Forestry Centre Culture and Heritage Language Departments of the provincial governments. It was not possible to include a chapter written on western environmental issues, again because of limited space.

There is little doubt that this book belongs mainly to those listed above. None is, of course, responsible for the views expressed in it except where they are directly quoted, or for any errors it contains.

Contents

Introduction

*T*HIS BOOK IS A CALL for full political, economic and cultural equality for Western Canadians within Confederation. It is a product of long observation. I have had the good fortune to know many Westerners and their communities, from Lake of the Woods on the Manitoba-Ontario boundary to Pacific Rim National Park on the west coast of Vancouver Island to Yellowknife, Northwest Territories. Hunting ducks, my father and I trudged through hundreds of marshes and barley fields, and we sat in farm kitchens across Manitoba and Saskatchewan many fall weekends during the 1950's.

My roots in prairie Canada were later extended by a period as Crown Attorney for Dauphin Judicial District in western Manitoba. In Alberta during the 1970's, court work took me from Fort Chipewyan near the sixtieth parallel (population 1,000, and essentially what it had been in 1800 — the local Hudson's Bay Company store manager still a recruit from the Scottish Hebrides) to Pincher Creek in the most southerly ranching region. Earlier, in British Columbia, I was a part-time residence master at St. George's school in Point Grey, and an assistant Vancouver City Prosecutor, travelled by canoe down the gorge of Vancouver Island's Nitinat Lake to the Pacific Ocean, galloped a horse at low tide along Spanish Banks near the University of British Columbia,

11

and ran for Parliament in 1968 in the Vancouver Centre constituency.

At the University of Toronto law school in 1962, I discovered that some Canadians were more equal than others. Later, as a University of Toronto delegate at a student conference in Quebec City, I watched with sadness how other student representatives and journalists appeared to defer to our delegation. What would be the long-term psychological impact of such attitudes on "outer Canadians" everywhere? I wondered then; I wonder now. With our self-proclaimed national media, publishing houses, theatres and so on, continuously under-representing most regions of Canada, as they do, what happens to regional pride and self-respect? Their failure, for instance, to tell Canadians at large about Frederick Haultain of Saskatchewan has caused this genuine regional giant to be all but forgotten, even to prairie Canadians.

This book is thus also meant to encourage Westerners to take greater pride in our contribution to Canada. For non-Westerners, it attempts to present the modern West free of dead stereotypes and cliches.

The book's title is intended to communicate the reality that, while almost all 7.3 million of us who live to the west and north of Lake of the Woods (Kenora, the Yukon, and the western half of the Northwest Territories are included here as parts of the West) love Canada deeply, many have serious misgivings about our past and present role within Confederation. *Uneasy Patriots* is written from the perspective of one who believes you can be both a good "regionalist," or "provincial," and a good Canadian. I make no apology for being a western nationalist in this sense; indeed, I believe it a major weakness of our current practice of so-called executive democracy in Ottawa that until recently fighting publicly and unapologetically for constituents' interests was the exclusive prerogative of Central Canadian MP's. Those who believe the weekly closed-door caucuses of any of our three national political parties adequately reflect, over the longer term, the priorities and legitimate concerns of the eight outer provinces are deluding themselves.

There is a distressing array of evidence, some of it set forth in this book, of Western Canadians not yet enjoying the same political, economic and cultural privileges their fellow Canadians enjoy who live in or near Ottawa, Toronto and Montreal. Few Westerners would feel the distinction is as great as between, say, Parisians and other Frenchmen. But the differences that do exist seriously harm national unity. The chapters on alienation, old and new, are an attempt to put this important question in perspective and to suggest some remedies. I hope public and private policy-makers in the three favoured cities who read this book will better appreciate the attitudinal and institutional nature of the problem. We Westerners are patient, but the time for addressing some basic issues effectively is long overdue.

Critics of my viewpoint will say that compared with Atlantic Canadians, non-metropolitan Quebecers, or northern Ontarians, Westerners "have it good." This misses the point. We Westerners want nothing for our region that we don't seek in equal measure for every part of Canada. Nor do we wish to weaken stable and diverse communities in Central Canada. We want prosperity, stability and opportunity promoted vigorously everywhere as a matter of basic national policy. How can Canadian officials continue to give speeches abroad on justice when some of our best-known national government agencies blatantly discriminate against Western Canada and other regions of the country?

Native peoples in both the West and the North have their own distinct reasons for feeling alienated from Confederation, and I have attempted to outline these in the chapter entitled, "Native Peoples: Civilizations Collide." "My West" gives profiles of a number of Westerners I have come to know personally over the years. Their individual stories are fair microcosms of Western Canadian life as a whole. "An International Community: The Peoples of the Region" attempts to reach the roots of our unique cultural mosaic and to explain what Westerners are all about. "Making a Western Living" deals with a subject of prime importance to the region and addresses the issue of diversification in an increasingly interdependent and competitive world economy.

The intermezzos on western giants feature five men and women from different places in the West who reflect well the frontier spirit of our region. Each of this group helped to create a Western Canada of which more than seven million of us today can be truly proud. All of them, including Riel, believed that it is possible to be loyal to one's region and to one's country. The West about which they dreamed often unrealizable dreams lives on for the better because of them.

At a dinner I attended with my wife at the home of an ambassador in Ottawa soon after the Calgary Olympic Games, two European ambassadors expressed astonishment at the nature and extent of the community spirit each had witnessed at those historic Games. One ambassador said he had been chauffeured by a volunteer who had devoted a two-week vacation to help out. A computer-expert volunteer said he had donated his two weeks because "Calgary has been good to me." Both diplomats declared no country in Europe hosting the Games could muster anything like the same level of resident commitment. There was later a general toast to the Calgary Games, and the host ambassador called upon Western Canadians to relocate to Europe.

Most Western Canadians are optimistic about our national future. Canadians everywhere have a well-deserved reputation for compromise and fairness. Westerners, moreover, are deeply committed to the proposition that we live in the most fortunate country on earth. This feeling has been demonstrated on myriad occasions, including a pre-Canada Day church service held in south-east Edmonton earlier this year. The building was filled with people of all ages and cultural backgrounds. A boy scout carried in the flag of each province in the order in which the ten provinces had entered Confederation. Patriotic hymns were sung and messages extolled Canada's many virtues. Not a single word was uttered on any western grievance. Readers might keep this snapshot in mind in reacting to parts of this book.

David Kilgour
September, 1988

ONE

My West
Personalities and Events

WESTERN CANADA IS MANY THINGS to all of us who live here; one is a strong sense of regional cohesion. This sense was reinforced while my family and I were driving from Winnipeg to Edmonton on the night the tornado hit Edmonton in mid-summer 1987. At a hospital in Saskatoon, where we stopped because of a child's worsening earache, the regional sense of the calamity was striking. The admissions officer, who was originally from Edmonton, the attending doctor, who had relatives in the Alberta capital, and others seemed as concerned as we were about what had struck a city four hours away by car.

Another is a strong conviction that our region is essential to the Canadian character. More than any other section of the country, we believe ours has fostered democracy and the democratization of our national and provincial institutions, a pluralistic society in which no cultural background is given preference, the right to oppose and dissent peacefully, and the opportunity for all to work directly to secure economic, social and other rights. The western and northern frontiers have long offered a new beginning for people from every corner of the country and world. In short, Western Canada, like the American West in the thesis of the historian Frederick Jackson Turner, explains much of Canadian development.

15

Mostly, of course, Western Canada is people and their relationships. One can speak of the great contributions and the tremendous potential offered by the interaction of the many ethnic groups peopling the West, a subject dealt with later in this book. But equally important to the West that I know are the individuals, their interrelationships, and the tremendous diversity of their experiences and perspectives.

Edmontonian David Bai, an anthropology professor at the University of Alberta, is one manifestation of that diversity. He was born in Chong-Ju, south of Seoul, South Korea, and studied philosophy and mathematics at Seoul National University before moving to Iowa and eventually to Edmonton, where in 1971 he obtained the first doctorate in anthropology awarded by the University of Alberta. He has a strong sense of the importance of community to the vitality and success of the West. In the face of an inhospitable climate, he states, ''it was through much community effort that agriculture became successful. With the increase in capital after World War II, mechanization began to ease some of the hardships of prairie farmers, at a cost, however, of the dissolution of the rural community.''

In Bai's view, most Albertans seem to want an administrative-minded government which will provide a stewardship function and tend to everyone fairly. In his opinion, the two-party system is more an Eastern Canadian phenomenon with its concomitant notion of corruption. In the West, many people view government as being a one-party system. Premiers Aberhart, Manning and Lougheed are thus all part of the habit of Albertans to coalesce around one political team on voting days.

He was particularly struck by the hospitality and openness of Albertans and our belief in free spirits and entrepreneurship. This mentality seemed to clash with a basic conservatism in Central Canada. The dominant western mood also matched the boom-and-bust nature of our resource-based economy.

Regional alienation is a growing rather than declining phenomenon now in Bai's view because most Westerners see our national institutions and policies as being fundamentally insensitive to our regional aspirations. Western Canada now occupies to him a psychological place in the nation similar to that of Quebec during the mid-1960's. Quebecers over two decades fought and won respect from the rest of the country. Westerners, he believes, must now in turn do the same thing.

The unique feature of the Prairies to Bai is the truly international nature of our communities. Westerners, he thinks, do not accept a "British, French and other" concept of multiculturalism. Instead, we see all of us standing together in a unique society. National institutions such as the Canada Council and the CBC must become more fully reflective of this reality in the four western and other provinces. Federal officials who still talk primarily about bilingualism and biculturalism miss this basic western reality. Bai worries that the concept of Quebec as a distinct society created by the Meech Lake agreement could become a major national problem. "If we fall back into 'deux nations' thinking again, the West could eventually secede."

Saskatchewan resident Procter Girard, though born in Montreal, is the quintessential prairie Canadian. During World War II, when his father was killed in an aircraft accident while on a training flight with the RCAF, his mother returned with Procter to her parents' home in Moosomin, Saskatchewan. In 1948 her father, Arthur Procter, who was a colourful figure in the provincial legislature, took a new appointment as a judge in the Saskatchewan Court of Appeal in Regina, and she then settled with young Procter in Moose Jaw.

Procter subsequently attended high school at St. John's Ravenscourt in Winnipeg, where we became classmates and later roommates. The headmaster, Dick Gordon, was enthusiastic about Procter's abilities and, at the request of his mother and grandfather, served as his surrogate father during his seven years at the school. Procter responded by graduating from St. John's Ravenscourt with its highest honours.

Like many others of his age, Procter began a difficult period in deciding what he wanted to do with his life. The ensuing years included a term in forestry at the University of British Columbia, a BA in English from the University of Saskatchewan and a

17

period of teaching English, Latin and football at St. John's Ravenscourt. These endeavours were followed by stints with the Saskatchewan Power Corporation and in the oilfields in southern Saskatchewan. After several years of uncertainty, Procter resolved to become a physician, and entered pre-medicine in 1969. Seven long years later he began his medical practice, and a decade after that he and a colleague opened their own clinic in Regina.

He believes the small-town atmosphere he grew up in was one of "'pitch in and help', communal values at a grass roots level and kinship with community and our friends. This is what fires our success. I think generally Westerners have a non-judgemental 'can do' attitude. Perhaps Easterners think us naive. We may be unsophisticated, but we are not naive. Recently, to support a Regina girl with terminal cystic fibrosis, this province raised $120,000 in an impromptu weekend radio campaign in two days! People I know here who have money and success could move but they love it here. Oh, they go to Hawaii, etc..., but they basically like Saskatchewan!'' What he says probably applies equally well to all communities in Western Canada.

Peter St. John and Barbara Huck, both happily married for a second time, are representative in many ways of the current generation of Winnipeggers. Peter, born in Victoria in 1938 of English parents and raised in Peachland in the Okanagan, describes himself as "growing more and more Western" in his outlook. He recalls from his British boarding school days the English schoolboy disdain for the "little colonial," an attitude which brought him back to this country a defiant Canadian at 18. Today, with a doctorate in international relations from the University of London, he has felt his sense of western identity deepen because of Central Canadian insensitivity towards the West.

Barbara was born in "pre-oil" Edmonton of parents who came West from Ontario, and she spent much of her youth in Regina, Saskatchewan, where her father, David Albertson, was for a time the only neurosurgeon in Saskatchewan. After studies at the University of Manitoba and a first marriage which ended in divorce in 1975, Barbara settled in Winnipeg with her four children and plunged into two full-time jobs: sports reporting for *The Winnipeg Free Press* and sports commentating for CBC Radio. In 1981, she became the first woman to win a National Newspaper Award for Sportswriting and in 1986 was named professional woman of the year in Manitoba. By 1987 she was looking for broader horizons, and she is now a full-time freelance writer.

Peter values the tolerance and moderation of Winnipeggers, "the last reasonable people in Canada," which he contrasts to "the strong British Columbian antipathy towards Ottawa, the extremism of some Albertans and the unbelievable smugness of Ontarians." Echoing historian Donald Creighton, he thinks Central Canadians believe that beyond the borders of Ontario and Quebec, Canada slopes gently to the seas, populated by half-fabulous creatures called Westerners and Easterners.

Barbara especially likes the stability of Winnipeg for raising children, the easy access to world-class ballet and top-flight sports facilities and the relative freedom from such problems as drug pressure on adolescents. "One can strive for excellence here as well as anywhere, but I'm not sure that is widely recognized," she says. "In the United States, there's a feeling one can achieve things virtually anywhere in the country; there's a world-class medical centre in small-town Minnesota, for instance, and a national centre of litigation in rural Tennessee. But in Canada, there's far too often a feeling that good work can only be done in Toronto and Montreal and that's completely counterproductive. Winnipeg is in fact a lot closer to the rest of the country than Toronto is."

Leo Mol is an artistic colossus of both Manitoba and Western Canada who now enjoys world-wide recognition as a sculptor. His major bronzes over three decades include sculptures of Queen Elizabeth, located in Winnipeg, John Diefenbaker on Parliament Hill in Ottawa, the Ukrainian poet and painter Taras Shevchenko in Washington, D.C. and Popes John XXIII, Paul VI, and John Paul II in the Vatican.

How he got to Winnipeg from a small village in Ukraine, where he worked with his father as a potter, is an odyssey of Homeric proportions. In 1930, when he was fifteen, his parents finally accepted his passion for painting and permitted him to go to Vienna. Supporting himself there with odd jobs such as painting and cleaning houses, he took evening classes in both sculpting and painting. In the mid-1930's he moved to Berlin because he was told that in Europe only there one could find commissions and a reputation. Just as his work was beginning to sell reasonably well, Hitler's war began. Mol, even as a Slav living in the bosom of the Third Reich, managed to survive from his sculpting and to marry Margureth in 1943. When Soviet troops approached Berlin in the spring of 1945, the couple quickly joined the stream of refugees going West. In a refugee camp in Holland, he prospered making ceramic figurines and found enough leisure time both to sketch and to return to the sculpting medium he loved. He also learned the craft of stained-glass making, which would later win him prominence in Canada. The four years in Holland, as he later noted, was ''a period of light, both spiritually and physically.''

Friends in Western Canada urged them to come there, stressing that the region contained many Ukrainians. Margureth's English was good, so together they chose Canada. They reached a friend's farm near Prince Albert, Saskatchewan, by train on a cold New Year's Eve, 1949. The celebration of the Ukrainian Christmas on January 7th and warm community spirit made the bewildered couple feel very welcome, but Leo realized immediately that he must find artistic work. Leaving Margureth behind, he set out for to Winnipeg as the closest big city. He recalls: ''It was a strange feeling stepping off the train and walking along Main Street. I could speak no English and I knew nobody. I explored the city until I came upon a church supply store.'' The owner hired him to do life-sized paintings of the Virgin Mary; he worked there for the next two years after Margureth joined him. He decorated numerous churches in Winnipeg and around the province while Margureth earned a teaching certificate from the Winnipeg Normal School and began to teach.

After a period making figurines on such local themes as square dancers and the Inuit, in the early 1950's Mol returned to bronze, producing dozens of small nudes and many examples of his real love, portraits. He also did a number of marble and limestone carvings in this period. In 1962, he won a world-wide competition to sculpt a large monument of one of his heroes, the Ukrainian poet and painter Taras Shevchenko. More than a hundred thousand people attended its unveiling in the American capital. He also completed a full length portrait of the Manitoba bush pilot, Tom Lamb, in 1974, one cast of which now stands in the Edmonton Municipal Airport. In 1980, his first major commission in Canada itself was a bronze of a father, mother and two children arriving from the Western Ukraine, which is now located at the Ukrainian Heritage Village near Edmonton. During 1987, his large bronze of John Diefenbaker, another of his heroes, was unveiled on Parliament Hill in Ottawa.

The Mols today are committed to both Winnipeg and Western Canada. Leo once told my father that after all his meanderings he needed, as an artist, to plant deep roots somewhere and to move no more. He chose Winnipeg.

Edmonton area resident Judith Kovacs, blonde, athletic and beautiful, was raised in Budapest, Hungary, and qualified as a dentist there in 1970. She accepted a dental position in a community of 35,000 in eastern Hungary where she met her future husband, Kalman Kovacs, after his presentation of a public lecture on music.

Kalman had grown up in eastern Hungary. His father, Jozsef, was removed from his job as a forester after being found "guilty" by a Communist court of giving some of his own wood to a local Catholic church for the building of a cross. During the national uprising in 1956, he was elected head of the provincial forest service, but was later removed by the government. Kalman showed musical talent at an early age and was allowed to study at the conservatory in nearby Debrecen. He became a teacher in Berettyoujfalu, 20 miles away from where Judith worked, and later principal of the school. During the two years before he and Judith fled Hungary, he was superintendent of all music schools in the province.

Kalman and Judith had remained single knowing that marriage

would make it forever impossible to obtain visas to leave Hungary simultaneously. After applying separately, Judith finally received one to visit her brother in the U.S. and Kalman got one to go to Vienna on a holiday. Not even telling their families about their plan, both left. They met in Yugoslavia and drove to Vienna for a month's visit. The weeks spent as tourists in Vienna settled the matter. Both had been taught that there were no medical, pension or other social programs in the West, which they soon realized was false. They had been raised in religious families and the care shown by some evangelical missionaries in Vienna also became a positive factor in choosing a new life in the West.

When the month was up, they reported to the Vienna police seeking refugee status and were soon en route to the United Nations-run Traiskrchen refugee camp. There they were finger-printed and photographed, and Kalman spent the next ten days in custody being investigated by Austrian police. Although they were both approved as refugees and found work in Austria, they were uneasy about their continuing proximity to the Eastern bloc.

In October of 1974, they were called to the Canadian embassy in Vienna concerning their earlier application to immigrate. They accepted an offer to move to Edmonton, although a Canadian Immigration official predicted correctly that both would have trouble with professional accreditation in Alberta. He nonetheless recommended Edmonton because our economy was then doing well and because it had an active Hungarian community. They landed at the Edmonton International airport on May 23, 1975, speaking virtually no English.

The immigration official had sent a note privately to my wife Laura, indicating that the Kovacs were coming, and we soon made contact. Both of them did meet severe difficulty in practising their professions. Judith, pregnant with their first child, narrowly missed passing a series of examinations in English, which, even if she had successfully completed them, would only have entitled her to enter the second year school of dentistry at the University of Alberta. For eleven years, Kalman supported Judith and their four children by up to 40 hours weekly of private music teaching. He became an elder and music director in an Edmonton church. All four children now speak Hungarian and English. The three oldest, Katherine, Gregory and Christina, are in a French immersion program and are already virtually fluent in three languages. Two years ago, Kalman was invited to join a life insurance company as a sales representative in Edmonton and has done well there since his first month. He maintains his love for music as a hobby.

Hilary and Patrick Oswald of Vancouver are old friends. She was born in Dublin, Ireland during World War II. Growing up in a small Anglo-Irish enclave, she encountered no friction with Roman Catholics and her parents instilled no negative feelings about Catholicism in her. She recalls, however, a protestant minister in Dublin cautioning her as a thirteen-year-old, "Don't bat your eyes at Catholic boys because if you marry one your children will be Catholics."

After high school, Hilary took a one-year secretarial course so as to have a "fall-back skill" and then pursued her love of horses at Dublin's famous Lt. Col. J. Hume-Dudgeon's Burton Hall Riding School. At 19, Hilary became First Whipper-in to the North Tipperary Foxhounds, a hunt south of Dublin. This meant that she was responsible for the hounds during regular live fox hunts.

In 1963, a Dublin friend just returned from a visit to British Columbia told her that the region was full of "tundra, wheat and people who know nothing of horses or fox hunting." Hilary was interested nonetheless and was soon on her way to becoming an assistant to Jean Dunbar of Victoria, who was training for the three-day equestrian event in the 1964 Summer Olympics. She enjoyed life with the Dunbars on Vancouver Island, but after 15 months returned to Dublin to complete her British Horse Society exams. While there, she received an offer from the Southlands Riding and Polo Club located on the flats beside the Fraser delta in south Vancouver to teach riding to younger members. "They imported me essentially for an air fare," she muses.

Six years later, she was teaching two hundred pupils and had been appointed Sports Director of the club. She and I met in 1966 and became engaged in 1968, but the romance did not survive a lengthy 3,000 mile separation. As an unemployed and defeated candidate for Parliament with election debts after the 1968 federal election, I accepted an offer to join the Justice Department in Ottawa. Hilary later married Patrick Oswald and is now the General Manager of the club. She began a disabled riding program which is available to anyone who can sit on a horse and has included blind, deaf and paraplegic riders.

Now a Canadian citizen, she thinks of herself as a Canadian first and British Columbian second. She values the lack of rigid conventions in Vancouver. "You can be what you want to be here. There is a niche for everyone." The physical beauty and climate of the province remind her a little of Ireland, although there are in British Columbia "more heat, more mountains and more potential prosperity." The province, she feels, tends to be toward the bottom of the barrel from Ottawa's point of view, but she empathizes especially with Atlantic Canadians for having an even worse position. In the horse world, she notes, international riders usually appear only in Toronto. Calgary's Spruce Meadows riding centre, she says, has been an enormous boost to Western Canadian riding generally.

Patrick, born in England, came to Canada to graduate in 1958 from Montreal's McGill University where his grandmother had taught Latin and Greek two generations earlier. Two years later, he moved to Vancouver as a manager with a paint company. Later, he became Master of the foxhounds at the Fraser Valley Hunt, but riding accidents were sufficiently hard on him that he later switched to sailing. He worked his way through numerous positions up to commodore of the Royal Vancouver Yacht Club in 1985. In his year the clubhouse figures moved into the black and he worked to develop racing by young people. He now works with the Vancouver region United Way which in 1987 raised $11.8 million for 86 agencies in eighteen lower mainland municipalities. This developed out of fund-raising he had done to establish the Western Institute for the Deaf in Vancouver.

Oswald clearly loves Vancouver and western life. Although research director for the British Columbia Liberal party in the mid-1960's, he strongly favours the proposed bilateral trade agreement with the United States. He thinks most Vancouverites do as well. He is proud of being a Westerner and like many British Columbians feels genuinely sorry for Central Canadians. "Here," he says, "you don't have to wait your turn."

Robert Engle's family were seventh-generation Yankees from New England and Pennsylvania who eventually moved west to Washington State. His maternal grandfather became a store-keeper on the Chilcoot Trail during the Klondike gold rush and his mother, now 91 and living in Santa Barbara, California, spent her school days in Dawson City. Bob, his brother and sister all went to school in Seattle, but he was sent off in his final high school year to Phillips-Exeter Academy in New England, and was admitted to Yale University in 1942. He soon withdrew for active naval service on a destroyer during the war, and upon discharge joined the largest freshman class (1,200) in Yale history in 1946 and graduated with a BSc degree in 1950.

A love of aviation drove him to seek a pilot's licence and in 1956 he made a personal survey of the Canadian North and Alaska in his Cessna 180 float plane to determine where he might best hang out his airline shingle. He concluded that the pioneer town of Yellowknife was the best location and settled there in 1958, becoming a Canadian citizen in the early 1960's. His first job was as a contract pilot for Max Ward of Wardair to fly a McGill University expedition to the High Arctic with his own DeHavilland Beaver. Until 1961, he cut his teeth in a single engine Otter and a twin engine Bristol Freighter flying for Ward throughout the North. When Ward left in 1961, Engle founded Northwest Territorial Airways. Today, he pays highest tribute to Wardair's founder, believing him to be the most astute individual he has ever met in Canadian aviation. "His ability to anticipate social, political and equipment changes is excellent." Engle still recalls the senior aviator's parting words to him when he left the North, "I wish you the best. In my judgment, the next decade will not be supportive to aviation in the North."

Ward's words proved prophetic indeed, because the Air Transport Committee of Ottawa's former Canadian Transport Commission made it as difficult as it could for Northwest Territorial to enter different routes in order to protect existing established carriers like Air Canada, Canadian Pacific, Pacific Western and Nordair. It took him three applications, two public hearings and seven years to win the right in 1975 to fly the Hercules which is now an essential supplier to many isolated northern communities across the North. He was required to attend so many public hearings over the years, usually without success, that he accepts a quip of the late Justice William Morrow: "You've had one of the most expensive legal educations I know." It was only his deep love of aviation, he maintains, that gave him the will to persevere.

Northwest Territorial began in 1961 as an all-charter line with a single Otter aircraft and Engle as its only pilot. In 12,000 hours of Arctic flying he never had an accident. By 1969, his company was flying scheduled routes from Yellowknife to Coppermine. It required another twelve years to persuade the Air Transport Committee to allow it to fly regularly from Yellowknife to Rankin Inlet, Iqaluit and Winnipeg, and another five years to win the right to fly on a scheduled basis between Edmonton and Yellowknife. In 1983, Northwest established an overnight freight carrier service across Canada. Today, it has two hundred full-time employees, including forty pilots and eleven aircraft, and carries 75,000 passengers yearly with annual revenues of $40 million. An affiliated company, Northwest Transport Ltd., provides highway transport and intermodal truck and air cargo from Edmonton throughout the Western Arctic.

Northwest Territorial Airways was recently sold to Air Canada with the understanding that Engle would remain its chief executive officer for at least three years. He feels responsible to his employees, to the North, to the level of service he has established, and to the continued growth of the airline. He sold out because he thinks it is now essential for the airline to be an alliance carrier with Air Canada. He became 65 years old in 1988 and clearly misses his family who live much of the year 2,500 miles away in California. He sees himself in the same light as a sea captain who comes home whenever his work allows him to.

His thoughts on the West and North as a Canadian by choice

are interesting. American Westerners no longer feel isolated, he says, except possibly Alaskans, because all regions of a large, essentially homogeneous nation are now developed. Professional services thus tend to be equally good in every corner of America, whereas from Northern Canada he still does his banking and legal work in Toronto. He recalls that as recently as the 1950's residents of the eastern Northwest Territories were unable to vote in federal elections because there was no system in place for distributing ballot boxes. He notes that in the Northwest Territories, comprising 1,300,000 square miles or one-third of the land mass of the entire country, "people have the least access to freehold land." Virtually everything outside centres like Yellowknife is still federal Crown land.

Engle observes that aboriginal peoples in the North relate very closely to land because their security is based on it. The entire region has the flavour of the old West because of the mixture of native peoples and numerous newcomers, except that airplanes fill the role that railways once had in the southern frontier. Devolution is now moving briskly, he feels, with a fully-elected Northwest Territorial council now in place. Health care has already passed to the Territorial Government and he thinks justice may follow before long. The transfer of natural resources to the Territorial Government is essential in his view to provide a Territorial tax base; the two sides are beginning to talk about it. A good precedent here is the Beaufort Sea settlement which provided a resource base to natives. Most Northerners, in Engle's view, clearly want self-government and provincial status. They are therefore concerned about the implications for them of the Meech Lake Accord and some are concerned that the existing provinces could eventually extend their boundaries northward as has been done before. "Southern insensitivity to the North remains," he notes, calling on Northerners to "stand tall with their regional identity."

My own parents were both born in Manitoba: Mother in Winnipeg, Father in Brandon. Her grandparents, Daniel and Helen Macdonald, eloped from their parents' homes on Prince

Edward Island. He, later joined by her, came West through the United States because the CPR line was not yet completed. They settled in Portage La Prairie, Manitoba, in 1883. Both believed correctly that the move would place them on the cutting edge of our national history, but they were dead wrong in supposing that Portage, today still only about 10,000 in population, would ever become a major city.

In 1906, the Macdonalds moved to Winnipeg when Daniel, despite being a quiet Conservative supporter (his wife Helen was much noisier about it), was appointed a King's Bench judge by Prime Minister Wilfrid Laurier. Later Mackenzie King as prime minister promoted him to Chief Justice of the same court. A family rumour persisted for years that he remained on the court until the year before his death in 1937 because there were then no pensions for judges and he badly needed the $4000 salary. Recently, I found an account of his career by a lawyer done shortly after his death in which Macdonald was quoted as saying, on reading a bill introduced in the mid-1930's to retire judges at the age of seventy-five: "If this law passes, what shall I do? My work is my life." When he died, there was evidently a request to have his body made available for a public funeral, but his children refused, one saying rather oddly to a reporter, "He belonged to the public in life. Now he belongs to us."

Mother's father, William Russell, who died before I was born, joined the turn-of-the-century flood of young Ontarians bound for Winnipeg. He soon met and married Nan Macdonald. In 1906, they built a home on Kingsway Avenue in south Winnipeg, a few hundred paces from her own parents' eventual home, and raised three daughters, Helen, Hester and Mary (my mother).

My father's father, James Frederick Kilgour, moved from Guelph, Ontario, to Brandon in 1901 to enter the bottom of the law firm which Clifford Sifton had founded and would soon abandon altogether in order to live grandly in Toronto. He married Geills McCrae, also of Guelph and a sister of the poet-physician John McCrae, and they returned to live in Brandon. During the 1911 national election, he as a strong Liberal campaigned hard in the Brandon area for Wilfrid Laurier and the

MY WEST

proposed reciprocity treaty with the United States. In 1927, when he was appointed a judge of the Manitoba King's Bench court by Mackenzie King, the family of six moved to Winnipeg.

There were four Kilgour children. Margaret, the eldest, became a secretary to John W. Dafoe at *The Winnipeg Free Press*, helping to do editorials before moving to the United Kingdom when she married. Katharine graduated in arts at the University of Manitoba but also left Western Canada, to marry and live in Hamilton. My father, David, and his older brother, Jack, now a retired doctor, remained in the West.

Jack is now nearly eighty, but his recall of life in Brandon remains virtually total. He boarded in Brandon College for a year when the rest of his family moved to Winnipeg. The residence monitors, the late Tommy Douglas and Stanley Knowles, who shared a room directly below his own, would levy fifty-cent fines against anyone arriving back at the residence even seconds after the 10 PM curfew. A consequence of this practice was some considerable friction between them and my uncle.

During World War II, Mr. Douglas as premier of Saskatchewan visited Canadian troops in Belgium. At a mess luncheon, the distinguished visitor turned to the person in uniform beside him and said, "Colonel Kilgour, where are you from?"

"From the West and Brandon!"

"Your sister, Margaret, was a year ahead of me at Brandon College."

"Yes," he replied. "And I was the guy in the room above you who used to drop his boots on the floor."

My father, on graduating from the University of Manitoba in the worst Depression year, 1933, felt himself extremely fortunate to find a trainee position in the Great-West Life Assurance Company in Winnipeg. Mother worked as a reporter at *The Winnipeg Free Press* for a few years before "retiring" in the fashion of the day in her early twenties when she married in order to raise three children. To the extent that one can be objective about one's home life, ours was clearly competitive, stimulating and demanding. We three children, Geills, Donald and myself, were expected to do everything well even if we had neither interest nor

29

talent in a particular activity. Several strongly-held views shared by both of our parents added another dimension. Mother still believes that one is either a sucker, who faces everything dutifully, or a ducker, who abandons a fight when the going gets tough. Father's views, containing more half-tones, were sometimes more nuanced than mother's but he lived by his principles and faith. Above all, he believed in leadership and teaching by example rather than by words. Both Mother and Father encouraged us to develop a religious faith.

Father's work caused him to travel a great deal throughout Canada and the United States because approximately half of Great-West's business was done in the U.S. Despite all his business travel, one of his favourite hobbies was duck-shooting and from the age of about nine I was often able to accompany him and others each fall, mostly by car, through what seemed like every town and village between Winnipeg and Grand Prairie, Alberta. We remembered many places by their proximity to good sloughs or to fields that held prairie chicken. During these outings, we met numerous farmers and discussed all manner of prairie matters. It was in a barley field in northern Alberta at the age of about seventeen that I began to question the sport. A family of five Canada geese flew directly into our decoys at dawn and our group of four hunters downed three of them. The remaining two then made a wide turn and to our utter astonishment returned to heroic and certain deaths. Never again did I want to shoot at a Canada goose and eventually gave up hunting altogether.

From the mid-1940's to late 1950's, a number of refugees, mostly from Central and Eastern Europe, became nannies in our home. Most told me something of what they had experienced during and after the war and my strong aversion to all forms of totalitarianism began at an early age. To my mother's considerable chagrin, my ongoing tendency to side with employees against employers developed during these years as well.

When my father died of lung cancer in the spring of 1973, a national CBC radio broadcast by Susan Hoeschen of Winnipeg read in part as follows: "David Kilgour... established a reputation as a tough, independent businessman with a strong regard for the rights of Western Canada. Mr. Kilgour was head of the West's largest life insurance company..., the Great West Life..., which is centred in Winnipeg. During his career, he never shirked a clash with the government over economic policy or with business over the rights of Western Canadians.''

My own affection and admiration for him grew continuously over the years except for the period between the ages of 16 and 21 when many children think they know more about everything than their parents do. He attracted people of all ages and backgrounds; children and adults alike could tell instantly that he liked them by the way he listened and spoke to them. If you did your best, and did it honourably, you kept his esteem; if you didn't, you could lose it – at least temporarily. He was the finest human being I have known anywhere.

Growing up in Winnipeg's south end in the 1940's and 1950's was to live on a rock of stability. At Grosvenor Public School, which my mother had attended a generation earlier, virtually every grade one to six student seemed to me to have two parents and at least one brother or sister. We all walked home for lunch because so few mothers then seemed to work. This prompted youthful disputes and on one occasion as a nine or ten-year-old I evidently protested that I just didn't have the energy to fight my way to and from school again.

My high school years spent at St. John's Ravenscourt independent school in the suburb of Fort Garry were a different experience. There were boarders and day boys — girls were admitted only some years later – and each community was understandably suspicious of the other. The boarders came from as far away as Vancouver Island and Inuvik, N.W.T. The school's antecedents in fact go as far back as 1820, when the Rev. John West opened a Protestant school in a log home in the Red River settlement. John and Vi Waudby arrived from London, England, in 1928, he to teach mathematics and Latin at a successor school to the one founded by West, St. John's. They had wanted to live abroad but under the British flag. In 1952, they moved to the amalgamated school. Teaching was always a high calling to both of them and never a mere job. They were a genuine Mr. and Mrs. Chips. Vi Waudby was a surrogate mother to every boarder who crossed her path. She loved us all openly; everyone knew it, and we loved her. All of us mourned the passing of both of them many years later.

Many of the other teachers were also dedicated and highly individualistic. Art Kroeger, currently Deputy Minister of Energy in Ottawa, flummoxed our entire French class one day by doing what no other teacher had ever dared to do: he simply walked out after announcing that we were unfit to teach. After moments of almost complete silence, most of us panicked, sending a small delegation of the most remorseful-looking pupils to urge him to return, promising, as he doubtless anticipated, to curb our unruly behaviour.

The headmaster, Richard Gordon, who like Kroeger was an Alberta Rhodes Scholar, during his twenty years at the school had an enormous influence on many of us. Though now dead, his influence continues in my own life because over the years I often find myself reacting to issues and people in the way I suppose he might have done. Father is probably the only other person who had a stronger influence. Mr. Gordon could see into our black hearts and stormy teenage moods at a glance. He also demanded from us at all times something most of us were otherwise very reluctant to provide: our best, whether in his English class, on a camping trip, or on the sports field. He saw the school's real job, as he said, "to set standards of work, conduct and morality and to help boys to attain those standards." He also taught tolerance, self-discipline, enthusiasm and good manners. By manners, he meant, in his words, "the enduring qualities of kindness, generosity, gentleness and self-sacrifice." Always optimistic and confident, Dick Gordon sought excellence in everything he encountered. He went to the Glenbow Foundation in Calgary after retiring from the school in 1969. Later he wrote a powerful and best-selling novel, *The River Gets Wider*, and another, *The Jesus Boy*, before dying in 1979 near Summerland, B.C.

Tom Bredin joined the school as a teacher after post-graduate work in history in Vienna, a period with the Winnipeg Rangers hockey team, and 13 operational missions as an aircraft navigator during World War II. He was the assistant headmaster and head of the history department for 25 full years. "The best decision I ever made at S.J.R. was to invite Tom Bredin to join the staff," admitted Gordon. Probably more than anyone at the school, he personified Western Canada. He once told a teacher freshly arrived from Britain that a unique North American culture had grown up different from any in the world. Colin Kiddell, the confronted newcomer, says, "He never really defined it except in the way he lived.... He was direct, unambiguous, tough in body and mind, physically and morally courageous, deeply scholastic, superbly athletic and...romantic." It was characteristic of the Bredin grit that near the end of his life, as he fought cancer in order to continue teaching at the school, he was obliged to teach his beloved history standing because he was unable to sit and incapable of walking without great pain, even supported by two sticks.

Bredin was truly a paradox: tenacious and blunt, letting everyone know always where they stood with him, yet simultaneously gentle, sensitive and always on the side of the underdog. His passion for history inspired students to develop and maintain an interest in Canadian history. He managed to bring names in dusty books to life, and was the author of several books on Canadian history. The early explorers of North America gripped our youthful imaginations even if philosophy or business were not yet of much interest. Part of his real teaching skill was in presenting Canada whole. No region or community was put down. Jacques Cartier and Samuel de Champlain were as much heroes to him as were Lord Selkirk and Gabriel Dumont. A strict Bredin teaching rule was to conceal his personal views on people and issues in the past unless pressed, so as not to unduly influence impressionable minds. When he died, a large part of the school died with him.

The individuals sketched above exhibit the strength, intelligence and confidence typical of those who commit their lives to the West. Such attributes have been essential in many instances, since Westerners have had to struggle for their successes against the indifference, insensitivity and outright resistance of the central governments which have formed, and still form, the backdrop against which we live our lives. Question a Manitoban, a British Columbian, or a resident of the Territories and you will probably hear a dozen instances in which hopes and aspirations were subordinated to those of someone in Central Canada. The unquenchable optimism, vigour and quiet satisfaction of today's Westerners meet regularly with disappointment, hardship, and the need for sacrifice – just as they have for more than a hundred and fifty years.

A long list of regional grievances against Central Canada and the national government existed long before "western alienation" was coined to cover a cluster of issues in the 1970's. Unhappiness with the political and economic realpolitik of Canada can even be traced back to the Selkirk settlers who first attempted to settle in the Prairies in 1812. The experience of western Indians and Métis is a less known part of the story here, but it has an important place. Farmers, consumers, business people, multicultural communities and virtually every other identifiable group of Westerners, including their provincial governments, have good reasons for concern about policy making in the heartland of the country. The West's grievances are clearly deeper than economic discontent. They flare even in boom years, and stem probably less from economics than from a deeply-rooted sense of the region's lack of political influence in Ottawa.

A young Quebec journalist, recently arrived from Quebec to live in Winnipeg, put the essence of the matter to me last summer, "I thought we lacked political clout in Quebec until I came to live in the West." A common quip in Vancouver catches the same point, "It is 3,000 miles from here to Ottawa and 30,000 miles from Ottawa to Vancouver." It is evident that many Westerners consider themselves to be treated as political and economic inferiors by our own national government and many of its agencies.

A Western Canadian conviction has persisted through the years that federal policies and practices have transferred opportunities, jobs, and people from their natural location in our region to

Central Canada. The consensus continues that the decision-making system, regardless of the political party in power, routinely discriminates against Western Canada. To take a recent example, the Industrial Regional Development Program (IRDP) of the now-defunct Department of Regional Industrial Expansion spent during fiscal year 1986/87 a mere 9% of its funds in Western Canada, a region holding about 30% of the national population and approximately 400,000 unemployed Canadians for much of that period. For the same year, the federal departments of government together purchased only 11.5% of their goods and services in Western Canada. Telefilm, the national film production agency, financed 22 films two years ago of which only one was made outside the two central provinces. Radio Canada International, which broadcasts Canada to the world in 16 languages, has one freelance journalist working full-time to cover events from Vancouver to Winnipeg. In short, discrimination against more than seven million Western Canadians by unelected policy-makers in many parts of the national government is still practised as a matter of both habit and ongoing indifference. This sense of continuing regional subordination is central to any definition of Western alienation.

The first reported public opinion poll on western alienation, conducted among Albertans in 1969, indicated that 55-60% of Albertans agreed with the view that the federal government neglects the West and benefits Central Canada, often at the expense of Westerners. During the early 1980's, four of every five Westerners agreed that the Canadian political system favours Central Canada to the detriment of the West. An opinion poll conducted shortly after the CF-18 contract was awarded by the Mulroney cabinet to Canadair of Montreal in the fall of 1986, notwithstanding a lower and technically superior bid by Bristol Aerospace of Winnipeg, demonstrated that fully 84% of Western Canadians believed the Mulroney Government plays regional favourites. The Prime Minister was genuinely surprised at the extent of the outrage. What he did not understand was that, having been abused by successive federal governments for generations and having largely placed their confidence in his team in the 1984 election, many Western Canadians naively expected that the bad old habits of Ottawa had finally left town. Roger Gibbins, a Calgary professor, noted in his discussion of western discontent that the election of a national Conservative government would in itself do little to reduce levels of western alienation unless that government were able to overcome the long-standing Western Canadian grievance. In that context, the CF-18 matter will long stand as a symbol of political expediency, national unfairness and regional impotence in the minds of many Westerners.

According to the Angus Reid Poll taken almost on the eve of the 1988 federal election, 73% of Western Canadians believe their region has been shortchanged by the Conservative government, and at the same time more than two-thirds of us think the federal government continues to favour Quebec.

We Westerners have long objected to the metropolitan-hinterland assumptions of the National Policy, which were put in place by Sir John A. Macdonald in 1879 and applied by successive governments of differing political complexions down to the present day. Our region was clearly intended under the railway, immigration and homestead policies involved to be Central Canada's colony. Westerners have asked for decades why there was never anything of real substance in the National Policy to strengthen the economies of Western and Atlantic Canada, Northern Ontario and non-metropolitan Quebec over the long term. Earlier on, Westerners protested high tariff and discriminatory transportation policies which caused the peripheral regions of the country to bear much of the cost of creating a diversified, stable and prosperous economy in metropolitan Central Canada.

In the 1970's and 1980's, tariffs have finally come down substantially in Canada as a consequence of the Tokyo and Kennedy rounds of the GATT multilateral trade negotiations. Systematic railway discrimination against the outer regions was removed by the Mulroney government in amendments to the National Transportation Act. Federal government procurement practices, regional development programs and the policies of a number of federal crown corporations have now moved to the first tier of sources of regional discontent.

William Morton, the Manitoba farm boy who became a major national historian, was probably our region's most eloquent 20th-century voice of protest, partly because he had such a strong feeling for the uniqueness, diversity and integrity of Western Canada. He became in the 1940's and 1950's the western foil to Harold Innis and Donald Creighton, the leading Central Canadian academics on the National Policy. (Even Innis, however, once wrote: "Western Canada has paid for the development of Canadian nationality, and it would appear that it must continue to pay. The acquisitiveness of Eastern Canada shows little sign of abatement.") Morton did not quarrel with their view of the dynamics behind Confederation and 19th-century Canada, but he denounced vehemently the corollary that because of earlier patterns, Central Canadians could remain indifferent to regional justice in the twentieth century. One of his objections to imperialism from the centre was that it reduced the self-respect of those who live in the hinterlands. In 1946, he wrote, "Confederation was brought about to increase the wealth of Central Canada, and until that original purpose is altered, and the concentration of wealth and population by national policy in Central Canada ceases, Confederation must remain an instrument of injustice." By 1950, he was complaining that metropolitan controls were stronger and more centralized and that the parliamentary system was less responsible to regional pressures than is a congressional system. More positively, he wrote during the same year that "in a federal union of free citizens and equal communities, there must be such equality of economic opportunity and such equality of political status as human ingenuity may contrive and goodwill advance." This has been the *cri de coeur* of hinterland Canadians everywhere for many years. Malign indifference in Ottawa skyscrapers remains the major obstacle to reform.

It would be foolish to ignore those who want to strike out for nationhood for Western Canada. Opinion surveys have rarely put their numbers at more than 10%, but if aroused sufficiently 10% of 7.2 million Western Canadians might transform themselves into a major political force. Nor is this a new phenomenon. Even in 1925, John Dafoe, editor of *The Winnipeg Free Press*, confessed to the paper's owner, Clifford Sifton, that "there is more secession sentiment throughout the West than I would care to admit."

It is clear that if the longitudinal centre of Canada in the 1920's was a little west of Winnipeg, before Newfoundland's entry into Confederation, the political-economic centre of gravity has since moved further into the Toronto-Montreal-Ottawa triangle. In consequence, we Westerners tend to be well informed about events in the triangle, even as Central Canadian indifference and ignorance about Western Canada continue to be a major irritation.

Regional estrangement has ebbed and flowed with circumstances, issues and personalities, but the common theme is subordination and exploitation by "the East." Roger Gibbins, the Alberta political scientist, concluded that the region suffered from economic and social marginality in the 1930's. In the prosperous 1970's, he writes, "the most prominent articulators of alienation in Alberta have tended to be individuals who have acquired wealth and success in oil, ranching, farming or construction." My own conclusion during the 1970's was that the most alienated Westerners were often people who had moved west from Central Canada with a continuous previous life experience as first-class citizens. Life on the political-economic periphery was bound to be psychologically difficult. When the prosperity vanished in many parts of our region in the early 1980's and did not quickly return, life at the margins for those who stayed was doubly difficult.

Alberta and Saskatchewan residents were in the 1973-1984 period required by Ottawa "in the national interest" to sell their oil domestically for about half of the prevailing world price. The National Energy Program is estimated to have cost Alberta alone in excess of $60 billion in terms of forgone revenue and subsidized oil consumption in the rest of the country. When the world oil price collapsed in late 1985, however, an estimated 40,000 to 50,000 men and women subsequently lost their jobs in the Western Canadian energy industry. Many Western Canadians felt that oil pricing had then become, in the minds of some Central Canadians at least, a regional issue only. The national issue appeared to a good many Westerners to be the threatened loss of 400-500 jobs at a Montreal oil refinery.

No thoughtful Westerner asserts that our region has received nothing from Confederation. The complaint is that we have over a long period received far less than our fair share of the benefits and have paid more than our share of its costs. Robert Mansell, a Calgary economist, looked carefully at the regional impact of federal spending, taxation and other policies since 1961 and pointed out serious regional inequities with the federal government collecting more than it spends in some regions and spending more than it collects in others. In his report, made public in late 1986, he concluded that since 1969 Alberta alone has transferred to Ottawa an astounding $90 billion more than it has received. His calls for a new national policy which will do fairness to the West and Atlantic Canada in a host of areas has widespread support in Western Canada. One of his proposals is that all federal policy and spending proposals should in future be assessed on the basis of their regional implications before enactment.

No fair-minded person would say that the West has not been treated a great deal better since September, 1984, than in the decade or so before. The NEP and the Petroleum Gas Revenue Tax were ended. The amended National Transportation Act should remove a good deal of the traditional practice by which our numerous captive shippers of potash, sulphur, coal, lumber and other products were required to pay essentially what the only railway going past their doors demanded. The plight of western farmers has clearly been recognized by the Mulroney cabinet in its spending priorities. Direct support for agriculture has increased by approximately 400 percent since 1984. The Western Diversification initiative, though inadequate in its funding, is certainly a modest step in the right direction. Within a year after its announcement in August of 1987, the WDI had provided funding for 503 Western projects worth $345 million and supported small and large businesses. More, however, is still needed.

Western Canadians have fought with successive Ottawa governments on many economic issues, including freight rates, agricultural issues, and resource control. Social and cultural issues have also contributed to discontent because most of Western Canada developed without the cultural-linguistic duality of Ontario and Quebec. Some observers, such as historian Doug Owram, have argued that the essence of the western grievance is more cultural than economic, the latter merely adding fuel to the first. He singles out such diverse matters as "the cultural centralism of the Canadian Broadcasting Corporation, bilingualism, markings on RCMP patrol cars and accusations of paternalism hurled against the East" to be as much the real base of the western grievance as economic issues.

Some people both in and outside our region are mystified by the entire notion of western discontent. How, they ask, can there be so much discontent in the West when even Manitoba, which was until recently the poorest economic performer among the four provinces, has a significantly higher standard of living than do the residents of Atlantic Canada? The reason might have to do with differing regional expectations. At the time of Confederation, parts of the three Atlantic provinces were as prosperous as much of Central Canada but circumstances since have caused their hopes to dwindle. Some western hopes and aspirations from the early decades of the twentieth century have clearly gone unfulfilled, yet a new self-confidence about the future emerged across the West during the 1970's. Many Western Canadians are convinced today that, if regional justice can be won from Ottawa in a new national policy, our full potential will be realized.

While a sense of regional discontent exists in all western provinces, it is clearly not the same in each. The British Columbian perspective on alienation appears to differ from the prairie view for various historical and structural reasons. Donald Blake, a Vancouver professor, concluded in 1979 that alienation in his province was linked to beliefs that the two central provinces have too much influence in national affairs and that the federal government was out of touch with provincial aspirations. The province's struggles, Blake went on, were "episodic rather than continuous, in part because the economic well-being of the province is not so directly dependent on federal government policies regarding resource taxation, transportation, energy exports and agriculture." Ottawa, he asserted, has rarely expressed any interest in the first two of the province's three major resource industries: forestry, mining and fishing.

A sense of frustration with Ottawa continues in British Columbia and occasionally surfaces as it did in the March 1988 throne speech given in the Victoria legislature. Prepared by Premier Bill Vander Zalm's cabinet and merely read by Lieutenant Governor Robert Rogers, it asserted bluntly that British Columbians are ready to put Canada's federal system of government on trial. "My government has been patient but we have seen too many inequities and the allocation of too many grants, subsidies and federal resources to Central and Eastern Canada. The result has been a deepening feeling of alienation in our Pacific Region. For too long, British Columbia has been out of sight and out of mind of successive federal governments. Even now, that vision of Western Canada appears to encompass only prairie grain and Alberta energy."

The exercise was quickly dismissed by some local political observers and a number of Central Canadian newspapers as self-serving "fed-bashing." Such observers failed to see Vander Zalm's complaint as a common one in the West – not merely one of an unpopular premier — based on the desire of Western provinces to achieve our full potential as full and equal members of Confederation. "The West wants in" may be the slogan of the new Reform Party of Canada, but it is a sentiment which still finds an echo in many parts of the region.

A qualifying word about the Yukon and the Northwest Territories is necessary. Tony Penikett, the current government Leader in the Yukon, used a typical northern mining project to characterize the territory's basic economic problems: "The ore goes to Tokyo, the profits to Toronto, the taxes to Ottawa, the jobs to Vancouver and we're left with a hole in the ground which, if the federal government gave permission, we could use as a garbage dump.'' In the Northwest Territories, Ottawa's paternalism is equally legendary because for many years the federal government operated virtually as a federal, provincial and municipal government all in one. To repair one's roof in the N.W.T. seemed to many northern residents to require a fiat from Ottawa. Many Northern Canadians sense that they continue to be treated as foolish children by their national government.

In short, the feeling persists among Westerners that our concerns are never or rarely an ongoing priority on any Ottawa agenda. On the relatively rare occasion when issues in our region do become a priority, as in the case of the National Energy Program of 1980, we have tended to suffer enormously as a consequence. When initiatives favouring the region are launched, they seem to be reactive rather than pro-active, usually done grudgingly, invariably late and often with more of an eye on short-term politics than the long-term interests of Westerners.

TWO

Frederick Haultain
Forgotten Statesman

*"I*F THE PRAIRIES EVER COME to the time for monuments to their statesmen, the first choice should be easy to name," said H.A. Robson, a Chief Justice of Manitoba and one-time leader of the Manitoba Liberal party, writing in 1944 of Frederick Haultain. Such a challenge directed at Western Canadians today would certainly fail to evoke his name because he seems mainly forgotten even in Saskatchewan. The first edition of *The Canadian Encyclopedia,* published in Western Canada in 1985, does not devote a single line to the individual who more than anyone achieved provincial status for Saskatchewan and Alberta in 1905.

Grant MacEwan laments this ignorance in his biography of Haultain, which was published in 1986, noting that he was stunned to see in a publication celebrating the seventy-fifth anniversary of Alberta that Haultain was not even mentioned among twenty-five early pioneers. To overcome such slights of a man who was one of the region's "best candidates for statesmanship" was partly why MacEwan wrote a study of Haultain's life.

Haultain, "the unsullied hero of the West standing up to the insensitivity of Ottawa," according to historian David Hall, was, at various periods, premier of the North-West Territories, leader of the opposition in the Saskatchewan legislative assembly, chief justice for Saskatchewan, and chancellor of the University of Saskatchewan.

The western period of his life began in 1884 when he stepped off a four-horse stagecoach in Fort Macleod, a small ten-year-old centre in the District of Alberta in the North-West Territories. He had been born twenty-seven years earlier in England into a family which had as Protestants fled France in 1572, becoming over two centuries chiefly officers in the British navy and army. His parents moved to Peterborough from Britain when he was three. There his father, only a year after coming to Canada, was elected as a Clear Grit member for Peterborough in the legislature of the Province of Canada. Later the family would move to Montreal for a number of years where the father was secretary of a Presbyterian missionary society before they all returned to Peterborough.

Frederick initially wanted to follow the family tradition of military service, but apparently financial difficulties caused him to abandon such a career. He graduated in classics at the University of Toronto and was called to the Ontario bar. His father's death shortly after his admission to practice touched him deeply. The shock appears to have been a major reason why he opted for an adventuresome life on the western frontier. He chose Fort Macleod because a university classmate who had settled there invited him to come out to discuss a partnership. None was forthcoming when he arrived, so Haultain's lawyer's shingle soon went out in the tiny community. In considering his prospects, he doubtless thought of the $40 in worldly possessions left in his pocket after the long train trip from Kingston.

Life in Fort Macleod, the district headquarters of the recently-established Mounted Police, was anything but dull. A flood of people was arriving in Western Canada from all over the world, some of them bringing with them contraband goods and illegal habits. Haultain was appointed Crown Prosecutor for the area soon after his arrival.

He became fast friends with James and Mary Macleod. Col. Macleod, another giant of the West and the renowned former Mounted Police commissioner after whom the town was named, had become the territorial judge for the district. His deep respect for Indians, personal courage and wisdom as both policeman and

44

judge did much to avert violence over many years. When he died in 1894, leaving Mary to support five children without any pension whatsoever, Haultain would help gather money for them and for one period even took one of the sons, Norman, to live with him in Regina. He raised money from local ranchers to send him to the same Toronto boarding school attended by his father.

Vast cattle ranches were being established in the foothills south and west of Macleod as a result of the virtually simultaneous completion of the western railway and arrival of refrigerated ships capable of moving large quantities of beef to Great Britain. Haultain wrote to his mother the spring following his arrival for a week-long vacation at the Cochrane ranch near what are now the Waterton Lakes: "Ranch hours are, breakfast at 4.30!!! dinner at twelve and supper at six.... I have been living a very pleasant life here with nothing to do but wander about and do as I please. There is a very large supply of novels in the home so that I have plenty of reading. My allowance is two and a half novels a day, which I get through religiously, besides riding about, shooting, walking and smoking...."

In his second year in the West, the North-West Rebellion erupted briefly near Prince Albert. Members of the Blackfoot, Blood and Piegan tribes near Macleod were clearly irritated and restless. The women and children of local pioneers were moved to much larger Calgary. Haultain, like every other able-bodied man, found himself participating in drill exercises by day and patrolling the town streets at night. Fortunately, no violence broke out in the Macleod area and life quickly returned to normal.

Clients began to appear at the door of his one-room office. His sense of fairness was such that even when he acted for the plaintiff in a libel action against, among others, *The Macleod Gazette*, the editor of the paper wrote afterwards that he had "conducted the prosecution in an impartial and able manner and we echo the feelings of all when we say: 'Well done, sir; you did your duty well.'" Clients with all kinds of problems came more and more frequently thereafter.

So, it appears, did mothers with daughters of marriageable age, but unsuccessfully. In fact he would not marry, and then only

45

secretly, until he was forty-nine years of age and living in Regina. The entire sorry subject speaks volumes about his character.

Briefly put, Haultain clearly became infatuated with Marion Mackintosh, almost twenty years his junior and daughter of a territorial Lieutenant Governor. She, however, married a Regina wine and tobacco wholesaler and eventually returned with him to his native England where he abandoned both her and their daughter, Minnie, to abject poverty. Discovering this a few years later, Haultain supported the two of them until she married again, this time an American who also abandoned them. Marion and her child were soon again depending on money from Haultain.

The prairies' historian Lewis Thomas wrote of the situation: "Haultain was now a forty-nine year old bachelor, and it appears that a single-minded devotion to politics and a degree of emotional immaturity handicapped his relations with women. His infatuation with Marion Mackintosh appears to have blinded him to the weakness of her character and her subsequent erratic behaviour."

Evidently, Marion's conscience finally got the better of her and she agreed to marry Frederick and settle in Regina after her health recovered in England. They did marry in 1906 but she never came West, much to her husband's inner sadness. He maintained his affection for her until her death in 1938. Throughout 32 years of marriage, he continued to send much of his income to support her at various locations.

As Grant MacEwan notes, the idea of keeping the marriage secret for so long was clearly distasteful to him, but he worried about gossip-mongers, especially while he was in politics. "Nobody," asserts his biographer, "could accuse him of legal or moral wrongdoing in the matter, and nobody could criticize him for his years of sacrifice to ensure the best medical attention and care for his ailing wife."

Nor would his code of honour permit him to marry again until Marion's death in Guelph, Ontario, in 1938. His marriage to a Montreal widow, Mrs. W.B. Gilmour, occurred only after Marion's death when he was 80 years of age.

Haultain's political career began in 1887, three years after his arrival, when he was elected to the council of the North-West Territories for the Macleod district. He defeated a Lethbridge "favourite son" candidate, C.P. Coneybeare by 301 votes to 156; thereafter until 1905 he was never again opposed by anyone. He soon became a positive and effective force on the Regina-based council. The governmental situation he and the other democratically elected members then faced was described colourfully by Frank Oliver in his *Edmonton Bulletin*: "While Canada as a whole, and the different provinces of which it is composed are united under a system of responsible government, the North-West is under a despotism as absolute, or more so, than that which curses Russia. Without representation in either parliament or cabinet, without responsible local government, the people of the North-West are allowed but a degree more control of their affairs than the serfs of Siberia."

The new member for Macleod was soon leading the crusade for responsible government against both the Ottawa government and its local lieutenant governors, who presided over the council and continued to take instruction from the federal minister of the interior on all matters, including the spending of funds. The population of the territory, which the 1885 census placed at 48,362, was rising steadily, and the move to responsible government was beginning to gather real momentum.

The Macleod Gazette reported in 1888: "The first question that Mr. Haultain referred to was that of self-government, and he literally wiped the floor with the Ottawa authorities over their new North-West Bill. He said that we had been dealt with like a parcel of political children. For three years the old council had sent memorials to the government demanding self-government, and each time the memorial had been acknowledged in the usual way of politicians or statesmen. It was now necessary to unite, and express a strong opinion in that direction not only through representatives, but by meetings all over the country.... We had asked for bread, and they had given us a stone; we had asked for a legislative assembly, and they had given us the shadow of self-government."

In 1888, an Ottawa measure by Sir John's government permitted the council to become a legislative assembly presided over by an elected speaker in place of the lieutenant governor. An advisory council of four was to be elected henceforth from its members to advise the lieutenant governor on spending matters. The new lieutenant governor, Joseph Royal, chose Haultain as a member of the council and he became its first chairman. He and other council members, quickly recognizing that the final spending decisions still rested with Royal, sent a resolution to Ottawa deploring the denial of financial responsibility to the territorial West's elected representatives. When Ottawa in effect ignored the resolution, the entire executive council resigned protesting that they were no longer willing "to accept responsibility without the corresponding right of control."

Royal then named more compliant individuals to replace them, but when it later became clear that the council's financial control applied to locally-raised revenues only and not to federal grants, Haultain and thirteen other full democrats in the assembly defeated the new council in a confidence vote. Another message was then sent by the assembly to Ottawa demanding full responsibility for all territorial spending. The constitutional crisis, wrote MacEwan, "became the favourite topic of conversation in towns and villages and over farm fences across the country.... It was bitter political fighting but remarkable in that it could be conducted without sacrificing friendships, without loss of honour, without accusation of dishonesty, 'kickbacks' and graft. The leading figures – Joseph Royal, Frederick Haultain and Dr. Brett could participate to the full without being in any way less the gentlemen."

Shortly thereafter, the assembly voted by a majority of fifteen to six to deny advisory council members the right to serve on assembly committees. Prime Minister Macdonald soon got the message and amended the North-West Territories Act to remove both the lieutenant governor and all non-elected persons from the daily business of the assembly. The issue of a four-man council was resolved in 1891 when the assembly passed a measure creating a four-person executive committee in its place. Haultain as the acknowledged assembly leader became its first chairman in late 1891. He would remain in substance, if not in name, the premier and spokesman of the North-West Territories until 1905 except for a short period in 1892-93.

Haultain dominated elected public life in the region by force of his character and intellect and his vision for a proud and democratic West. When Hugh Cayley of Calgary resigned as deputy chairman of Haultain's executive in 1892 to lead the perhaps inevitable group of assembly dissenters, Haultain and his cabinet resigned immediately after they narrowly lost a confidence motion. The respected speaker of the assembly, James Ross, quickly resigned his position in order to vote with Haultain; Cayley's group could no longer obtain a majority in favour of their choice for speaker. The assembly was soon prorogued rather than dissolved for an election by Royal acting on Cayley's advice. The affair expired when a member of the Cayley faction died and a supporter of Haultain was elected in a fiercely contested by-election. The lieutenant governor then invited Haultain to resume his position as leader of the assembly and government.

In 1898, a year after the Laurier government in Ottawa granted the final vestige of full responsible government to the territories, R.B. Bennett, the future prime minister, was elected to the assembly. The new Calgary member, although only 28 years old and a resident of Western Canada for only about a year, quickly appeared to be gunning for Haultain's job as premier. The issue he chose to attempt to topple the ''punctiliously honest'' premier was an alleged discrepancy of $20,000 in the public accounts for 1896. The territorial auditor, J.C. Pope, explained to an assembly committee that $45,000 had been promised by Ottawa in 1895 so that sum was entered as a credit but only $25,000 was actually received by the year's end.

That would have been the end of the matter, but the headline of Regina's newest newspaper, *The Standard*, soon roared: ''Cooked accounts – how the territorial treasurer made $20,000.'' A select committee of the assembly, which was immediately struck to investigate the matter, reported that Bennett was the source of the statements published by the paper and that his allegations were without foundation. Thirteen assembly members voted to support the committee's conclusions and three, including Bennett, voted against. The Calgary member's quest for the premiership thus ended quickly.

Haultain showed his mettle later when a brisk movement developed in Manitoba to annex part or all of the territory which now comprises much of eastern Saskatchewan. Events climaxed in 1901 when he met at Indian Head east of Regina to debate the issue with Rodmond Roblin, premier of Manitoba. Roblin made an effective case for annexation, but Haultain appealed strongly to the shared experiences of the local residents to join his western vision of a new province stretching to the Rockies. "If you form part of what I would like to see — one big province in the West you will have unlimited resources; you will be able to do things no province in Canada has even been able to do and you will have no need to ask your brother Manitoba to help you." The appeal to local pride appears to have carried most of the audience of 1,000 and the annexation movement soon died out.

Haultain's most important accomplishment in politics was winning provincial status for the territories. His five-year campaign began formally on May 2, 1900 when he spoke in the assembly for four hours on the unsatisfactory constitutional situation of the territories. Along with his speech, the assembly sent a draft bill to Ottawa, intended to grant provincial status. The federal Interior Minister, Clifford Sifton of Brandon, whose brother Arthur served as Haultain's minister of public works between 1899 and 1903, sent the limp reply that the entire subject would have to be considered fully. This caused Haultain, who admired both Siftons, to query how "such a man [could] become a mere tool of the Ottawa government."

Everyone but the Laurier cabinet appeared to understand that Regina's surging population faced a critical need for new services. When Laurier and Sifton again refused to move, Haultain decided to attend the founding Conservative Convention in Moose Jaw in early 1903 to present his case. Though a steadfast opponent of party politics, he let himself be made the honorary president of the organization by Senator James Lougheed, R.B. Bennett and others. He objected to the nomination of Conservative candidates for the upcoming territorial elections, but applauded the call by the party's national leader, Robert Borden, for immediate provincial status for the region.

The full consequences of his first entry into partisan politics were difficult to detect at first. Clearly, Haultain was convinced that the good of the territories and entire country now required the defeat of the Laurier government; on the other hand, some Liberals both in Ottawa and in the territories now wanted the most popular public figure in the West defeated because he had publicly identified himself with a competing political party. The first partisan attack came in late 1903 when the federal government offered Haultain an appointment as a judge, with the hope of removing him from a political arena in which he was the dominant player. His political opponents also wished to discredit him by creating the false impression that he had sought such an appointment. The ugly affair ended when Haultain refused the offer, saying that he had no intention of "deserting the ship." The entire incident only solidified in the premier's mind the view that political parties corrupt public life and reinforced his opposition to the introduction of federal party names and divisions to the provincial sphere.

In mid-1904, Haultain, aware that a general election was coming, wrote again to the prime minister, noting that the assembly's submission and a draft bill of 1901 to him were still unanswered. Laurier responded only after the Commons had been dissolved for the election to say that, if re-elected, his government would grant provincial autonomy. Haultain campaigned hard for Borden's Conservatives regardless, believing they were more sincere on the issue. In fact, the election proved an easy victory for Laurier, who had become, in popular opinion, the embodiment of both national development and national unity. Laurier won 139 of 214 seats in the House of Commons, including 7 of the territories' 10 seats, 7 of Manitoba's 10 and all of British Columbia's 7 seats. Although Haultain was disappointed by the election results, Laurier did honour his provincehood pledge with the creation of two provinces, Saskatchewan and Alberta, which officially came into being on September 1, 1905.

It seemed to be a virtual certainty that Haultain would be offered the premiership of one of the new provinces. In the end, however, in the words of *Saturday Night* magazine, "this strong, straight, able man who has locally directed nearly every good thing that has been done for the Territories [was] to be ousted from any share of the government of either of the two new provinces." Walter Scott, the provincial Liberal leader, was called on by Lieutenant Governor Forget to form the first government of Saskatchewan, the province Haultain chose for his future political activity. Certainly, Haultain's support of the Conservatives was detrimental to his candidacy for the premiership, but it may also be assumed that his unqualified opposition to the treatment of natural resources and separate schools in the autonomy bills worked against him.

Why, if Haultain was such a popular premier of the greater territories, did he subsequently lose the 1905, 1908 and 1912 elections in Saskatchewan as leader of a provincial rights party? It has been suggested that the patronage and power of the Walter Scott provisional government and the influence of the Laurier government and its Interior Department played significant parts. Or, as J.W. Brennan suggests, it may have been the tendency of new immigrant settlers to vote for the party that had brought them to Canada. Haultain's opposition to separate schools also provoked a letter by Archbishop Langevin to Catholic voters in favour of the Liberal party. Balloting irregularities and corrupt returning officers were reported as well.

When he lost in the 1908 provincial election, Haultain was quite content to return part-time to the practice of law in Regina. His ninth election campaign in 1912 he considered to be the most vicious of all, largely because of the doings of the two old political parties. By that year, there were half a million residents in the province, many of them newcomers, who found themselves looking at headlines in the Liberal papers such as: "Endorsement of the Haultain Conservatives Would Mean Surrender to the Eastern Trusts," and "Haultain would demean the province.'' This time he and his non-partisan followers could win only seven seats against the 40 Liberal MLA's elected.

Late that year, Prime Minister Borden appointed Haultain Chief Justice for Saskatchewan, which post he filled with distinction for the following 25 years. John Diefenbaker remembered him as ''an amazing person, a cultured man who never lost the common touch and an eminently just judge....'' Four years later, he was knighted by the King. In 1917, he was elected as the second chancellor of the University of Saskatchewan, a post he retained until 1939. That year, at the age of 80, he retired from both positions and moved to Montreal, the home of his new bride. He received also an honorary chieftainship from Saskatchewan Cree Indians and the name Winter Star. When he died in 1942, the provincial Chief Justice and former Premier, W.M. Martin said: ''No judge in Western Canada was held in higher esteem by his brothers of the bench and the members of the bar.''

Haultain's biographer, Grant MacEwan, a one-time Liberal leader in Alberta and a federal Liberal candidate in Manitoba, quotes fellow Liberal John W. Dafoe, editor of *The Winnipeg Free Press*, writing in 1937: ''The most interesting 'if' in the history of the West is, what would have happened 'if' Haultain had won and not lost his controversy with the Laurier government thirty-two years ago?'' MacEwan goes on: ''It takes very little imagination to see Haultain, if premier of Saskatchewan in 1911 and willing to adjust to such degree as the federal arena seemed to demand, being summoned to Ottawa to become Prime Minister Borden's minister of the interior. Then, if his judgement and skills were still adequately recognized, he would, in due course, have been a candidate for the party leadership in the 20's and probably prime minister.''

Instead, Haultain has become a forgotten giant of Western Canada.

THREE

A History of Anguish
The Roots of Western Alienation

A WESTERN POLITICIAN, Otto Lang, speaking in the House of Commons in the spring of 1974, said: "The grievances, the inequities, the discontent, the so-called alienation, are real. In Western Canada the problems have been growing steadily for some considerable length of time. This goes back through a succession of governments involving different political stripes."

Westerners can still trace the roots of the feelings Lang was voicing in 1974. Identifying and understanding the regional discontent and how it began and developed is necessary to the central message of this book: a century of subordinate status for Western Canada must end. The Frederick Haultain experience illustrates only one aspect of a deeply-set pattern of regional alienation. Discontent reaches deep and spills into many spheres of western life. Whether a western politician, a women's rights activist, a struggling artist or a native leader, we have all experienced the feelings of helplessness, frustration and anger with our regional lot in Confederation.

What follows are some earlier experiences which help explain current western attitudes. A historical pattern of subordination and resulting grievance constitutes the basis of the western alienation which continues to the present day.

Farmer Fury

The first albatross from Ottawa was hung around western farmers' necks in 1879 when Prime Minister Macdonald began to enact the high tariff feature of his National Policy. A 20% tariff imposed on farm implements in 1879, for example, was raised to 35% in 1884. The aim was to encourage new Ontario and Quebec manufacturers by penalizing the entry of competing products primarily from the United States and Britain. For western farmers, however, the result was that they were forced either to pay high duties on imported farm machinery and the like, or to buy substantially more expensive substitutes from Central Canada. For almost a century afterwards, Westerners, who obtained no visible benefit from high tariffs in terms of manufacturers locating their plants near their most important customers, believed that they were paying for most of the elegant mahogany in the homes and offices of manufacturers in Toronto and Montreal.

The western complaint remained until well into the 1970's that world export realities required Westerners to sell our agricultural products, notably wheat, into highly competitive world markets, but that we were obliged by Ottawa to buy necessities in a domestic market made less competitive by protective tariffs. The tariff quickly became in the late nineteenth century a key point of confrontation between the prairie farm community and, as the economists W.T. Easterbrook and Hugh G.J. Aitken have put it, "those who viewed the wheat economy as a hinterland to be exploited...."

The Saskatchewan economist V.C. Fowke asserts that Canadian farmers generally were no more free traders than protectionists. Until the 1840's, many were protectionists, just as 150 years later some would express fear that a Canada-U.S. comprehensive bilateral trade agreement would threaten their livelihoods. A reciprocity agreement with the U.S. in agricultural products in effect between 1854-66, however, benefitted Central Canadian producers of oats, rye and barley handsomely. One reason the Americans abrogated the treaty after their Civil War, concludes Fowke, was because the legislature of pre-Confederation Canada raised tariffs during 1858 and 1859 on products which were important to American exporters. The Manufacturers' Association of Ontario was also formed at about this time with the sole purpose of seeking high tariffs, and one of its officers would boast later that the high tariff proposal of the Macdonald government in 1879 was with very few exceptions "the same as suggested by the Manufacturers' Association." A majority of Ontario farmers appear to have voted for Macdonald and high tariffs, including those on grains and wheats, in the 1878 election.

Seven years later, however, delegates from the West, Ontario and Quebec voted at a farm conference for the removal of tariffs on farm machinery and other necessities. In 1883, one of the first agricultural producer organizations formed in Western Canada issued a declaration of rights which included a call for the removal of duties on farm machinery and building materials. Western wheat growers were clearly more united against the tariff than were those from Ontario and Quebec. Unfortunately, Central Canadian manufacturers, merchants, bankers and railroaders, fearing competition in the West from American suppliers and railroads, lined up on the side of tariff protection as the general election of 1911 approached.

If the Conservatives were unmovable on the tariff, the Liberal party was little better in practice. In 1894, the Liberal leader, Sir Wilfred Laurier, declared to attentive Winnipeggers: "I denounce the policy of protection as bondage – yea, bondage; and I refer to bondage in the same manner in which American slavery was bondage." This was consistent with the low-tariff platform of the Liberals in the previous national election, but once elected in 1896, Laurier's government repudiated both the 1893 platform and his Winnipeg comment. No major change to Macdonald's tariff policy was made. By 1905, Prime Minister Laurier could even tell the Canadian Manufacturers' Association: "They (western settlers) will require clothes, they will require furniture, they will require implements, they will require shoes.... It is your ambition, it is my ambition also, that this scientific tariff of ours will make it possible that every shoe that has to be worn in those Prairies shall be a Canadian shoe; that every yard of cloth that can

be marketed there shall be a yard of cloth produced in Canada....''
Both national political parties had lost all real interest in tariff
reform by 1905, despite the ongoing preoccupation of western
agriculture with the issue.

Several factors resuscitated it. First, Prime Minister Laurier
during his famous prairies trip in the summer of 1910 heard
repeated calls for reciprocity with the U.S. In December of that
year, a large delegation of both Western and Central Canadian
farmers went to Ottawa stressing both the tariff and reciprocity.
Second, as Fowke points out, the Prairies, which held only about
8% of the national population in 1901, contained about 18% by
1911. These factors, plus the government's uncertainty of winning another term for other reasons, appear to have persuaded
Laurier to seek reciprocity with the U.S. Following months of
heated debate in the House on a bill to implement the agreement,
Laurier, confident victory awaited him, called an election on the
single issue of reciprocity.

The Liberals entered the 1911 election campaign with 133 MPs
and came out with 87; Robert Borden's Conservatives began
with 85 and finished with a comfortable majority of 134. The
campaign has been thoroughly discussed in numerous places, but
a few points about the western perspective are in order because
the two parties surprisingly ended about evenly divided overall in
the West.

Initially, as political scientist Murray Beck notes, none of the
sitting western Conservative members expected to hold their
seats if they opposed reciprocity. Soon, however, the nation's
manufacturing, transportation and banking establishments, whose
well-being was thought to depend on continued protection, rallied against the agreement in the name of national loyalty. On the
other side of the issue, advocates of reciprocity pointed out that
people like Edmund Walker, the president of the Canadian Bank
of Commerce, could do business in New York City without a
disloyalty charge but a Saskatchewan farmer could not sell a load
of grain in Minneapolis ''without selling his country and his soul
with it.''

All but one of ten seats in Saskatchewan went Liberal; in

Alberta, the Liberals won six of seven. In B.C., where there was a strong British sentiment, voters were asked by Borden's supporters to choose between the Union Jack and the Stars and Stripes; the Conservatives in consequence won all seven seats. In Manitoba, the Conservatives won eight of 10 seats. Their campaign proved successful for a number of reasons, largely having to do with the strong political organization of the provincial Conservatives led by Premier Rodmond Roblin; the Manitoba campaign turned only partly on the reciprocity issue.

One of the ironies of the 1911 election was that the reciprocity agreement in issue in the campaign dealt with natural products and not manufactured goods. In Fowke's words, Central Canadian business had rallied to defeat ''an agreement which in itself asked practically nothing of them. They fought it for what it might lead to, a later agreement which might not leave their position of economic privilege untouched.''

Western farmers returned to the attack on the tariff in the 1920's without success and in the worldwide trade wars of the 1930's most Canadian tariffs rose by 50%. Only in the 1970's, after the Tokyo and Kennedy Rounds at the GATT, did tariffs begin to go down.

"Damn The CPR"

Another major farm issue in Western Canada over many decades was the railway monopoly in general and freight rate equalization in particular. It began when the CPR printed its first freight schedule in 1883 and, except for a few items, the rates were 50% higher than the Grand Trunk Railway's rates for Central Canada for the same services. Westerners soon noticed that while the CPR pooled its income and expenses nationwide, wheat travelled 200 miles for ten cents a bushel in Ontario and Quebec but for twice that in parts of the Prairies. In fact, as the late transportation economist Howard Darling observed, Manitobans paid a higher rate than Central Canadians, residents of what is now Alberta and Saskatchewan a higher rate than Manitobans, and British Columbians paid the highest rate of all. Ottawa rail officials would later approve this as ''fair discrimination.''

Westerners argued in vain during most of a century thereafter that there should be equalization of rates in the sense that all Canadians should pay the same rate for the same distances for the same kind of material shipped in any part of the country. Struggling settlers in the West deeply resented that they alone must carry the cost of building and maintaining the less productive section of the CPR line lying between Kenora and Sudbury. Convincing Ottawa's Board of Railway Commissioners that different rates for the same goods in different regions constituted unjust regional discrimination would prove to be a crusade not for the faint-hearted.

In Manitoba, widespread objections to the early CPR monopoly, which had included massive land and cash grants, a monopoly on western rail construction, and in effect control over all products moving to and from the province, led in 1882 to the first recorded western threat of secession from Macdonald's Canada by some angry Manitobans. Their provincial government had attempted to build a rail line from Winnipeg to the U.S. border, but was not permitted to cross the main CPR line. When Manitoba's Métis premier, John Norquay, who was in fact supportive of Macdonald's own party at the federal level, vowed in 1887 to build the Manitoba Red River Valley Railway to the U.S. boundary, the prime minister used his connections to prevent a bond sale in New York and London. He then ousted Norquay as premier by spreading rumours, probably false, to the Lieutenant Governor of Manitoba about alleged financial irregularities. Within two months of Norquay's resignation as premier, Liberal Thomas Greenway, who had earlier been a Macdonald MP in Ontario but broke with him over the tariff, took the job in 1888. Macdonald soon swallowed his decade-old view that the transcontinental line of the CPR was the heart of his National Policy and he granted to Greenway the right for Manitoba to create rail competition. The CPR monopoly was ended in 1888 in return for substantial financial compensation.

The CPR sought and won a further cash grant from Ottawa in 1897 to build a spur line from Lethbridge, Alberta to Nelson, British Columbia, through the Crow's Nest Pass in the Rockies.

Neglecting to specify a termination date for the agreement, the CPR voluntarily agreed, in exchange for its access to some very rich minerals in southern B.C., to reduce its existing freight rates on "settler's effects" moving west. More importantly, it also agreed to reduce its existing freight rates by about 20% on grain moving eastward from Winnipeg to Thunder Bay. This was the first of the fixed Crow rates which to some Westerners made, in W.L. Morton's words, "the burden of the tariff tolerable on the Prairies." In fact, the first Crow rate was no gift at all to Westerners because in the 1903-1918 period the CPR agreed to an even lower rate for wheat moving east. In 1922, the final Crow regime was set at 1/2 cent per ton-mile for grain shipped from Regina to Thunder Bay. Five years later, it was also extended to grain shipped to Vancouver and to Churchill.

Eventually many western farmers and ranchers, along with the rest of the consumers and manufacturers in the region, realized that they had paid a steep price for the "Holy Crow." This was partly because its existence allowed other freight rates to continue to discriminate against the West. A study by economist Thomas Schweitzer indicates that before 1914 the general freight rate on the Prairies was fully 30 to 50% higher than in Central Canada and Ontario. An additional surcharge for British Columbia was not finally abolished until 1949 when the cheaper prairies rates were extended to B.C. by Ottawa's Board of Railway Commissioners.

During the 1920's, British Columbians took the leadership in the western freight rate issue by arguing that the province should not have to pay higher rates for the same service because of the presence of the Rocky Mountains. Residents of the three other western provinces returned soon to the rail war as well. The *Calgary Albertan* in a piece entitled, "Freight Rates Throttle the Prairies," argued that "The main blame probably rested on greedy eastern manufacturing and commercial interests determined that the West develop as a sort of colony of Ontario and Quebec, dependent on them for manufactured goods...." By the time the CPR and CNR announced in October of 1946 that they had applied for a 30% increase in freight rates, seven of the nine provincial governments were ready for a major confrontation, none more vehemently than the four western ones. Only Ontario and Quebec did not protest. Ultimately the Mackenzie King government allowed a 21% increase and only in 1949 was the Mountain Differential for B.C. freight abolished.

Over the years, the Crow Rate arrangements have been the subject of numerous government enquiries, first by the MacPherson Royal Commission on Transportation in 1961, and then by the Snavely Report in 1976, the Hall Commission in 1977, and the Snavely Update in 1982. The 1982 Gilson Report led to the 1983 Western Grain Transportation Act replacing the Crow's Nest Pass Freight Rate.

John Whalley and Irene Trela, authors of a 1986 study commissioned by the Macdonald Commission on the economic union and development prospects for Canada, concluded their discussion of the Crow Rate with the following statement: "The Crow Rate will not be as important a policy element within Confederation in the years ahead as in previous decades, since it will be slowly phased out as inflation reduces the real value of the benefit. However, the sense of regional grievance in the West over the recent action on the Crow is real. Following its removal these feelings will no doubt remain, especially as the benefits to the West from the Crow Rate have traditionally been seen as counterweight to benefits accruing to central Canada from the tariff."

A fascinating case study of the situation today involves an experience last year by Alberta Gas Chemicals Ltd. in Medicine Hat. The company was exporting methanol, made from natural gas, from its plant in southern Alberta in rail tank cars. CP Rail has the only rail line entering or leaving Medicine Hat, one line of which travels south to the U.S. boundary where it connects to the American-owned Burlington Northern Railroad. Long anxious to increase its sales in the U.S., Alberta Gas tried repeatedly, without success, to get CP to quote a rate to Coutts. Finally, it simply shipped a car of methanol to Coutts — a distance of 178 miles — only to receive a preposterous bill from CP for $13,000.

In mid-1987, Sam Egglestone, a spokesman for Alberta Gas,

gave evidence to a Senate Committee on behalf of the company on the consequences of having earlier outlined the episode to a House of Commons Committee. He told the astonished senators:

"You might be interested in how the CPR responded to the submission we made to the House of Commons standing committee on March 17. The next morning they were on the phone from the senior level of their company telling us they are very unhappy with us, that they did not like our submission, that they did not like the way we got the rate, and that we did not tell the whole truth.... Just in case we did not get the message, they informed us on May 8 that they were increasing all our rates to Chicago and west of the Mississippi by 23%. They were going to remind us who is running the show. They put that rate increase through."

CPR management is clearly still hard to like in Western Canada but CN is at times little better. Why, Westerners ask, does the federal Crown Corporation have only 37% of its active rail employees living in the four western provinces when it does two-thirds of its entire freight business in Western Canada?

Champion Forest Products operates a pulp and lumber mill employing 750 men and women on the CN line west of Edmonton. Most of the output is sold to the United States where substitute products come from American, Brazilian and Scandinavian mills. In order to become more competitive, Champion proposed a $285 million modernization which would both secure the present jobs and create up to 400 permanent new ones. According to Ken Hall, the company president, CN as a captive shipper unilaterally raised the cost of moving their products 19% between 1983 and 1987, compared to a 6% increase over the same period by American railroads. No thanks to CN greed, the plant expansion is proceeding.

Pushing Wheat

The historic attitude of many western grain growers to the marketing of their wheat is well phrased by Gerald Friesen: "The business of the Prairies during the half-century after 1880 was, first and foremost, agriculture. Crop prospects, the weather and wheat prices were part of daily conversation because they affected the fate of the region. In these years, a complex system for raising, handling, transporting, and marketing grain was built on the foundations provided by village and farm residents. And when farmers believed the system to be unfair or inefficient, they united in protest. As a result, discussion of economic issues became, willy-nilly, partisan political debate. King Wheat, as he was known, inspired intense disagreements among his subjects.''

A major problem for early wheat growers was the monopoly of grain elevators at many rail points. This meant that farmers were obliged to accept the local elevator agent's terms for the price, storage, weight and grade of their crop. Complaints about these practices led to the appointment of a royal commission in 1899 and the Manitoba Grain Act by the Laurier government in 1900. Many farmers believed, however, that the elevator abuses at which the new legislation was aimed continued due to limp-wristed enforcement by federal agents. The economic historians Easterbrook and Aitken concluded Ottawa's enforcement of the act led to the founding of the Territorial Grain Growers Association in 1901 and the Manitoba Grain Growers Association in 1903. Before long, the Grain Growers Grain Company began as a producer cooperative to compete directly with the private grain companies and the Winnipeg Grain Exchange, both of which were hugely unpopular with many grain producers throughout the West. By the time World War I began, producer cooperatives in all three prairie provinces were competing effectively against the private companies by both handling and selling up to a third of all grain sold on the Prairies.

Events during and after World War I confirmed again for prairie farmers that their national government was not really concerned about their problems. First, despite the vigorous opposition of prairie producers, government control of grain marketing in war-time was discontinued by Prime Minister Arthur Meighen, himself first elected to Parliament from Portage La Prairie, Manitoba. World export conditions thereafter quickly obliged Ottawa to create the Canadian Wheat Board as the exclusive domestic and export marketing vehicle, but it ceased to operate in 1920. Many prairie wheat farmers believed that the hand of the Winnipeg grain barons was behind Ottawa's decision. When Western farmers were unable to persuade Ottawa to revive it, the three prairie wheat pools came into being to market wheat. They were highly successful during the decade. Easterbrook and Aitken note that when the Depression struck more than one half of prairie wheat acreage was under contract to the three pools.

The total collapse of grain prices in 1930 ended the period of the pools as international marketers of prairie wheat. It also led to the appointment of a royal commission into the operations of the Winnipeg Grain Exchange. Nothing, however, of substance was changed for the producer; again the Winnipeg middlemen appeared to have carried the day against the producer interest. Only in early 1935 was a re-created Canadian Wheat Board proposed by Prime Minister R.B. Bennett of Calgary. In what many saw as a deathbed conversion inspired by a looming election disaster, Bennett first proposed in effect to nationalize the entire elevator system and to have the Canadian Wheat Board become the only dealer in all major crops both domestically and abroad. But, again in Friesen's language, "when the private traders had completed their lobby, the board was a shadow of its former self: it became a wheat, not a grain marketing agency; its elevator system was never created; and its compulsory features were eliminated, leaving it to establish an annual minimum price for wheat that farmers were free to accept or to reject in favour of the offers of private companies."

The resulting vexation of financially-desperate prairie farmers with a self-proclaimed prairie prime minister was clear. When Bennett's Conservatives were thrown out in the 1935 election in favour of Mackenzie King's Liberals, many prairie residents were again hopeful. Four years later, however, the King government planned to eliminate the Wheat Board until the rage of prairie producers stopped him cold. Another so-called national government had wanted to abandon the business of selling western wheat but, for once, the prairie view had prevailed in Ottawa.

Prairie Political Inferiority

The ongoing problem of political inequality for prairie Canadians has probably generated as much alienation as tariff and freight rates combined. The issue surfaced nowhere as strongly as in disputes over natural resources ownership and the setting of provincial boundaries.

Manitoba barely crawled into being as a province in 1870, lacking control of even its crown land and resources, and it did not succeed in obtaining them until sixty years later. The Macdonald government had concluded that providing Manitoba a constitutional status equal to the five existing provinces, including tiny Prince Edward Island, would deprive the federal government of much of the rich lands in the Prairies. The Manitoba Act of 1870 declared that crown lands in the new province were reserved "for the purposes of the Dominion." The same principle was applied in 1905 to Saskatchewan and Alberta when they, after much difficulty, also won provincial status. British Columbia maintained control of its resources on entry to Canada in 1871, presumably because no one in Ottawa would have dared to try to take away what was already won.

The eventual success of the three provinces in obtaining control of their own resources probably had more to do with political clout than the merits of the matter. In 1901, only 8% of Canada's population lived in the Prairies, but by 1931 the number had grown to almost 25%. More than 300,000 farms were using 60 million acres of improved prairie land by 1931. As V.C. Fowke notes, by 1929 the country was exporting an average of one million bushels of wheat per day, having a total value that year of half a billion dollars. Some still argue the transfer symbolized the end of the establishment phase of the first National Policy. Many weary Westerners concluded at the time that the real reason Ottawa transferred land and resources was because Ottawa felt neither was worth keeping. In Fowke's words: "The remaining natural resources which were transferred to the prairie provinces in 1930 would not have tempted any railway company, nor any hard-bitten farmer from Ontario, or scarcely even the unsuspecting immigrant."

Between 1918 and 1920, Manitoba's provincial government had, once again, unsuccessfully attempted to obtain a transfer. W.L. Morton noted that one of the obstacles in that period was the claim to compensation by the governments of the provinces which already owned their resources if the prairie provinces received theirs; a second was the demand for compensation by all three prairie provinces for the loss of their lands. Only when a federal Royal Commission finally reported favourably on the issue in 1929 ("the railways had been built and the lands settled"), was the transfer made and modest compensation paid. "After two generations of subordination to the needs of Canadian nation-building," Morton wrote, "the once small province of 1870 had come into its own. Sprung from resistance to Canadian authority; blocked in its hopes of expansion into a great mid-western province, it had seemed doomed to play the part of the 'Cinderella of the Confederation'."

In the two sister prairie provinces, feelings ran equally high on the resources issue. The *Calgary Herald* described the Laurier government's 1905 refusal to accord Alberta and Saskatchewan equality with the original provinces on the resources issue as an "autonomy that insults the West." To this day, some prairie Canadians believe that this act of gross discrimination by Ottawa demonstrated clearly that the West was regarded as an exploitable colony. It is with this sorry historical background that prairie residents judge contemporary slights such as the awarding of the CF-18 contract.

Ontario Beats Manitoba

The Manitoba-Ontario boundary dispute, which has surprisingly been very little examined as a historical subject, is instructive. When it became the "postage stamp" province in 1870, Manitoba consisted of the small area around the Red River Settlement. Being without land or resources, it was simply not viable. John A. Macdonald's government, returned to office in 1878 after defeating the Liberal one of Alexander Mackenzie, was sympathetic, and extended Manitoba's western boundary to its present location and northward to the fifty-second parallel. A board of arbitration appointed by Mackenzie had accepted Ontario premier Oliver Mowat's view that the Manitoba-Ontario boundary should be west of Lake of the Woods, but Macdonald refused to ratify the finding.

The case was in fact strong for extending the eastern boundary of Manitoba to a north-south line in the vicinity of the present location of Thunder Bay. The prime minister championed this location against the Ontario Liberal premier partly because he wanted to keep federal control of the rich timber and mineral resources west of Thunder Bay. If Mowat won the region, Ontario alone would inevitably own the resources. In addition, as Ina Elizabeth Hutchison pointed out in a 1986 thesis written on the dispute, the Red River Basin clearly extended "to approximately fifty miles west of [Thunder Bay] at Lac des Mille Lacs," and the original Selkirk Grant from the Hudson's Bay Company included Kenora and well beyond. The fact that Ottawa had purchased from the Hudson's Bay Company all the land drained by rivers flowing into Hudson's Bay (which watershed ended at Lac des Mille Lacs) was also in Manitoba's favour.

Ontario's claim to the land mass west of Thunder Bay was historically weak on other grounds as well. The western boundary of Quebec had been defined in the Quebec Act of 1774 as "running 'northward' from the junction of the Ohio and Mississippi Rivers," a point which lay well to the east of Thunder Bay. Both the Constitutional Act of 1791 and the Union Act of 1840 put the Ontario boundary at an identical location, a little west of Thunder Bay: presumably at Lac des Mille Lacs. In short, the eventually successful Ontario claim to the large territory reaching to the present location of Manitoba-Ontario boundary was anything but firm at the beginning of the dispute.

The completion of the CPR rail line to Lake of the Woods and the discovery of gold near the present site of Kenora brought an influx of approximately 1,000 miners and rail workers to the region by the late 1870's. Premier John Norquay of Manitoba was moved by the resulting liquor-induced violence in 1881 to incorporate the disputed area as far east as Kenora (then known as Rat Portage) as part of Manitoba with Prime Minister Macdonald's blessing. A more determined Manitoba premier would have sought to include most if not all lands as far east as Thunder Bay, especially given that the federal Dominion Act passed the same year said, in effect, that the western boundary of Ontario was the eastern boundary of Manitoba.

In any event, as of 1881 the governments of both Manitoba and Ontario were policing the Kenora district. A general riot erupted in the summer of 1883 when constables representing the two provincial governments attempted to arrest one another. Norquay himself went to Kenora with his provincial police to arrest the persons who had broken into Manitoba's local jail. Both governments held provincial elections on September 28 that fall and the same voters elected two representatives for the same district, one going west to the legislature in Winnipeg, the other east to Queen's Park in Toronto. Finally, a truce was called and a joint Manitoba-Ontario Commission attempted unsuccessfully to administer the region for a period before the boundary issue was sent off to Britain for the Judicial Committee of the Privy Council to resolve.

Mowat won the case for Ontario in 1884 before the Committee, whose members knew little or nothing about the issues or terrain. More accurately, the counsel for the governments of Manitoba and Canada lost it through lack of preparation and incompetent advocacy. Mowat, who was familiar with both British legal circles and the issues of the case, prudently had a map prepared which was very favourable to Ontario's position. Even counsel opposing Ontario fell into the trap of referring the jurists to it. Once the map was in effect accepted by everyone, Ontario's case was all but won. In 1889, Macdonald reluctantly confirmed the Privy Council decision and extended Ontario to Lake of the Woods and James Bay. The final Manitoba-Ontario boundary to Hudson's Bay was finally set in 1912. The entire issue ended Manitoba's historic ties with Thunder Bay and plainly constituted another put-down of Manitobans. In Morton's words, "It ended, moreover, the possibility of Manitoba's becoming a great central province in Confederation with an east to west orientation... the developing tradition of grievance was reinforced."

Once again, Ottawa had let down the West on a matter of major importance. Even today, many Kenora residents consider themselves residents of Western Canada.

More Than Full Term Babies

The births of Alberta and Saskatchewan are inseparable from that of Frederick Haultain, who has been portrayed earlier in this book as a Western Canadian giant. One of his major goals in public life was to achieve provincial status for the vast North-West Territories lying between the present western boundaries of Manitoba and British Columbia. As chairman of the territorial assembly based in Regina from 1892 to 1905, he was both premier and the region's most respected elected politician for all of that period.

The pressures for provincial status within the North-West came from every direction and group in the region. The regional population had grown enormously in the 1890's. The territorial treasury was severely strained by new demands for all manner of services, including roads and schools. Only provincial status could provide residents with a chance to obtain larger federal grants; the existing government lacked even the power to borrow money. Once the issue managed to catch the attention of the national political parties, real progress was made: Robert Borden committed his Conservatives to establishing provincial status in 1902; Laurier his Liberals in 1904.

Haultain favoured one strong and large province for the region and became convinced that the movement for two provinces stemmed mainly from the ambitions of some Edmontonians and Calgarians to have a provincial capital. The proposal of his cabinet to Prime Minister Laurier in 1901 was for one province going as far north as the 57th parallel. When four years passed without even a reply from Laurier, Haultain went to the capital for a conference in early 1905. The re-elected Laurier indicated to Haultain a preference for two provinces and rejected his demand that crown lands and natural resources must belong to the new province or provinces. Friesen suggests an explanation: "The decision to retain the lands in 1870 may have been prompted by

70

Macdonald's distrust of the Métis; no such excuse was available in 1905. Presumably, the wishes of [Interior Minister Clifford] Sifton and his federal bureaucracy had prevailed over British constitutional practices.''

Haultain found it unthinkable that the entire jurisdiction for education, a very sensitive issue, would not be transferred to the new provincial government by the British North America Act. Laurier's bills provided for separate schools, which did not then exist in the North-West. Clifford Sifton, one of Laurier's stronger ministers and a Westerner, resigned from Cabinet over the issue.

Two weeks of unsatisfactory negotiations ended when bills providing for the creation of Alberta and Saskatchewan north to 57 degrees, essentially in their present form, were introduced by Laurier. Each contained about 6% of the total land mass of Canada because the national government felt that one big province of 506,985 square miles would have been too large. This was nonsense, of course, as Haultain's biographer Grant MacEwan pointed out, because Ontario and Quebec at the time already respectively had 10.7 and 15.4% of our total land area and ''the senior government had no such hesitation some years later in authorizing extensions of provincial boundaries for both Quebec and Ontario.'' Gerald Friesen concluded that Laurier simply did not want to grant Haultain, who had supported Borden's Conservatives in 1904, the premiership of a single, large western province. Friesen writes: ''Far better, the prime minister reasoned, to create two provinces of equal size divided by the fourth meridian, and to ensure that the Liberal party controlled at least one of the governments.''

Haultain put his objections to the proposed legislation in a letter to Laurier before he left Ottawa. He objected strongly to the formation of two provinces because of the ''consequent duplication of machinery and institutions. The provincial machinery is elaborate and expensive and is more suitable for large areas and large populations. The Territories have for a number of years been under one government and legislature, performing most of the duties and exercising many of the more important powers of provincial governments and legislatures. There has never been any suggestion that the territorial machinery was in any way inadequate for the purposes for which it was created.'' He was particularly concerned about the provision for separate schools because, as he wrote, ''your proposition was not laid before my [western] colleagues and me until noon of the day on which you introduced the bill. Up to this time, the question had not received any attention beyond a casual reference on the previous Friday.''

The outrage of the western representatives at Laurier's refusal to turn over natural resources and crown lands to the two new provinces was equally acute. MacEwan quotes Haultain as saying on his return to the West, ''The Government has been acting like a big pig trying to keep the little pigs from the trough.'' The new provinces were to be denied even the right to control water running across their territory. Haultain had warned the federal government that its policy would cause division in Western Canada. MacEwan notes that his warning came well ahead of a time in which some Westerners would even talk about political separation.

More abuse from Ottawa was still to come even as the seventh and eight provinces opened their new eyes. A few days before the inauguration ceremonies in each, Ottawa announced that the lieutenant governor of Saskatchewan would be A.E. Forget; Alberta's, G.H.V. Bulyea — both friends of Laurier and having Liberal leanings. In the presence of Governor General Earl Grey, the prime minister and approximately twenty thousand instant Albertans, Bulyea took his oath of office in Edmonton. The same process was repeated with Forget three days later in Regina. There were plenty of flowery speeches in each new capital but as MacEwan, himself a one-time federal Liberal candidate in Manitoba and leader of the Alberta Liberal party, writes: ''In the list of speakers [in Regina] on that historic day there was one amazing omission: the name of the long-time premier of the North-West Territories, the man with the best claim to statesmanship was conspicuously absent.'' It was true that Haultain, who believed in non-partisan governments in the territorial and provincial legislatures, had attended a Conservative convention at Moose Jaw in 1903, but this display of malicious and petty partisanship by the prime minister in 1905 was thought outrageous by many Western Canadians.

More pettiness was still to come when Bulyea chose as first Alberta premier Alexander Rutherford of Strathcona. All four of his choices for provincial cabinet ministers were, like himself, Liberals. In Saskatchewan, Forget outrageously chose Walter Scott as provincial premier instead of the man who had served as premier for 13 years, doubtless for the reason that Scott was first, last and always a Liberal. The two new premiers were victorious in the subsequent elections. Friesen notes that an ''army of Liberal homestead inspectors and highway supervisors no doubt assisted the two Liberal governments to convincing victories in the 1905 elections....'' Before the Saskatchewan Liberal jugger-naut, which won 16 seats, Haultain's provincial rights' group only managed to win nine. A bad taste was left in many Western mouths by the political tactics Ottawa had sent West. Indeed, W.L. Morton noted that two decades later it was precisely this sort of ''machine politics which the Progressives hoped to de-stroy, politics rendered noisome by the corruption arising from the scramble for the resources of the West, and the political ruthlessness of the professional politicians of the day.''

Regional Political Parties

A number of political parties have emerged in the West in recent years, most to disappear quickly without trace. Many if not all of them were inspired by the spectacular, if short-lived, success of the Progressive party in the West during the 1920's. The movement deserves a closer look.

The leading authority on the Progressive movement in Western Canada, W.L. Morton, concluded that it was both an economic protest to Macdonald's National Policy of 1878 and a political revolt against the two old parties, both of which were perceived by many Western Canadians to be equally committed to main-taining the high tariff and other basic features of the Old National Policy. Many prairie wheat farmers who had begun by clearing trees and breaking the soil felt engulfed by railway charges, interest rates, elevator rates and crop costs by the 1918-1921 period. The tariff was the most visible feature of the National Policy and, as Morton noted, ''it became the symbol of the wheat growers' exploitation and frustration, alleged and actual.'' When the Laurier government, elected in 1896, repudiated the Liberals' earlier low tariff policy and appeared to appropriate all of Macdonald's National Policy for itself, many western wheat growers decided that both national parties were ''organized hypocrisies dedicated to getting and holding office.''

The climate in the West for both old national parties deteriorated even further when a three-level tariff was completed by Laurier's government in 1909. When the prime minister returned to his party's low tariff position in the reciprocity election of 1911, the strain, as Morton notes, was ''too severe for a party which had become committed as deeply as its rival to the National Policy.'' The defectors to the Conservatives included Clifford Sifton who had until 1905 been the second most influential Liberal in the entire country. In the West, the Conservative party in both Alberta and Saskatchewan was wrecked by its high tariff stance in 1911, and in fact began a long-term decline in all three prairie provinces. Agriculture dominated most aspects of life in the prairie West during the first third of the twentieth century, and in the decade after the 1911 setback, many grain farmers still wanted Ottawa to accept Washington's offer of reciprocity, which remained on statute books there until 1921.

Another factor favouring the creation of a new party on the Prairies was the arrival after 1896 of thousands of Americans from the Midwest who were well versed in third parties and the influential farmers' organizations south of the boundary. Immigrants from the United Kingdom who were well schooled in protest politics provided both a language and much of the organizational effort toward an occupational and doctrinal, but thoroughly democratic, third party. Morton believed that the Progressive Movement was an authentic expression of ''Jacksonian, Clear-Grit democracy, reinforced by American populism and English radicalism,'' and based on a difference between the political temper of Central Canada and that of the Prairies. The first, he wrote, ''is Whiggish. Government there rests on compact, the vested and legal rights of provinces, of minorities, of corporations. The political temper of the West, on the other hand, is democratic; government there rests on the will of the sovereign people, a will direct, simple and no respecter of rights except those demonstrably and momentarily popular.'' Morton's view of western politics is probably equally true today.

Laurier's hold on the support, if not the personal affections, of many Western Canadians collapsed during the 1917 national election. It was the first since 1911 because of the outbreak of World War I in 1914 which had caused an extension of the Parliament elected six years earlier. Virtually its sole issue was whether conscription was necessary to win a grisly war. Certainly, the win-at-any-cost philosophy of the all-party Union government of Robert Borden, including its War-Time Elections Act, which both enfranchised the female relations of soldiers on active service and disenfranchised many citizens of foreign birth or first language, helped create the Unionist majority of 71 MPs. Unionist candidates won 57% of all votes cast across the country. Some Liberal MPs supporting conscription both joined Borden's cabinet and ran as Union candidates in the election.

In Western Canada, Laurier's view that voluntary enlistment would work, if given a genuinely fair choice, was unacceptable to many despite the warm welcome he received during his western tour in the dying days of the election campaign. His promise to remove duties on farm implements was largely swamped in the West by the manpower issue, especially when, as Murray Beck reminds us, the Unionist Minister of the Militia and Defence asserted that he would himself see to it that ''farmers' sons who are honestly engaged in the production of food will be exempt from military service.'' All four premiers in Western Canada, each a Liberal, had become Unionists. When Arthur Sifton, premier of Alberta, Thomas Crerar, president of the United Grain Growers, and J. A Calder, a Saskatchewan cabinet minister, entered the Union cabinet, Laurier's low-tariff commitment lost most of its impact. In Saskatchewan, for example, Calder took the entire Liberal organization over to Unionists. In consequence, only two of 57 western constituencies returned Liberals in 1917.

How did the Progressive party manage to elect 39 of its 64 MPs from Western Canada in the 1921 election? W.L. Morton's answer is probably the best: the Union government created the necessary conditions for an independent political party. "The electorate of the West," wrote Morton in 1950, "came out of the election of 1917 purged of old party loyalties. It had undergone a political emancipation, and thereafter the old traditional ties of party were to remain permanently weak across the West." It is, of course, unclear whether this analysis is applicable in the remaining years of the twentieth century.

Morton concluded that the serious price-inflation across Canada following the conclusion of the 1914-18 war, which had been fought without price or wage controls, was another major cause of the Progressive Movement. Rising post-war prices, he wrote, were the root of the "general unrest of the day, and the influence of the Russian Revolution, the radical tone of many organizations and individuals, the Winnipeg strike, and the growth of the labour movement are to be ascribed to inflation rather than to any native predisposition to radical courses." A second factor, according to Morton, was the revocation during 1918 of the order-in-council exempting farmers' sons from military service, which invoked "a bitter outcry from the farmers, the great delegation to Ottawa in May, 1918, and an abiding resentment against the Union government and all its works...." Two further nails in the coffin of the Unionists in Western Canada were the severe prairie drought in the years 1918 to 1921 and the refusal of the Borden government to continue the Wheat Board beyond 1920, an element of national policy designed, for once, to assist prairie farmers.

During 1918, a number of farm organizations adopted "The New National Policy" which rejected the National Policy of 1878 and demanded large reductions in tariffs. In mid-1919, when the Borden government refused to reduce tariffs, T.A. Crerar and ten other farmer MPs broke ranks with the cabinet and in early 1920 formed the National Progressive Party. Arthur Meighen, a Westerner by adoption but protectionist by conviction, succeeded Robert Borden as prime minister for the 1921 general election, but all of these factors ensured a Progressive near-sweep in the West when Meighen in effect attempted to make protection the sole issue in the campaign. In Morton's words, "Prime Minister Meighen, first of those western men with eastern principles to be called to head the Conservative party, put on the full armour of protection and fought the western revolt in defense of the National Policy.... His party attacked the Progressives as free traders seeking to destroy the National Policy for selfish class advantage. Mr. W.L.M. King stood firmly on the Liberal platform of 1919, which, marvelously contrived, faced squarely all points of the political compass at once." The Progressives, with 64 seats, beat Meighen's Conservatives by 14 and would have become the Official Opposition in the House if they had opted to do so. Thirty-nine of 57 western and northern seats were won by the party.

It is interesting that the Progressives on the Prairies chose to root out the old parties at the provincial levels as well. Partly, says Morton, it was out of the conviction that defeating machine politics in Ottawa required beating the old parties in their citadels in the provinces. In both Alberta and Saskatchewan, Liberal governments had ruled since 1905 but the Progressives regarded them, in Morton's words, as "examples of the machine politics which Progressives hoped to destroy." In Saskatchewan, the Liberal administration of William Martin survived the Progressive tide of 1920-21 by severing its ties for the time being with the federal party. In Alberta, however, the United Farmers of Alberta under Henry Wise Wood won a majority of the seats in the Alberta legislature in 1921 as a farmers' only party. In Manitoba, the United Farmers of Manitoba won the largest number of seats, if not a majority, in the 1922 provincial election.

FOUR

Emily Murphy
Person For All Seasons

THE STATURE OF EMILY MURPHY as a Western Canadian giant has grown in recent years. A recent biographer, Christine Mander, in *Emily Murphy: Rebel*, concludes she was an individual "for all seasons" and this is probably the best explanation. Beyond any doubt, she was unique, someone whose inner force no part of Canada or any nation produces in either sex more than once or twice in a generation. Among her many roles were those of a judge; wife, mother and neighbour; crusader for equal rights; author and journalist; and social reformer extraordinaire. Her story embodies a large measure of the determination exhibited by so many individuals who settled in the West.

She was born Emily Ferguson in 1868 at Cookstown, about 60 miles north of Toronto, and raised in a tradition-minded and prosperous home. Her father, Isaac, had arrived from Ireland at the age of twelve, stepping ashore with his mother, who had been widowed on the trip across the Atlantic, and five other children. Her mother, Emily Gowan, was also from an Irish-Canadian family, whose patriarch, Ogle R. Gowan, was a twenty-seven year member of the provincial parliament and the founder of the Orange Order in Canada.

All of the six Ferguson children were raised on an estate with access to ponies and other luxuries. Their parents insisted on equal sharing of household duties, and all were taught to write and speak well. Emily particularly enjoyed tree climbing, sucker and sunfish fishing and cricket. She was known as "Sunshine." Three of her brothers would become lawyers and the fourth, Gowan, a doctor. She performed as a youthful actress in their Conservative home in front of visitors such as Sir John A. Macdonald and Sir Charles Tupper. Mander sums up her early family life as being one of "affluence, accomplishment, affection and high ideals."

At fifteen, Emily was sent as a boarder to the fashionable Bishop Strachan School for Girls in Toronto. She was homesick initially, but soon became an earnest and capable student, assisted considerably by an extraordinarily good memory which would serve her well throughout her life. One day, two of her brothers came by the school to introduce her to Arthur Murphy, the man who would become her future husband, who was eleven years her senior. Murphy, who was studying for the Anglican ministry, had decided earlier as a neighbour of the Fergusons that he wanted to marry Emily. He instigated the first meeting and then persisted in his efforts to win her. They met as frequently as possible despite the school rules forbidding such meetings. On their first encounter, he said, "Hurry and grow up so I can marry you." Although Emily evidently continued to fall in love with others over the next four years, she would insist many years afterwards that "there was never anyone, really, but Arthur." They were married at an elegant wedding the summer after she graduated and established their first of several homes near Lake Simcoe where Arthur had his first parish church.

The nineteen-year-old bride threw herself into the role of minister's wife: Bible classes, the presidency of the missionary society, playing the organ and organizing bazaars. She was, as she later noted, "acquiring a stability that fitted me for half a dozen other duties." Over the next decade, there were other moves for the family in south-western Ontario. At a church in Chatham, which had earlier been a refuge for blacks fleeing American slavery, she spoke out for understanding. Three daughters had arrived by the time they left Chatham, Kathleen, Evelyn and Madeleine, but Madeleine, who had been born prematurely when her mother walking down the stairs tripped over her nightgown, left heartbroken parents when she died at nine months. The next move was to a church at Ingersoll, where the Murphys' fourth daughter, Doris, was born. Emily, now 25 years old, was becoming more independent. She joined firmly on the affirmative side in a raging controversy on the issue of women serving on church vestries, arguing that "women could contribute much to the administrative body of the church." Also at about this time she entered what she herself termed "the loneliest place on the curve of her religious life," when she found herself deeply involved in a skeptical phase of her intellectual development. Her honesty, which was characteristic of her entire approach to life, continued both to bind people to her with hoops of iron and to vex her opponents.

She began to use her gifts with words and prodigious memory to help Arthur with his sermons. Life for the family was full and good until the day Arthur's bishop asked him to become a missionary in Ontario without either a set salary or a home. For the next two years, the entire family moved about from parish to parish. With time on her hands, Emily began to nibble on sweets, little knowing that diabetes would later strike her and probably contribute to her death. The missionary years opened her eyes to the very bad social conditions of the Ontario poor. She began to write about what she saw in her diaries; these entries would later became the basis for numerous articles.

In mid-1898, the Murphys eagerly accepted an invitation to preach in England. On board ship, while enduring patronizing comments about Canadians from English and American passengers, Emily resolved that in future she would write under the name "Janey Canuck," that being the female equivalent of "Johnny Canuck." In Liverpool and later in the East End of London, she was deeply disturbed by even worse conditions than she had seen in south-western Ontario: prostitutes, beggars, and "poverty-distorted children."

In late 1899, the Murphy family crossed back to Canada. Emily was extremely happy to be home: "... once more in the first, best country, God's fairest gift to man – the land of the Maple." The couple bought a home in Toronto, and Arthur continued to do missionary work with a comfortable salary paid from England. A mood of buoyancy came to both Canada and Britain with the succession of the dour Queen Victoria by her fun-loving son, Edward. Emily's first book, *The Impressions of Janey Canuck Abroad*, was published and became an immediate success in Britain and Canada. She soon became a regular contributor to a popular magazine, *National Monthly of Canada*, and eventually became Women's Editor. One piece she wrote at the time pleaded for the suspension of the ban on immigrants to Canada from China.

In 1902, Arthur and then Emily contracted typhoid, which brought them close to death. But both recovered and Arthur secured a church near his family's farm where his mother sought to restore some meat to his bones. While he was gone, six-year-old Doris caught the dreaded diphtheria and died just after asking her mother to sing her favourite hymn, "The Little Lord Jesus." Her mother's grief knew no limits when they buried her next to Madeleine at Cookstown.

With the catastrophe a little behind them, the Murphys accepted a medical opinion that Arthur should seek exercise, fresh air, and a changed environment. Emily reluctantly agreed to move to Swan River (population 1,300) in north-western Manitoba where Arthur had earlier bought some timber land. Leaving their remaining two girls at a boarding school in Toronto, the couple in 1903 joined the international sea of humanity sweeping into the Prairies. Her first impressions of bustling Winnipeg, the urban gate through which virtually every newcomer was then obliged to enter Western Canada, were extremely favourable.

She wrote: "How the sun shines here in Winnipeg! One drinks it in like wine. And how the bells ring! It is a town of bells and light set in a blaze of gold. Surely the West is golden – the Sky, flowers, wheat, hearts.

"Winnipeg is changing from wood to stone. She is growing city-like in granite and asphalt. Hitherto, banks and hotels were run up overnight, and had to pay for themselves in the next twenty-four hours.

"Winnipeg has something western, something southern, something quite her own. She is an up-and-doing place. She has swagger, impelling arrogance, enterprise, and an abiding spirit of usefulness....

"On the streets of Winnipeg, there are people who smile at you in English, but speak in Russian. There are rushful, pushful people from 'the States', stiff-tongued Germans, ginger-headed Icelanders, Galacians, Norwegians, Poles and Frenchmen, all of whom are rapidly becoming irreproachably Canada. In all there are sixty tongues in the pot....

"Every Mother's son of them is a compendium of wordly wisdom and a marvel of human experience. What more does any country want?"

Swan River, at the time two days by train beyond Winnipeg, must have been a severe disappointment for the newcomers, but Emily tried everything — even duck shooting. One day at forty-eight below zero, they set forth in a horse-drawn sleigh to inspect the timber field, spending the night at a Doukhobor village. While in camp, Emily met a number of Cree and Chippewa Indians, gaining a respect for their independence and forest skills.

Gradually, Arthur's timber operation began to produce some income and he made more money in land speculations. Emily began to review books for *The Winnipeg Tribune* newspaper as well as sending pieces to *The National Monthly*. Her work in helping to manage the timber operation, which soon included five employees and seventeen horses, kept her away from the "Votes for Women" issue which in 1906 was beginning to preoccupy fellow western women, such as Winnipeg's Nellie McClung. Four years later, when Arthur decided to seek new business opportunities further west in Edmonton, Emily was not in the least sorry. She had experienced enough of bitter cold, wolves and bears. She longed for the "sweet security of streets, the pushing crowds, the call of the latest editions, the velvety sweep of feet, the whir of the automobile, the glare of the stage, the long rows of horses, and all else that once I hated."

The years 1907-1916 in Edmonton were golden ones for the entire Murphy family, and Emily became a convinced Westerner. As the new capital of a new province, Edmonton's population was diverse and growing rapidly from the eighteen thousand there when the Murphys arrived.

Arthur engaged in coal mining and later speculated in city real estate. Kathleen and Evelyn were rapidly growing up when their mother first took aim at the dower issue. Under the Alberta law of the time, a husband could legally sell his land and pocket the proceeds without sharing a dime with his wife and children. Emily quickly marshalled the facts of the issue, wrote articles and otherwise started the campaign rolling across the province. Several times, the provincial legislature turned down a Dower Bill to award a third of common property in a marriage to wives, but finally passed it in 1911. Many Albertans were delighted with the success of Emily's campaign.

During this time and until 1912, she was literary editor of *The Winnipeg Telegram*. She also completed in 1910 her next book, *Janey Canuck in the West*, which was such a success that it remains in print today. Becoming the first woman member of the Edmonton hospital board, she filed a devastating report on the conditions of a local hospital. She became president of the Canadian Women's Press Club. She published two more books, *Open Trails* in 1912, and *Seeds of Pine* in 1914, both of which sold well. She later reported for *Collier's Magazine* on a five-day steamer trip up the Athabasca river to Lesser Slave Lake. In 1911, she became a good friend of Emmeline Pankhurst, the English suffragette, during her second North American speaking tour. When Nellie McClung, founder of the Political Equality League in Winnipeg, moved to the Alberta capital in 1914, she and Emily became friends and allies in the cause. They had the satisfaction in 1916 of seeing Alberta become the third province in the nation to provide the franchise to women. The Canadian frontier was establishing itself as fertile soil for democratic reforms.

In 1916, urged by the local Council of Women, Emily went to the office of the Alberta Attorney General, C.W. Cross, to request him to establish a women's criminal court presided over by a woman. Soon afterwards, she was appointed by the provincial Liberal government of Arthur Sifton to be the first female judge in what is now the Commonwealth. Congratulations flowed into an ecstatic Murphy home from seemingly everywhere. The new police magistrate was soon studying books of court procedure and law. Her first anxious day in court, which she later said with her characteristic good humour, was "as pleasant an experience as running rapids without a guide," was a unique experience. The police and lawyers, being unsure what to call her, mostly called her "Sir."

On that very first day, defense counsel Eardley Jackson objected to her right to hear his client's case because she was not 'a person' within the meaning of the relevant statutes. He was in effect arguing that the nineteenth century English common law, which astonishingly had ruled that women were persons in matters of pains and penalties but not in matters of rights and privileges, barred her from being a judge. Emily noted the objection without ruling on it and heard his case. The Alberta Supreme Court later ended the dispute, but only within the provincial boundaries, when it ruled that no judge could be disqualified from holding public office on account of sex.

This was scarcely the end of the obstacles to her successful judicial career in the Women's Court. People opposed to her appointment created frequent annoyances. For example, she would arrive at her court to find that it was booked to another judge. She faced all such attacks with dignity, firmness and good humour, knowing that her enemies were hoping for an over-reaction or other mistake with which they could berate both her and all of her sex as judges.

She was by no means unduly lenient with accused members of her own sex. She spoke bluntly about the difficulty in obtaining convictions against female law-breakers, noting that often "the woman's part is that of complicity. She instigates the crime, receives the goods after the man has stolen them, procures the girl for his immoral purposes, or carries the noxious drugs which he disposes of. It was probably an observer of this combination who gave expression to the odious dictum 'cherchez la femme'.'' In time, she became a good judge.

Another problem she met in the courts, narcotic drug trafficking, affected her deeply. Her studies on the subject, which indicated that Canada on a per capita basis led the world in 1919 in narcotic drug trafficking, became a series of articles in *Maclean's* magazine, subsequently published together in 1922 as *The Black Candle*. It became a text book in the Narcotics Division of the League of Nations.

Her best known crusade was establishing that women were persons for the purpose of appointments to the Senate. The British North America Act provided that ''Properly qualified persons may from time to time be summoned to the Senate.'' On what constituted qualification, it said only that a senator must ''be a British citizen, at least thirty years of age, and possess four thousand dollars in real property.'' As absurd as it now seems, she and her supporters were obliged to do battle off and on for twelve full years before triumphing. The first skirmish occurred in 1917 when she allowed some Alberta women to put her name forward as a candidate for the Senate to Prime Minister Robert Borden. Borden rejected both her name and those of other women on the basis that under Canadian law women were simply not ''persons.'' In 1921, his successor as prime minister, Arthur Meighen, rejected a request by the Montreal Women's Club to appoint Emily to the Senate, saying that government lawyers said that it was impossible to nominate a woman. In 1922, she herself wrote to the new prime minister, Mackenzie King, asking for an appointment. King did nothing but declare his good intentions about a possible amendment to the BNA Act during his second period as prime minister between 1926 and 1930.

In 1927, one of Emily's lawyer brothers, Bill, noticed that a provision of the Supreme Court of Canada Act then gave to any five interested persons the right to petition the federal government to seek a ruling from the Supreme Court of Canada on a constitutional issue. The four others she recruited were Nellie McClung (a school teacher, homemaker, MLA for five years until defeated for her pro-prohibition stand in 1926, author, and comrade-in-arms with Emily on issues until her move to Calgary), Louise McKinney (the first female MLA in the Commonwealth and a crusader against alcohol and tobacco), Henrietta Edwards (a social reformer and author of two books on the legal status of women), and Irene Parlby (a former president of the United Farm Women of Alberta, MLA and Minister without portfolio in Alberta for fourteen years).

"The Alberta Five," as they came to be known, signed the petition which would soon be known throughout Canada, in the Murphy home in the late summer of 1927. "Does," it asked simply, "the word persons in section 24 of the BNA Act of 1867 (re senate appointments) include female persons?" The Justice Department in Ottawa quickly accepted the petition and agreed to pay the legal costs of an action in the Supreme Court of Canada of whichever lawyer the five might choose. The highest Canadian court heard their case in the spring of 1928 and woodenly decided that they were obliged to interpret the BNA Act in light of the legal conditions applicable when it was first passed in Britain in 1867. It was then an easy step for the five Canadian judges to hold unanimously that it was not intended for women to sit in the Senate. It was not in Emily's nature to accept defeat; she soon resolved to carry the case through the only stage left: an appeal to the Privy Council in imperial London. It was largely because of her efforts, as her biographer indicates, that the "person case" did not expire at this point. The outcome of the final appeal was hard to predict. The Attorney-General of Alberta supported their position, but counsel for the governments of both Canada and Quebec argued that the earlier decision should be upheld.

The Canadian Press reporter, Lukin Johnson, wired a pithy eyewitness account of the polite legal fight underway at number one, Downing Street: "...five great judges, with the Lord Chancellor of England at their head, and a battery of bewigged lawyers from Canada and from England, are wrestling with a question, propounded on behalf of their sex, by five Alberta women.... Deep and intricate questions of constitutional law are debated back and forth. The exact shade of meaning to be placed on certain words is argued to the finest point. And so it goes on, and probably will continue to go on for several days. At the end of all these endless speeches, lessons on Canadian history, and questions by five great judges of England, will be decided, if one may hazard a guess, that women undoubtedly are Persons. Which one may say, without exaggeration, most of us know already!''

Three months later, on October 18, 1929, the Lord Chancellor, Lord Sankey, strode back to the court to deliver the patently obvious and unanimous decision: women are Persons and are thus able to become Canadian senators. Significant history had been made. Congratulations came to Edmonton from around the province and country. Nellie McClung issued a statement giving the full credit for the victory to Emily, who in turn tactfully declared that in future Canadian women could say '''we' instead of 'you' in affairs of State.''

A public campaign quickly began for the leader of the five to become the first woman senator, but it was not to be. Prime Minister Mackenzie King appointed Cairine Wilson from Ottawa in 1930. The Alberta Five received a bronze plaque in their joint honour in the Senate which was donated in 1938 by the Federation of Business and Professional Womens' Clubs. In addition, since 1979 five awards have been made annually to Canadians who have fought for sexual equality. In fairness to Mackenzie King, it would appear that there was no Alberta vacancy in the Senate in 1929-30 before he lost the general election. There was no excuse whatsoever for his successor as prime minister, R.B. Bennett, also an Albertan, for not supporting Emily (who doubtless wanted the appointment) because an Edmonton vacancy did occur in 1931. It was simply sophistry of the basest kind for Bennett to refuse her on the basis that the new senator must be a Roman Catholic. Years later, an Edmonton senator probably provided the real reason in quipping: ''Oh, we never could have had Mrs. Murphy in the Senate. She would have caused too much trouble. ''

In late 1931, Emily, aged 63 years, retired as a judge, confiding to a friend that she had promised her family that she would retire after fifteen years of service. Policemen, bailiffs, librarians, clerks, reporters, lawyers – all were sorry to see her go. Perhaps sensing that her health was going, she wrote a farewell letter to her family in late 1932 and placed it in her safety deposit box. Twelve months later, when she dropped in to visit a court, she had the quiet satisfaction of hearing Eardley Jackson, her enemy from her first day on the bench, spontaneously salute "the kindly smiling countenance of this beloved lady." That night, October 26, 1933, she died in her sleep. As she had said long ago when her daughter Doris died, "life is lent and not given." Her friend, Nellie McClung, among countless mourners around the world spoke of her "burning love of justice, a passionate desire to protect the weak, and to bring to naught the designs of evil persons."

FIVE

The Pattern Continues

Western Alienation in the
1970's and 1980's

*T*HE WEST'S EXPERIENCE in Confederation has centred on protest, disappointment and constant indications that Canada's parliamentary system of government is tilted in favour of Ontario and Quebec. The subordination of the West persists and Westerners in the 1980's feel as strongly about it as our parents and grandparents did, possibly the only difference being our increasing determination to affect politics, to be more vocal, to get things changed at last.

The reality of our political system is that Central Canada is where national elections are won or lost. Successive federal governments have thus tended to identify the interests of the voters living in Central Canada with those of all Canadians. In late 1987, Ontario Industry Minister Monte Kwinter, while criticizing Canada's proposed free trade agreement with the United States, asserted: "... if it's a bad deal for Ontario, by extension it's a bad deal for Canada." His quip indicated that little had changed in a century-old attitude held by many Ontarians that what is good for them is also good for Canada as a whole. How can Canadian federalism preserve and protect regional interests and unite Canadians everywhere, if it is constantly undermined by the assertion that what suits one province suits all?

In a speech on "The West in Confederation" last year, I quoted two prominent Westerners to contrast the past and present in our region in terms of expectations, hopes and realities of life. In the mid-1970's, Peter Lougheed described the Western Canada he saw developing: "I think it will be a stronger part of Canada a decade from now, both in terms of population, in terms of distribution of income, in terms of spending in a more balanced industrial economy. I think the West will have more confidence and hopefully more input into decision-making nationally.... Canada will be a stronger nation, because we'll be a stronger West."

The Edmonton publisher and western nationalist Ted Byfield described our region's situation in mid-1987 thus: "...something is grievously wrong in Western Canada. Farmers can't afford to seed their crops, mines are closed, oil rigs lie derelict, shipyards are idle, food banks are besieged, the savings of many lifetimes have vanished, homes have lost their value, and a host of unemployed burst the welfare rolls of every town and city. "

The creation of the Reform Party of Canada in the West under the slogan "The West wants in" reflects the disillusionment of some Westerners with all three traditional parties. It is also another cry of frustration from a forgotten child of Confederation. Earlier efforts to bring the region fully into national decision-making have failed, for some Westerners at least. Central Canadians, they say, will not even try to understand western alienation. There are, and always have been, more important matters of national interest to most residents of Canada's heartland.

A number of issues arising in the 1970's and 1980's ominously increased western discontent with the federal government. The following is a discussion of some selected policies of governments of different political colours that have particularly intensified alienation in Western Canada. Essential to western objections to all of them was the conviction that each was decided by a central government, centrally controlled, for the benefit of the centre – Ontario or Quebec or both — and imposed by Ottawa on the western provinces regardless of the legitimate needs and wishes of Western Canadians.

Energy Blitzkrieg

It is often forgotten now that the national Liberal party was historically strong in Western Canada; as recently as the 1953 election, it won 27 of 59 western seats. Pierre Trudeau and his Just Society and One Canada, blended with his iconoclastic personal style, were attractive to many Westerners during the 1968 election campaign. Trudeaumania in fact won for the Liberals 16 of 23 seats in B.C., 4 of 19 in Alberta, 2 of 13 in Saskatchewan, 5 of 13 in Manitoba and the only seat in the Northwest Territories. Winning eleven seats on the Prairies, which during the previous four elections had voted almost as one with John Diefenbaker, provided an excellent opportunity for Pierre Trudeau to break the existing political mold in the West.

How the Liberals destroyed their political base both federally and provincially in Western Canada between 1968 and 1980, when they won but two of the West's seventy-seven constituencies, has been well chronicled. More than anything else, their National Energy Policy (NEP) and constitutional package reinforced the western suspicion that Pierre Trudeau and his party regarded our region as a continuing colony of Central Canada.

In 1974, as the Arab and other oil producing countries began to raise oil prices from about $4 (U.S.) a barrel to $11 and later much higher, oil became the focus of western differences with the Trudeau government. Ottawa's initial response to oil-related events in the world was to impose an export tax on the more than one million barrels of oil a day which Western Canada was selling to the U.S., and to freeze temporarily the domestic price of oil. Alberta premier Peter Lougheed replied that the only reason for exporting oil to the U.S. at all was that, continuously since the 1960's, successive federal governments had refused permission to extend a western oil pipeline to Montreal on the premise that it was a little cheaper for Canadians east of the Ottawa River to buy oil from the Middle East or Venezuela. A consequence of this myopia in Ottawa, argued Lougheed, was that a number of Canadian-owned oil companies which could not afford to operate at other than full capacity had been forced to sell out, mostly to American oil companies.

Lougheed noted that as recently as January of 1973, the federal Energy Minister, Donald Macdonald, had again refused an Alberta government request to extend the oil pipeline with the usual reasoning that it was cheaper to buy offshore oil. "It is my understanding," wrote Macdonald to the Alberta government, "that the relative cost disadvantage of using Western Canadian crude in lieu of offshore crude at Montreal refineries at the present time, is greater than when this matter was considered by the Borden Commission."

"What the federal government said in effect," concluded the Alberta premier, "was that it had weighed Alberta's needs for markets against the economic advantages to Eastern Canada, and decided against us."

On the principle of an export tax on oil itself, Westerners wondered why the non-renewable oil of Alberta and Saskatchewan was the sole Canadian export to be subject to a federal tax, when renewable energy exports such as electricity were not similarly taxed. The federal government's reply was essentially that oil was unique; Westerners, having been discriminated against so often in the past by Ottawa, were mostly unconvinced. At the federal-provincial conference on energy held in Ottawa in January, 1974, the shared scepticism of all three prairie delegations, headed by Peter Lougheed, Edward Schreyer and Allen Blakeney, grew. The federal participants were, among other things, badly prepared. Only Premier Dave Barrett from British Columbia remained apart from the other western premiers. He called, as did the national NDP leader David Lewis, for the gradual nationalization of the Canadian oil industry.

The National Energy Program

The National Energy Program (NEP) was introduced in the House of Commons by Marc Lalonde eight months after the Liberals defeated the Conservatives in the 1980 general election.

The Clark government was thought by many Westerners to have lost the election because of its campaign to move the domestic price of oil and gas toward international levels. Progressive Conservative proposals to soften this by subsidies to farmers and fishermen were doomed from the start by a quixotic proposal in the defeated Crosbie budget to increase taxes on gasoline by 18 cents a gallon at the pump. Most residents of Ontario, Quebec and Atlantic Canada, and some from Western Canada, understandably voted for the more comforting "made-in-Canada" price promised by the Liberals.

The Liberals' NEP contained both an announced and an undeclared set of objectives. The four public ones seemed the soul of reason: greater energy self-sufficiency, conservation, "nation-building" and Canadianization. The unspoken goal was clearly continued Liberal party hegemony in Central Canada at the expense of Western Canadians generally and Albertans in particular.

The program would achieve energy self-sufficiency partly by incentives intended to redirect exploration and development away from the western provinces toward areas in the North and off our coasts, which were controlled by the federal government. This was hazardous because it requires several years to bring an oil well into production and very few commercially-recoverable discoveries have been made in the Beaufort Sea, the Canadian Arctic and off the coast of Newfoundland and Labrador. As these tax incentives were unavailable to foreign-owned firms, a number of companies moved approximately 200 drilling rigs (each employing about 200 persons) to the United States. This caused some observers to conclude that the NEP was not concerned with petroleum self-sufficiency at all. The real goal was for Ottawa to continue to purchase off-shore oil at $37 (U.S.) a barrel as of 1980 from sources such as Libya and Venezuela while at the same time refusing to buy it from a good number of capped western wells for $18 a barrel. When the international price of oil fell in 1982, this view became especially plausible in Western Canada.

The NEP's conservation feature was praised initially in every part of Canada, including the West. Both Western Europe and Japan were demonstrating that nations could reduce their energy consumption without reducing significantly either their manufacturing efficiency or their standard of living. Some of the NEP programs, such as grants for better home insulation and for converting to natural gas heating, were excellent. Unfortunately for the authors of the NEP, price is the major factor determining the amount of oil and gas used by both individuals and commerce. In keeping domestic oil prices across Canada at about half of international levels between 1980 and 1984, the government ensured great waste. A longer term consequence of this cheap energy to both industry and agriculture was that both sectors were able to postpone investing in the more efficient machinery with which competitors around the world were retooling. The future international competitiveness of the exports from every region of Canada was harmed by the NEP.

Defenders of the NEP agree that one of its objectives was to establish the leadership of Ottawa in the energy sector. The means chosen was a bold attempt to create a new community of energy leaders with a primary loyalty to the federal government. This group was to join industrial-financial elites in Toronto and Montreal who have historically identified closely with Ottawa because of various federal measures such as the Bank Act. The NEP was thus profoundly anti-western because until 1980 our energy industry was one of the very few sectors centred in Western Canada. It was, to many Westerners, as if a national government with no elected representation on either coast had told our east- and west-coast fisheries that they should relocate their industry decision-makers to Ottawa.

A major goal of the NEP was the reorganization of energy industry ownership. As other governments of energy-producing nations had done during the 1970's, the NEP took advantage of the rapid rise in world petroleum prices to buy out some foreign-owned parts of the Canadian energy industry. To persuade those unwilling to sell to do so, the NEP went well beyond what other programs of industrial democracies had done. It created tax incentives and prohibitions which favoured locally-owned oil firms. The best known of these was the 25% "back-in" provision through which Ottawa took an automatic fourth of the revenues from any oil or gas discovery made on lands controlled by Ottawa. Among other things, the government of Canada was accused of legislated theft. Following an avalanche of protests when the back-in was initially applied to expensive discoveries already made, compensation for approximately a quarter of such expenditures was made by the government.

During the first ten months of the NEP, the outright discrimination against foreign-owned firms was so successful that foreign ownership dropped from 74% to about 66%. Canadian companies, such as Dome Petroleum, the Canada Development Corporation and Petro-Canada, made huge buy-outs of foreign-owned oil and gas properties. The means used to achieve this Canadianization were judged by the American and British governments to violate Organization for Economic Cooperation and Development (OECD) resolutions on investments, which clearly banned member discrimination against foreign-owned companies. As the American academic Charles Doran put it, "The American counter-response was that Canada was now 'on the varsity', meaning Canada now had full economic summit membership, and it therefore had to abide by the rules that the majority of the OECD countries observed in investment and trade matters." Many foreigners concluded that the NEP was part of a general campaign against foreign investment of any sort.

In many western minds, the key goal of the NEP was to keep Central Canada on the Liberal side of the political fence by pursuing a consumer-oriented oil strategy. Rather than creating a policy which attempted to balance the interests of both the producing West and the consuming East, Trudeau's government came down all but entirely on the consumer side. The Liberal party, having learned to govern with virtually no representation from the West, wished to be seen as the defender of Central Canada regardless of economic consequences in Western Canada. Indeed Marc Lalonde in a candid moment later confessed: "The major factor behind the NEP wasn't Canadianization or getting more from the industry or even self-sufficiency. The determinant factor was the fiscal imbalance between the provinces and the federal government.... Our proposal was to increase Ottawa's share appreciably, so that the share of the producing provinces would decline significantly and the industry's share would decline somewhat." The Calgary economist Robert Mansell has calculated that the artificially low domestic price of oil since the early 1970's cost Albertans approximately $60 billion.

The results were devastating. The number of oil wells drilled throughout Canada dropped from 9,188 in 1980 to 7,186 in 1981, and the number of drilling rigs in service across Canada fell from 650 to 450 fairly soon after the NEP was introduced. Thousands of jobs in Western Canada were lost, primarily in the drilling and service sectors of the energy industry. Proposed mega-projects such as the Alsands plant at Fort McMurray were cancelled. Numerous western businesses went into bankruptcy. Many careers and families were broken; home mortgages were foreclosed in large numbers. The respected *Economist* magazine of Britain during the summer of 1982 summed up the NEP in politely brutal language: "The NEP has come close to wrecking an industry that until October, 1980 was drilling like fury finding enormous volumes of gas and much new oil, creating jobs and investment all over Canada and increasingly using Canadian-owned capacity in exploration and management.... The NEP drove Canadian exploration and service companies into the United States until only 150 drilling rigs were left, the lowest number since the 1960's deCanadianization, in effect. Owners of capped-in gas wells had big debts and no cash flow. Oil serving companies in Alberta withered into bankruptcy."

The NEP was loathed even by Western Canadians who had no direct daily contact with the energy industry. It provided a major impetus to both separation and alienation sentiments in the West. As a federal program which blatantly discriminated against the western provinces, maintained the domestic price of conventional oil and gas resources at about half the world price, and subsidized the consumption of imported oil, it probably dashed for a generation the political hopes of federal Liberals throughout Western Canada. In fact, however, the NEP was in significant respects an intellectual product of the New Democrats, particularly the Canadianization provisions. For a short period after its introduction, the NDP energy spokesman in the House of Commons, Bob Rae, had a difficult time in distinguishing his party's policy from that of the Liberal government.

James Laxer, the Research Director of the federal NDP, described his party's dilemma over the NEP in a 1984 report to its federal caucus as follows: "The NDP faced a dilemma. Should it allow a progressive, nationalist policy to become intolerable because it received only criticism and no support? Or should it give the programme critical support and face the renewed Tory charge that the NDP was in bed with the Liberals? Already under fire because of its stand on the constitution, the NDP chose the first option. It attacked the NEP as 'phoney nationalism', charging that the programme was simply a corporate giveaway because it included the Petroleum Incentive Programme (PIP) grant to Canadian owned companies."

By the time of the 1984 general election campaign, the NEP had become an orphan to both Liberals and New Democrats, although by 1988 a position paper of the federal New Democrats appeared to some Westerners to call for the resurrection of the NEP.

CF-18 Debacle

The CF-18 aircraft maintenance contract issue today continues to trouble residents of all four western provinces, primarily because most of us placed our confidence in Brian Mulroney at the end of the 1984 election campaign, hoping that justice for all regions would result. Much of a positive nature has been done by his government. The NEP was removed in favour of the Western Accord, the Federal Investment Review Agency was defanged, the problems of western agriculture received new attention, and Western Canada generally for the first time since 1958 enjoyed a place in the political sun.

The CF-18 issue arose during 1986 after the British-owned Ultramar Canada closed a 65-year-old Montreal refinery it had bought from Gulf Canada. The resulting loss of 350 jobs in East Montreal caused an uproar for weeks afterwards in the House of Commons. Prime Minister Mulroney appointed a ministerial committee, headed by Robert de Cotret, to consider ways of fostering growth in the Montreal region. The pending contract to maintain 138 CF-18 jet fighters, which had been purchased from the United States in 1980, became for de Cotret a convenient means of creating future-oriented jobs in Greater Montreal. A major obstacle was the fact that a team of 75 technicians from the three federal departments involved had already decided that the tender by Bristol Aerospace of Winnipeg, a 1,500-employee business owned by Rolls Royce, was better in terms of demonstrated expertise and about four million dollars cheaper than the competing bid by Canadair of Montreal.

Westerners know that the aircraft industry in the U.S. is almost entirely located in western states, mostly Washington and California, whereas in Canada most of it is now in Toronto and Montreal. Air Canada, for example, began in 1937 in Winnipeg as the geographical centre of the country but later moved its head office to Montreal. It also moved a maintenance base to Montreal from Winnipeg in the late 1960's, uprooting several hundred Winnipeg families in the process. That Western Canadian sensitivities about the industry were acute was something many members of the Mulroney cabinet simply never seemed to understand.

In the spring of 1986, following the inter-departmental assessment, de Cotret as president of the Treasury Board overruled the recommendation, and ruled that Canadair would obtain the contract. Almost four months of feverish lobbying by Quebecers followed. Quebec Premier Robert Bourassa met with the prime minister in the early fall about the matter. The full Treasury Board of six ministers, including only one from Western Canada (Frank Oberle), decided finally in October that Canadair should have the contract. The decision was announced by de Cotret.

The reaction in the West was both immediate and uniformly vehement. Had the integrity of the tendering system disappeared? Had Bristol not submitted both a cheaper and technically superior bid? The president of the Winnipeg Chamber of Commerce, John Doole, declared: ''Winnipeg has a good sense of what's right and wrong and we have long memories...nothing has changed. The basic political system still heavily favours the mass block of the eastern provinces.'' Bristol indicated that it would be required to lay off 100 employees in its Winnipeg aircraft maintenance division, and that it would probably sue Ottawa for the $5 million it had spent in preparing its bid in good faith. More bad news came when it was revealed that Canadair, whose competence was in building aircraft rather than maintaining them, would have to spend $30 million to purchase the technology from Bendix-Avelex of Toronto, which itself had been an associate in the Bristol tender. The taxpayer would have to pay for this. Many Westerners concluded that on this issue at least the Mulroney government was indistinguishable from the regime it had succeeded. James Richardson of Winnipeg, a former Liberal Defence Minister, was blunt: "The CF-18 decision is going to be one of the landmarks leading to a greater degree of independence. Westerners are being prevented by the greed of Ontario and Quebec from building an advanced, industrial and technological society on top of their great agriculture and energy base."

Every indicator of western public opinion on the decision taken afterwards showed overwhelming rejection. An Environics Research Group poll done not long after the CF-18 decision was announced found that "84 percent of Western Canadians — the highest of any area of the country — think the Government does not treat all parts of Canada equally." An Angus Reid poll released in November 1986 showed that in B.C. 71% of those surveyed said it was an unfair decision and in the Alberta and Manitoba-Saskatchewan region, 60 and 67% respectively condemned the decision. Only six percent saw it as fair in both Manitoba and Saskatchewan. The only national survey indicated that 46% of the people across the country felt the award was unfair, while only 29% said it was fair. *The Calgary Herald*'s editorial comment indicated the bitterness in the West: "Once again, the West is excluded by the power brokers.... Instead of a national government, we have national decisions made on a selfish regional basis for purely political reasons. There is nothing unusual in that. Just add it to the long catalogue of injustices done to the West."

Peter McCormick and David Elton, Alberta professors of political science and serious spokesmen for the West, singled out the National Energy Policy (1980), and the CF-18 contract decision (1986) as the issues in this decade "which have particularly infuriated Canadians, and which highlighted with unusual clarity the West's powerless quasi-colonial status within Confederation. For many, they have come to symbolize national unfairness and regional impotence. Both decisions dealt a serious blow to the region's economic future, and both were made by a federal government to whom other considerations were simply more important than the economic prospects of the West." Additional salt was added to the wound earlier this year when departmental documents indicated that the additional cost to all taxpayers of awarding the contract to Canadair over Bristol was approximately $26 million dollars, not the much smaller amount implied by de Cotret's comments at the time of his announcement. In early 1988, a $250 million contract for heavy duty military trucks was awarded to Urban Transport Development Corporation of Kingston, Ontario. Another bidder, Bombardier Inc. of Montreal, had committed itself, if successful, to build the vehicles at Cochrane, Alberta. The bidding process functioned cleanly on this occasion, but many Westerners noted that when a western firm had submitted a better and cheaper bid on the CF-18 contract, special considerations were invoked to site the work in Central Canada.

Broadcasting Central Canada
Many Westerners think the English language television service of the Canadian Broadcasting Corporation should be called the Toronto Broadcasting Corporation. Although the CBC's overall appropriation from all Canadians for 1986/87 was $782.7 million, approximately 10% of the complete English television programs shown nationally originated from outside Metropolitan Toronto. As of late 1987, CBC president Pierre Juneau conceded to me that only 16% of the Canadian Broadcasting Corporation permanent staff lives in the prairie provinces and British Columbia. Based on the corporation's operating budget, 10.7% of its funds were directly allocated to components west of Ontario.

The corporation's local stations are permitted only about an hour daily for local news and current affairs in contrast to CBC English radio, which allots seven or eight hours daily in prime time for local programs. The result is that virtually everything appearing on the screen in prime or any other time is chosen by CBC staff in Toronto. "The Canadian Broadcasting Corporation has an important and unique task – guarding our cultural heritage and explaining us to ourselves," observes western historian David Bercuson. "It is difficult to see how this can be done as long as the corporation continues to dictate taste and ideas from Toronto."

The virtual elimination of regional television broadcasting has evolved gradually. Locally planned programs that reflect the real flavour of life in each region and reflect community creativity nationally have all but vanished on our so-called national broadcasting network.

A Committee of Inquiry on the National Broadcasting Service was established by the CRTC in March 1977 to determine how the CBC was fulfilling its mandate, particularly with respect to public affairs, news and information programming. The Chairman of the CRTC at the time, Harry Boyle, concluded: "By overcentralizing production and programming in Toronto and Montreal, and by the orientation of the CBC to events in and around those centres, the CBC has failed to serve 'the special needs of geographic regions'.... The CBC has thereby, in the Commission's view, failed in its very important responsibility to 'contribute to the development of national unity'."

The chapter of Boyle's report entitled "Cultural Apartheid" includes the line: "The regions of English Canada, from sea to sea, exist chiefly during the summer vacation." The Commission inquiry judged that centralizing the CBC in Montreal and Toronto was one reason for its failure to include adequately all parts of the country. Some letters from citizens across the land were also quoted in Boyle's report. A British Columbia resident wrote: "Regional access, at least in the West, has become more limited with each passing year. It is now practically non-existent. Local writers and producers have largely disappeared. Toronto selects, Toronto dictates, Toronto produces, and the talent pool shrinks accordingly.'' Another voice from British Columbia put his point even more forcefully: "They have sowed alienation, and will reap full-scale separatist movement eventually in every region."

More than ten years have passed since the Committee of Inquiry published its report saying clearly that the CBC was failing to foster Canadian unity. Has the Corporation taken the necessary actions to respond to the criticism expressed both by the CRTC and the public? The Caplan-Sauvageau Task Force on Broadcasting Policy reported to the Minister of Communications in 1986. "No experience during our year-long work," it said, "touched us as deeply as hearing the submissions on our tours of eastern, western and northern Canada. The notion of regional alienation so often invoked as a bloodless, abstract cliché in Toronto, Ottawa and Montreal, came alive with passion and visceral reality."

The Task Force spoke of the current concerns of Canadians everywhere who want to be better reflected by the public broadcasting system and who want more opportunity to participate in it. It went on: "There is widespread feeling that our broadcasting system, like so many other Canadian institutions, reflects reality largely as it is understood in Toronto and Montreal. Similarly, there is strong belief it also reflects the mainstream elites of central Canada. As a result, Westerners, Easterners, Northerners, women, natives, ethnic groups and minority groups in general feel that Canadian broadcasting neither belongs to them nor reflects them."

During 1985, Calgary political scientist Barry Cooper supervised five students who during a four-month period monitored four of the corporation's major AM radio network shows: As It Happens, Sunday Morning, Morningside, and The House. Over 78% of the 1,400 stories examined originated in Central Canada. The obvious solution, notes Cooper, is to allot all regions more input into national shows in both production and broadcast.

Charles Feaver, senior policy advisor to the Manitoba Communications Department, complained to the House of Commons Communications Committee in mid-1987 of excessive CBC program centralization in the two central provinces. According to him, "Ontario and Quebec, with 62% of Canada's population, spent 81% of CBC-TV's combined network and regional budget. By contrast, Manitoba, with 4.2% of the population, spends 2.6% of the budget, primarily on programs produced for distribution within this region. Manitoba's weekly contribution of regularly scheduled programming...for the network totals an hour and 15 minutes, with none scheduled in prime time."

Douglas Smith, Associate Deputy Minister of the Saskatchewan Communications Ministry, also confronted the House Committee on regionalism in national broadcasting. "How," he asked, "can we exercise our right to express ourselves to the rest of the country when the CBC, for example, spends 70% of its program production budget in central Canada and a paltry 30% on regional broadcasting in the rest of the country? The CBC's own budget figures show that Saskatchewan's taxpayers contribute nearly 3% of CBC's budget, yet the television program costs by province show that less than 2% of the programming budget is spent in this province."

Canada's aboriginal peoples voiced concerns about the failure by the CBC to reflect their unique identity. Maria Campbell, a producer and writer with Saskatchewan's Katip Aim Media Production, said: "We find that as an independent native production house we really are the forgotten people.... A real problem for us as an independent house [is] the availability of developmental moneys, the unavailability in a lot of cases for broadcast time." Northern Canadians had only a slightly different perspective. Ernie Lennie, Vice-President of the Native Communications Society of the Western N.W.T. (serving 28 western Arctic Dene and Métis communities), told the same hearing: "Communications in our region are dominated by forces and agencies that do not reflect the culture and the society of the Dene and Métis people who are in the majority."

The same basic message was heard at hearings at eleven public forums sponsored by the Canadian Association for Adult Education in the Spring of 1987. Audiences in Western Canada evidently returned again and again to the need for our national public broadcasting network to reflect local needs and regional aspirations. Fil Fraser, an Edmonton broadcaster and a member of the Caplan-Sauvageau Task Force on Broadcast Policy, spoke of his experience as a CBC broadcaster when Alberta was first made a separate CBC region in 1972-73: "The net result of the whole initiative, which was supposed to bring more programming to this region, was that they built another storey on the building out there on 75th Street and added another layer of bureaucracy. No more programming was made. In fact some disappeared. So the reality that we face in this country about CBC regions is that it's a sham. The regions are not producing programming because they have no access to the network's schedule and they don't have any money with which to produce."

In December, 1987, the CRTC granted the CBC a three-year licence to provide a national, 24-hour all-news cable television channel. Even as staunch a defender of Toronto interests (if not of the CBC) as *The Toronto Sun* was moved to call the decision "a massive insult to independent broadcasters, to Westerners and all people whose hunger for round-the-clock news this channel is supposed to satisfy." Edmonton broadcaster Charles Allard, who also applied for the licence but was turned down by the CRTC, spoke for many in the region afterwards: "An historic opportunity to decentralize and diversify electronic news and information has been lost. The CBC now has a stranglehold on television news and public affairs information in Canada and this is not in the best interest of our country."

The CBC's dominant role in the news and current affairs field of English television broadcasting continues essentially undisturbed and so do its cultural and regional biases. Its mandate to foster a national spirit, to recognize the truly multicultural nature of the country and to contribute to building national unity continues for the most part to be honoured more often in the breach, except for those viewers who live near Highway 401 in southern Ontario. The indifference of senior CBC management to the other regions has encouraged the same attitude toward the corporation among at least some Western Canadians, myself included, who would prefer to be its friends.

1982 Constitutional Cake

It is difficult to isolate the full regional consequences of the 1980-82 constitution-related events, partly because many Westerners concluded that Pierre Trudeau's constitutional goals were closely allied to those of his detested NEP.

An opinion survey of 1,370 residents of Western Canada in October 1980 at about the time the NEP was introduced indicated that a disturbing 28% of them agreed that "Western Canadians get so few benefits from being part of Canada that they might as well go it on their own." By March of 1981, the mood had deteriorated so much that a second survey of Westerners on the same question indicated that 36% agreed. In British Columbia, support for this view had risen from 29% in 1980 to 37%; among Albertans the increase over the same period was from 30% to an ominous 49%. Among Saskatchewan and Manitoba respondents, agreement actually declined a little from 25% in October, 1980, to 23% in March, 1981. Of equal concern, 61% of persons in all four western provinces surveyed in March, 1981 agreed with the statement, "The West has sufficient resources and industry to survive without the rest of Canada." Seventy-nine percent of all Westerners agreed with the companion statement, "The West usually gets ignored in national politics because the political parties depend upon Quebec and Ontario for most of their votes." Between October, 1980 and March, 1981 support for outright western independence grew from five percent to seven percent, and eleven percent in Alberta. Part of the worsening western attitude doubtless came from both the process and the substance of Trudeau's constitutional package.

What happened between referendum day in Quebec on May 20, 1980 and March, 1981? Almost immediately after the rejection of sovereignty association by a majority of Quebecers, Liberal Justice Minister Jean Chrétien visited all provincial capitals except Quebec City. All ten premiers and Prime Minister Trudeau agreed the next month on a twelve-item agenda to be studied over the summer. In early July, however, the federal government revealed its new demand for greater powers over the economy if any other powers were to be surrendered to the provinces. A memorandum from Michael Pitfield, clerk of the Privy Council, was leaked in the late summer outlining a federal strategy for unilateral patriation of the constitution by Ottawa.

The atmosphere darkened further a few weeks later when the eleven first ministers met in Ottawa. A confidential memorandum prepared by Michael Kirby, an advisor to the Prime Minister, giving some constitutional options for Ottawa, was also leaked, causing a major uproar both among the premiers and afterwards with the public across the country. Part of it suggested that Alberta might be isolated on the very sensitive western issue of control of natural resources on which the western provinces were otherwise united if the cabinet could strike a deal with Premier Blakeney of Saskatchewan. It also outlined a strategy by which the prime minister might patriate the constitution unilaterally, and attempt to avoid a court challenge as to whether unilateral patriation was constitutional. The Kirby memorandum implied anything but good faith in the process by the federal cabinet. The televised first ministers' conference, whether in consequence of this, or because of competing visions of the country, or both, ended in a stalemate on all twelve agenda items.

In mid-September, 1981, a caucus meeting of Liberal MPs and senators ended with a declaration by its chairman that the caucus was "ready to go to war." A few weeks later, Prime Minister Trudeau indicated on national television that he would patriate the constitution without provincial consent and simultaneously have enacted by the British Parliament a charter of rights which would apply in both the federal and provincial jurisdictions. Joe Clark on behalf of the Progressive Conservative Opposition denounced the proposal on the same evening; Edward Broadbent of the New Democrats indicated general support for the package, thereby splitting his own caucus on east-west lines. Premier William Davis of Ontario was so enthusiastic about the prime minister's proposals that he urged Conservative MP's to break with their leader on the issue, a suggestion that would not soon be forgotten by Western Canadians.

In mid-October, all the ten premiers met; five of them, including western premiers William Bennett, Peter Lougheed and

Sterling Lyon, said that they would challenge the government's constitutional proposal in the courts. A Gallup poll released in early December indicated that 58% of Canadians opposed Ottawa's plan to patriate without first obtaining considerable provincial support.

As 1981 began, Trudeau's government rewrote part of the charter of rights to strengthen it. The Conservative opposition in the House moved at the end of January that the government's constitutional resolution before Parliament be amended to specify that the charter would not apply to provincial jurisdiction until the provincial legislatures approved it by means of a new constitutional amendment formula. A committee of the British Parliament considering the issue recommended at about the same date that the Thatcher government reject the package because of the indicated lack of provincial support. In mid-February, four New Democrat MPs from Saskatchewan announced that they would vote against the constitutional resolution, now through public hearings at committee level, for the same reason. Premier Blakeney, whom the federal cabinet had attempted unsuccessfully to win over with an additional natural resources amendment, announced that he too would oppose the resolution.

By mid-March, 1981, the New Democrats dropped four points in the Gallup poll and the PCs were only five points behind the Liberals. When the government introduced a form of closure in the House of Commons in mid-March on its constitutional resolution, Conservative MPs began a filibuster that lasted for two entire weeks. It ended only when the Newfoundland Court of Appeal, differing sharply from the majority view of the Manitoba Appeal Court on the same issues, ruled unanimously that the resolution was unconstitutional. The government immediately agreed to put off a final vote until after the Supreme Court of Canada decided the issue. A Gallup poll published in mid-May indicated that 66% of both prairie and B.C. residents in effect opposed the government's proposal that the British Parliament should be asked to amend our constitution and add a charter of rights, before sending it to Canada.

In mid-April all of the premiers except for William Davis and

Richard Hatfield of New Brunswick (the "Gang of Eight") met and produced an agreement calling for patriation alone, the Alberta amendment formula (which required, for constitutional amendments, resolutions passed by Parliament and the legislatures of seven of the provinces containing fifty percent of the national population), and no charter of rights. Under the amendment formula favoured by Pierre Trudeau and Edward Broadbent, the legislatures of Ontario and Quebec alone would have vetoes on any constitutional amendment, whereas full legislative support in fully three Western and three Atlantic provinces would be required to stop a proposal. The Federal-Provincial Relations Office in Ottawa conceded to me at the time that it knew of no other federal democracy in the world which assigned, as proposed, differing weight to residents of different provinces for constitutional amendment purposes. The notion offended Western Canadians deeply.

The Supreme Court of Canada ruled at the end of September, by a majority of seven to two, that the Trudeau package was legal, but six of the nine judges also said that it was contrary to our constitutional conventions. A first-ministers' conference was set for early November, 1981 to attempt one last time to seek an agreement. During the late night of November 4th, a compromise was reached which was acceptable to all first ministers except René Levesque. This package quickly passed the House of Commons, Senate, and British Parliament and was proclaimed by Queen Elizabeth in mid-April 1982 at a large outdoor ceremony on Parliament Hill in Ottawa.

The price in terms of national cohesion was painfully high in the West. Even those of us who favoured an entrenched charter of rights, on the premise that some basic rights should not depend on the result of any elections, were deeply troubled. We felt that a so-called national government which held our region in barely-concealed contempt had tried to relegate us to second-class status in its preferred amendment formula. Not very many Westerners cheered the proclamation of the new constitution despite the widespread western support at the time for an entrenched Charter of Rights and Freedoms. The active role of Saskatchewan's Allan

110

Blakeney and Roy Romanow in the final compromise and the insult thrown at them – "Western Liberals" – contributed to the overwhelming defeat of the Blakeney government in the April, 1982 Saskatchewan election. A separatist MLA, Gordon Kesler, who campaigned in part on the view that the new constitution would remove Canadians' right to own property, was actually elected in an Alberta by-election in Olds-Didsbury. Peter Lougheed later recognized that the federal government's refusal under New Democratic pressure to include a property rights' provision in the Charter of Rights contributed to Kesler's victory.

The issue of an "alternative constitutional vision," in Roger Gibbins's phrase, was probably nowhere a burning western issue during the 1980-82 period because of our severe economic difficulties. The long-standing inability of majoritarian parliamentary government to address the problems of the West had not yet ignited a movement to reform central institutions such as the House of Commons and Senate. A consequence of this was that none of the western premiers sought institutional reforms; nor did either of the opposition parties in the House of Commons. The British Columbia government did push for Senate reform, but won little support from any other quarter. The earliest constitutional proposals of Prime Minister Trudeau, most notably his amendment formula, did nothing but entrench regional conflict. The final amendment formula endorsed by all four western premiers reinforced the perception that provincial governments alone speak for their voters in national affairs because future constitutional amendments became solely the prerogative of the eleven legislatures. Any citizen participation in the process as present in other federal democracies (Australia and Switzerland, for example) was excluded.

In terms of the more fundamental problem of effective western representation in national institutions, the Constitutional Act of 1982 achieved absolutely nothing. The subject was not even on the agenda. Nothing was done to initiate a more effective role for western MPs in policy-making, to weaken party discipline, or to ensure that national institutions became more sensitive to regional concerns. Nor did it set in motion the process of meaning-

111

ful reform to the Canadian political system. "In the Constitution Act," concludes Gibbins, "we missed the opportunity to organize regional conflict out of the political system, or at least to reorder our institutional life so that regional conflict could be moderated and contained. Instead, the Constitution Act takes a troubled political past and casts it in constitutional cement for an uncertain future." Many Westerners agree.

Meech Lake

The Meech Lake constitutional accord, which achieved the very important goal of bringing Quebec into the constitutional family, represents the loss of another opportunity to reform national institutions so that regional interests can be represented effectively by national politicians within national institutions. As a result, many Western Canadians feel strongly that the 1987 accord does not adequately address our own long-term concerns and aspirations.

A process by which eleven first ministers, relying on party discipline to obtain majority support in their legislatures later on, exercised exclusive control over constitution-making should be unacceptable to all Canadian democrats. Western Canadians who know our own constitutional history can only say "Amen" to the objections raised by the Yukon and Northwest Territories governments and by native leaders. The Report of the Special Joint Committee of the Senate and House of Commons examining the Meech Lake proposal, perhaps acknowledging that their public hearings had been little more than a charade, conceded that in future both "legislators and the public must be encouraged to participate in the process of constitutional change before and not after First Ministers meet to make decisions." The constitutional process is too important to be left to first ministers exclusively ever again.

In replacing the seven-province amendment formula of the 1982 agreement – with a unanimity rule for all changes involving institutions like the Senate – each province now has an absolute veto over Senate reform. In practice, this could freeze the status quo for institutions which Western Canadians want reformed, so that Canadians in all regions will for once feel themselves to be full and equal partners in Confederation. The Meech Lake accord also says that the government of a province "may" submit names to fill Senate vacancies arising in the interval before our first ministers can achieve the Senate reform which is mandated in the accord. The federal government, says the agreement, "shall" appoint new senators from the names submitted by the provinces. What happens if a province refuses to submit any names is left unsaid.

The constitutional reform committee of the Canada West Foundation says that "giving the premiers a share of the Senate pork barrel represents more than just the tragedy of a squandered opportunity: it is the Achilles heel of the Meech Lake Accord, a move that will seriously limit the capacities of Canada's national government while paralyzing any attempt to repair or contain the damage." The committee thus urged all provincial governments to provide no names of would-be senators until meaningful reforms "have been ratified, and tied to a timetable and a procedure for drawing up those amendments." Others, myself included, have argued that if one province would fill its next senate vacancy by means of a province-wide election, then other provinces would soon be obliged by public opinion to follow suit as proved to be the result when progressive Oregon first began to elect its U.S. Senators in state-wide elections. The momentum toward a fully elected Senate might quickly become unstoppable. Should this occur, one of the major weaknesses of Meech Lake might be overcome.

SIX

Emily Carr
Solitary Genius

*F*ORTY-THREE YEARS after her death, the reputations of the complex personality of Emily Carr are numerous: Western Canada's best-known painter as virtually a textbook example of struggling artist; a memoirist of real charm, individuality, and skill; a traveller whose health broke down when she stayed in two of the world's most glamorous capitals; an individualist about whom legends, true and false, have multiplied almost continuously since her passing in 1945.

Born in 1871, Emily was the youngest of the five daughters of Richard and Emily Carr, who also had a son. The other children were obedient to their sternly Victorian father, but from her childhood Emily was a disturbing element, always in revolt against authority and discipline. Clearly her father's favourite child, Emily went with him everywhere. Her interest in art began when she took lessons once a week at a private school. Her father later found private art lessons for her when she began attending a public school which did not offer art. At the age of nine, she produced a reasonable sketch of her father's profile.

An undefined incident between Emily and her father when she was in early puberty permanently soured their relationship and probably had a lifelong effect on her. Whatever it was, her beloved father became an object of utter contempt until his death

115

from a lung ailment in 1888. The full consequences of this possible act of child abuse during an era decades before such things were acknowledged to occur are of course impossible now to measure. Her mother pre-deceased her father by two years, probably from tuberculosis. Emily, aged 18, quit Victoria High School the year after her father died leaving an estate of fifty thousand dollars.

Emily clearly loved art from childhood days on, but she turned to it for a career because she was unhappy at home under her eldest sister's rule and because it was the one activity which she did well. She went to the California School of Design in San Francisco with a small monthly allowance from their guardian, James Lawson. Her prudery soon deprived her of the best teacher at the school because he used nude models. Without completing her third year, she returned to Victoria when Lawson insisted on it, saying that she had "played at Art" long enough.

She won two first prizes in the Victoria Fall Fair and began to teach art. In the summer of 1898, she journeyed alone by steamer to visit the Ucluelet Indian Band and was struck, having an idealized view of Indians, by their severe economic problems and the current epidemic of German measles and whooping cough. She quickly made friends with those she met. They allowed her to sketch them throughout the summer and she left with a number of drawings and watercolours. On board ship on the way back to Victoria, she met Willam (Mayo) Paddon who would later try very hard to marry her. He found her to be deeply religious and to regret being her family's "black sheep."

Despite her platonic romance with Mayo, she saved her money from teaching and left the next summer by ship to study further at the Westminister School of Art in the British capital. She dropped her reluctance to paint nude models, now finding them beautiful. The students were more serious than those in California, and she missed San Francisco's fun. Other students were critical of her because she did not yet smoke and wore dowdy clothes. She met a number of Canadians, and on one memorable occasion rented a canoe with Sammy Blake, son of Edward Blake, the former national leader of the Liberal Party of Canada. "Canada still peeped out of Sammy," Emily noted, evidently both somewhat infatuated with him and having an active disdain for other Canadian visitors who attempted to be more English than the English. A year later, Mayo came 5000 miles from Victoria to press his marriage proposal, even though she had previously rejected it in a letter. Together they saw London in September; he proposed on average five times a week. The fall term activities and Emily's cooling toward him soon made him a nuisance. Finally, in December, he left with a thoroughly broken heart. She was also upset for she noted much later, "It does not hurt the killed, it hurts the killer." Towards the very end of her life, she would write to her friend Ira Dilworth words which bitterly describe her only romantic involvements, "Love can be unfair. I've been loved furiously and not able to pay back, and I've loved furiously with cold response."

After many months of painting the human figure, she began to do landscapes. In 1901, she moved to the Cornish village of St. Yves, already a well known English art colony, where she spent eight months painting the sea, cliffs, beaches and fishermen. In a haunting wood above the village, her love for forest painting began, far from the B.C. rain forests, which she would only conquer gradually during the rest of her life. Unfortunately, her health broke down several months later, and she entered a sanatorium north of London for a 15-month stay, admitted for what is now termed psychoneurosis and was then termed hysteria. Eventually she returned to Victoria after five and a half years abroad.

Overweight and smoking heavily, Emily was lonely in Victoria, and not long afterwards accepted a teaching post at the Vancouver Ladies' Art Club across Juan de Fuca Strait. Optimism was everywhere in Vancouver as she arrived in 1906, and the absence of an entrenched English élite rendered the city far more agreeable to Emily than Victoria. More important, many Vancouverites had become interested in art. Unfortunately, the Ladies' Art Club was then merely a social club useful for passing time. Emily characteristically would brook no frivolity from her students. She and the club parted after a month, Emily resolving to teach only children in future because they were more pliable. Within a year or so, she had about 75 eager pupils coming to her rented studio and she threw herself into the work. She was also asked to give lessons at what is today Crofton House School for Girls. The students there loved her too. In 1909, she did so well financially that she was able to buy five city lots, but she worried that her teaching was interfering with her own painting. What she did manage to complete, however, won uncritical praise from other prominent artists on the lower mainland.

During a boat trip to Alaska in 1907, she painted her first totem poles and became captivated by the Indian art. Ever afterwards, the "Indian stuff" was to remain, besides forests, a major focus of her artistic expression.

When an experienced American artist, Theodore Richardson, complimented her first piece, she decided to return each summer to paint Indians and their totem poles "before they are a thing of the past." Her paintings have become a precious record of a way of life rapidly disappearing. The next summer, travelling by boat, canoe and stage coach, she painted the Kwakiutl Indians 150 miles north of Vancouver. Emily's strong temperament was clearly causing her problems in polite Vancouver circles, but she had a moderately successful auction of some of her pieces, which would help with the expenses of a trip to Paris.

Emily and her sister Alice arrived in Paris in the summer of 1910 with a letter of introduction to an English artist, Phelan Gibb. At Gibb's suggestion, she joined the private studio of the Scot John Ferguson, who taught Emily to notice rhythm in nature. Unfortunately she soon drove herself too hard, and suffered further attacks of hysteria and influenza.

After her recovery, Emily joined Gibb's landscape painting class outside the city for four months. It was the highlight of her year abroad. She did quaint villages, farms, and local people. Gibb taught her to juxtapose cold colours with hot to give natural objects greater depth. He also told her that she could become one of the great woman painters of the day. Under him, she grew much artistically and yearned to try out her new techniques on the "bigger material of the West." Just before leaving Paris, she was quite overjoyed to see two of her paintings exhibited in the Salon d'Automne in the Grand Palais just off the Avenue des Champs Elysées.

If Emily half expected to set the west coast afire with the new techniques of the French impressionists, she was deeply disappointed. Back home, even her sisters and favourite friends turned only icy silence toward the canvases she had done in France. Despite public scorn and poor reviews, however, she opened a studio on West Broadway Avenue in Vancouver and exhibited seventy of her oils and watercolours. Although several visitors gasped at her new indifference to detail and very aggressive colours, a number of pieces were sold. No one in the entire city seemed to realize that the old art order had passed.

She developed an original Post-impressionist style and later adopted some elements of Cubism to express "the bigger things" in nature. By a skilled juxtaposition of colours, and ignoring details when aiming at achieving a light effect that would reveal things in nature not seen by the average person, she achieved her finest pieces. As a leader of creative art, bringing emotion and movement into a scene that no camera could catch, she was half a century ahead of her time, overlooked by most of her contemporaries.

She eloquently defended her new artistic credo: "Pictures should be inspired by nature but made in the soul of the artist.... Extract the essence of your subject and paint yourself into it; forget the little petty things that don't count; try for the bigger side...."

After further instances of rejection, she journeyed north in 1912 to try her new techniques on her beloved totem poles, and the following winter she moved back to Victoria.

Emily soon entered the lowest period in her entire life as she established a boarding house to provide an income to support her art. She was able to supplement her meagre income a little by selling paintings, but in Victoria the general hostility to her new style remained strong. In 1913 and 1914, she made no trip north and produced few new canvases. As her biographer Maria Tippett puts it, Emily's life after 1913, her forty-second year, was for the first time no longer dominated by her art but instead by her boarders. "I loathed being a landlady," she said.

When the war finally ended, and the local economy improved, she began to spend more time at painting. In the summer of 1920, she went to the west coast of Vancouver Island to do landscapes and painted briefly in southern British Columbia. In late 1921, Mortimer Lamb, a promoter of Ontario's Group of Seven artists, viewed and was greatly impressed by her entire personal collection of art. Lamb later wrote about her to Eric Brown, director of the National Gallery in Ottawa. Brown did nothing during the next several years as the National Gallery continued its practice of essentially ignoring Western and Atlantic artists.

Only in the summer of 1927 was Emily finally "discovered" by Brown, during his visit to Victoria in search of pieces for an upcoming exhibition of West Coast Indian art. He was overwhelmed by her sketches, oils and watercolours of Indians, totem poles and Indian villages. The next night, speaking as if he had never heard of Emily Carr before, he told a Victoria audience that their local artist's work was "as good as anything that is being done in the country."

Emily sent 27 watercolours and eleven oil paintings immediately to Ottawa and journeyed east herself by train for the exhibit. Stopping in Toronto, she made one of the most important friendships of her life with the acknowledged leader of the Group of Seven, Lawren Harris. It was Harris whose work struck her dumb. His paintings, she noted, played deep "into the vast lovely soul of Canada; they plumbed to her depths, climbed her heights and floated into her spaces."

Brown and Marius Barbeau gave her a royal welcome in Ottawa: teas, dinners, drives. On the glorious day when the exhibit opened, her pieces sparkled. Although only a few people attended the opening, her six-week trip, during which she passed her fifty-sixth birthday, elevated her work to national stature. The leading members of the Group of Seven had accepted her and the National Gallery bought three paintings from the exhibit.

In 1929, accepting Harris's suggestion that she choose subjects other than totem poles for a year, she began to paint the B.C.

forests, feeling for the presence of God in them. Though she never thought of herself as a religious woman in an orthodox sense, she had always carried with her a strong sense of God. She felt that God was always present in the forest and attempted to reach out and up to Him through her paintings. During her spring trip, this time to Nootka Island, she did one of her most famous paintings, *Indian Church*, and later that summer she painted *Grey*, depicting a terrible almighty in a vast forest.

No other Canadian has succeeded so well in capturing the deep silence of West Coast forest, the surging rush of living stretches of green and grey and brown, or the towering majesty of trees reaching up to the light. Her forest is silent, dark and awesome in its powerful swirls and strong rhythms. The light is shadowy and slants down the long brown trunks of trees in shifting yellow patterns. Far above, the tree tops sway majestically. Down below it is tangled at its edge with the deep, lush green underbrush bursting with vitality and growth. This was essentially the vision of our western forests which Emily Carr loved and whose essence she caught on her canvases and on paper.

The first years of the Depression were very productive ones. Though the reception of her work in Vancouver remained so cool that she stopped exhibiting there, Victoria and Seattle were much more welcoming. But Emily's problems were never absent for long. By 1934, her relationships with both the National Gallery and the Group of Seven were deteriorating. When she wrote asking for the return of some watercolours, the Gallery's assistant director, Harry McCurry, demonstrated the procrastination and insolence of office for which officials in every capital are known. She was understandably indignant that for many years the National Gallery owned only three of her paintings, created in 1912.

For two full years after 1933, she refused to send a single piece to exhibitions in Central Canada. In fairness to the Gallery, it did direct her pieces to many exhibitions and the Depression severely reduced its budget.

Predictably, Emily soon turned her cold shoulder to the Group of Seven one by one. She wrote in her journal that for years she had been at the mercy of the East; ''Now they are far away and I stand alone on my perfectly good feet,'' and from now on she would ''push with my own power, look with my own eyes.'' The years 1934-37 were ones of fruition for Emily. Her two surviving sisters, Lizzie and Alice, who for years had remained indifferent to her art, began to show a genuine interest. She gave many showings in her studio, where, if she wished a visitor to stay, she would lower a chair from the ceiling using a rope and pulley.

In the summer of 1933, Emily travelled to Lillooet and Pemberton. Her art was reaching its best. She left her Hill Home apartment for a cottage, where at first she felt very lonely. In 1936 she wrote, ''I seem to be enveloped in a dull ache composed of tiredness, homesickness, and loneliness.... I don't feel as if I belonged to a soul or mattered on earth.''

Lizzie died and Emily herself had a heart attack in early 1937. News of her illness and critical financial position prompted Eric Brown to arrange to purchase eight of the paintings. Harris and a number of art galleries and individuals also rallied, and provided in all almost $3,000. She could now pay her hospital bills; suddenly she had supporters everywhere.

Emily had become virtually an invalid. Angina and cardiac asthma where now added to all her other health problems: stiff knees, rheumatic hip, partial deafness, weight problems and others. She exhibited frequently in 1937, including a solo exhibit at the Toronto Art Gallery, and her work was compared favourably with even that of Vincent van Gogh. In the fall of 1938, several of her paintings were featured by the National Gallery at a showing in London called ''A Century of Canadian Art.''

Eric Newton's review of the exhibition for Canadians included the following passage: ''If the word 'genius' (a word to be jealously guarded by the critic and used only on very special occasions) can be applied to any Canadian artist it can be applied to her. She belongs to no school. Her inspiration is derived from within herself. Living among the moist mountains and giant pines of British Columbia, a country climatically different from the rest of Canada, she has had to invent a new set of conventions, a personal style of her own. Where the Eastern Canadians have been content to stylize the outward pageantry of the landscape, she has symbolized its inner meaning and in doing so has, as it were, humanized it.''

The next triumph was in Vancouver, where in the fall of 1938 the Vancouver Art Gallery exhibited twenty-nine of her forest scenes. Eleven of them sold. After so many years of neglect, the Gallery wanted Emily, now past sixty-five and in poor health. She continued to work too hard and suffered a slight stroke in the spring of 1939, but was back in the woods at her rented cottage by summer.

Between 1930 and 1940, she made four sketching trips. The quality of her work, however, was worsening and this caused her to become discouraged.

Of Carr's numerous paintings, the ones I find most moving are *Indian Church, Grey*, and *Blunden Harbour. Indian Church*, painted on one of her trips to Nootka Island, depicts a one-room church all but engulfed by a primeval forest. A fragile symbol of faith in the form of a white building is set against a towering green tapestry of forest. The contrast of green and white implies an alien element in the woods: man's intrusion into nature's domain. At the same time, God's presence is sensed in the vast entangled interior of the forest.

Grey is considered one of the most remarkable paintings of Carr's entire career. It is a poetic vision of a forest at night with the dark tree forms and a faint light glowing from an opening in the central conical tree. The mood is inviting yet fearful, with an almighty spirit strongly implied in the vast forest.

Blunden Harbour is an excellent portrayal of the spirit of the totem poles which project feelings of mystical proportions. The powerful, inscrutable figures of the poles against the harmony of the sky, water and hills face the unknown in a timeless confrontation.

Carr is now recognized also as a remarkable Western Canadian writer. Her diaries, entitled *Hundreds and Thousands* and published twenty years after her death, made it clear that her desire to express herself in words came early. She was always attracted to writing. When she was a student she would make up little rhymes about her friends and illustrate them with pen-and-ink drawings.

In her sketch sack, when she was leaving for field trips, she always carried a notebook. She used an interesting technique, "wording," as a means of clarifying her thoughts before painting. She insisted that it was the handling of thoughts, rather than the handling of paint, which overwhelmed her. In her notebook she explained to herself why she wanted to paint a particular subject: what attracted her to it, and what meaning in the subject she was trying to express. She found that this system — an articulation in words, as well as in colour and form – gave her a double approach to her subjects which she found helpful.

Her approach to painting and to writing was similar. In writing, she stuck to two guiding principles; first, to get to the point as directly as possible, and second, never to use a big word where a little one would do. She was persuaded, correctly as it turned out, that while her mechanics and spelling were poor that if she were "ultra-honest, ultra-true, some deep realizing of life" would overcome other writing deficiencies. She spoke many times in her diaries of the difficulties she had to overcome in writing. "There's words enough, paint and brushes enough and thoughts enough. The whole difficulty seems to be getting the thoughts clear enough, making them stand still long enough to be fitted with words and paint. They are so elusive, like wild birds singing above your head, twittering close beside you, chortling in front of you, but gone the moment you can put out a hand. If you ever do catch hold of a piece of thought it breaks away leaving the piece in your hand just to aggravate you."

Sincerity and honesty are closely related characteristics of her writing. She believed that an artist must speak clearly to people in terms of her own actual experience, enriched with the spirit and the soul. "Be careful that you do not write or paint anything that is not your own, that you don't know in your own soul. You will have to experiment.... But don't take what someone else has made sure of...." Consequently, Carr's literary style is characterized by complete independence, a great simplicity and directness.

Her written words are the equivalent of the brisk, sure brush strokes and splashes of dramatic, strong colours which are so characteristic of her canvases.

Writing was both less physically difficult than painting and less likely to lead to criticism because she originally wrote with no thought of publishing. When her health prevented trips to the forests, Emily turned to writing with zest. She wrote *Klee Wyck*, about her youthful years of travels among Indians, and then *The Book Of Small*. "Small" was the name Emily gave herself when she was a child; this book brought to life her recollections of Victoria in the late years of the last century. Her next book, *The House of All Sorts*, presented a bitter picture of her life as a boarding-house manager, when she struggled to make ends meet and tried to cope with the petty details of running a boarding house.

Maria Tippett notes that most of her writing was done between the ages of sixty-three and seventy-one: "[Her stories] have in common many characteristics — crotchetiness, alienation, exaggeration and sentimentality — that had always been part of her personality but had become more pronounced in her old age."

Of her writings Tippett says, "One feels her intense love for the West Coast in her evocative descriptions of the scent of salt air, the sting of campfire smoke in the eyes, the push of growth in the tangled forest, or the forest's overwhelming silence. Emily makes the reader share not only the things she loved but her dislikes – the thoughtlessness of tenants, the hypocrisy of the English, the cruelty of her sisters – all of which she was able to treat comically. Finally, she reveals herself in her stories: her morality, her sentimentality, her prejudices, her love of nature, even her meanness and the childlike side of her character, all are present."

The recognition of Carr as a writer came even before her full acceptance as a painter. *Klee Wyck*, made up of sketches written at various times when she penetrated forests and visited Indian villages on the British Columbia coast, was a great success. "Klee Wyck" was the name the Indians gave Emily at Ucluelet. It meant "Laughing One" and was given to her not because, in the words of Ira Dilworth, "she laughed a great deal — as she herself would say, there is not much of a giggle in her. But her laughter in Ucluelet went out to meet the Indians, taking the place of words, forming a bond between them. They felt at once that the young girl staying in the missionaries' house understood them and they accepted her.''

Both Macmillan and Ryerson presses initially rejected *Klee Wyck* for publication, but Ira Dilworth, the regional director of the CBC in Vancouver, was so impressed by her stories that he broadcast some of them in 1940. He also succeeded in persuading Oxford University Press to publish *Klee Wyck*. The first printing, dedicated to her Indian friend Sophie Frank, sold out. The Women's Canadian Club of Victoria celebrated the publication on Emily's seventieth birthday. Congratulatory letters arrived at the gathering from many people, including the B.C. premier and Lieutenant Governor. The B.C. Indian Commissioner thanked her on behalf of the Native people. Emily herself was above all grateful to Dilworth. Like her, says Tippett, he was deeply religious, proud of being a Western Canadian and resentful of Central Canadian dominance of the country. The two of them opened up to each other fully, mostly by letter, and he outlined his inner thoughts, including his concern about head office control of the regional CBC. Both were ecstatic when *Klee Wyck* won the Governor General's Award for non-fiction in 1942. Dilworth remained her most loyal friend and continued to edit her writing.

There were three further books. *Growing Pains*, about her youth, appeared in 1946. *Pause: A Sketch Book*, about her period in the sanatorium, came out in 1933. *The Heart of a Peacock*, more Indian and bird sketches, was published in 1953. When Dilworth, her literary trustee, died in 1960 only a portion of her writings had been released, and in 1966 a new literary executor published a selection of her journals as *Hundreds and Thousands*. The notebooks were as she said, "to jot me down in, unvarnished me, old at fifty-eight.'' There she poured out her private thoughts, doubts and inspirations. The form a revealing self-portrait depicting an artist often tired and discouraged yet always honest and true to her ideals, and a lonely woman.

In the early spring of 1942, Emily sketched the forest again at Mount Douglas Park near Victoria and later produced a number of oils. She was rushed to the hospital with a clot on her heart and later moved to a nursing home. Recovering in hospital she wrote: "I must go home and go sketching in the woods. They still have something to say to me." She was in fact preparing for her end from 1942 on. She asked a friend, Carol Pearson, to bury a number of personal items in Victoria's Beacon Hill Park that year: they were never recovered afterwards. She gave away many of her art pieces as gifts. At Lawren Harris's suggestion, she set aside forty-five paintings for Western Canadians. Dilworth and Harris, as trustees of the Emily Carr Trust, chose the pieces with her assistance. As Tippett says, "the public was informed that Miss Emily Carr had given the paintings to the nation, or more specifically to the Vancouver Art Gallery, on permanent loan." In her will, she also indicated that some of her paintings should be sold to provide for a scholarship fund "to enable art students residing in British Columbia to study art at some school or art schools to be selected by the trustees." Dilworth was made her literary trustee and Harris and Willie Newcombe her artistic ones.

Her affairs settled, and the University of British Columbia wanting to give her an honorary degree at their May, 1945 convocation, she died on March 2nd, 1945 of yet another clot on her heart.

Today, 43 years after her death, Emily Carr enjoys the recognition and admiration that eluded her during her lifetime. Her artistic bequest constitutes another chapter in the history of our cultural heritage. So uniquely "Western" in spirit and determination, she eventually succeeded in passing to Canadians from all parts of the country her artistic vision of the great West — her West.

Above everything else, Emily Carr was a truly great British Columbian and Western Canadian. "I am a Westerner," she wrote, "and I am going to extract all that I can to the best of my small ability out of the big glorious West." It was her single purpose to share and express through her art the experiences of her life in the West she loved. "There is something bigger than fact: the underlying spirit, all it stands for, the mood, the vastness, the wildness, the western breath of go-to-the-devil-if-you-don't-like-it, the eternal big spaceness of it. Oh the West! I'm of it and I love it.''

She was not interested, as she said in one of her books, in the stories brought by the people from their trips to the Old Country, as she found that ''These wild, western things excited me tremendously. I did not long to go over to the Old World to see history, I wanted to see now what was out here in our West. I was glad Father and Mother had come as far west as the West went before they stopped and settled down.''

''I want my work to be typically Western,'' she said, and consequently all her life she tried to make ''western places speak'' to people who were to see her paintings or read her books. With courage and devotion, she continued to dispel the absurd myth that the West was unpaintable.

''Oh, just let them open their eyes and look! It isn't pretty. It's only just magnificent, tremendous. The oldest art of our West, the art of the Indians, is in spirit very modern, full of liveness and vitality. They went far and got so many of the very things that we modern artists are striving for today.''

Ira Dilworth captured the greatness of this amazing woman when he said, ''I am convinced that Emily Carr is a great genius and that we will do well to add her to that small list of originals who have been produced in this place and have lived and commented in one way or another on this Canada of ours.''

SEVEN

Civilizations Collide
Native Peoples

A MAJOR THEME OF WESTERN HISTORY is local subordination by outsiders. Indians and later the Métis provide especially
good case studies in alienation because no other groups of
Westerners were treated worse, or subjugated for longer, by
successive governments in Ottawa. Oddly, native concerns have
only rarely been included as part of the western alienation issue,
but there is clearly a common cause. This linkage continues
despite less-than-warm attitudes demonstrated by western provincial governments of different political colours over the decades.

Until the mid-seventeenth century, prairie, British Columbia
and northern aboriginal peoples lived well as hunters and gather-
ers, some probably as comfortably as Europeans did before the
Industrial Revolution. Gerald Friesen, the prairies historian,
concludes that between 1640 and 1840 relations between Indians
and European fur traders on our plains were notable for "adaptation, peace and cooperation." Cultural autonomy and a real sense
of social equality with Europeans prevailed among Indians with
only minor setbacks until well after the merger of the Hudson's
Bay Company and Montreal's North West Company in 1821.
Admittedly, a Métis party led by Cuthbert Grant had killed 21
supporters of the Governor of the Red River Settlement in 1816
("The Seven Oaks Massacre"), uniting the Métis people in the

129

process, but Lord Selkirk himself re-established the settlement and peace the following year. Selkirk with his strict Scottish sense of propriety also signed a treaty with local Crees, Ojibwas and Assiniboines.

The Métis

The emergence of Western Canada is closely linked with the history of the Métis people. They did not come centuries ago from a distant part of the world: Prairie Canada alone witnessed their birth as a new people.

The Métis nation began in the late eighteenth century as the result of unions between French and English fur traders and Indian women. Indian women were essential for European survival in the West because they made pemmican, moccasins and snow shoes and could act as both guides and interpreters. Their offspring, the Métis, both bilingual and bicultural, became the archetypal voyageurs and were active as interpreters, traders, canoeists and fur packers at numerous western trading posts. During a century and a half, their pivotal role in the fur trade enabled them to become a self-confident community within Western Canada. This was most noticeable at Red River, where in the mid-1820's many Métis began to take up subsistence agriculture as a supplement to the buffalo hunt.

The next two decades in the western interior were prosperous and peaceful. The harmony began to unravel only in the 1840's when corrosive notions of race and class from Victorian England and elsewhere began to seep into the Red River community. Contrary to its earlier practice, the Hudson's Bay Company, restored as a monopoly in the fur trade, stopped permitting ambitious Métis to enter its officer ranks. The Company governor, George Simpson, stood adamantly against the promotion of Métis even though there were virtually no "European" children in the overwhelmingly native region and most officers therefore had to be brought in from outside. Numerous Métis who would earlier have enjoyed good careers with the company were driven to trade outside the company. Ultimately, when one Métis trader was convicted of illegal trading in 1849 but not fined, the monopoly collapsed because the law enshrining it had become toothless. Approximately 6,000 Métis, divided about equally between French and English-speaking groups, had regained a viable — if short-lived — niche in the fur trade and buffalo hunt. A new period of prosperity began as Métis operated a freight service by ox cart between Red River and St. Paul, Minnesota. Their final golden age ended with the decline of the fur trade and the coming of the steamboat.

Disaster for prairie Indians and Métis alike began during the 1850's, when their region came to be seen in what is now Ontario as a place for the land-hungry to establish a new civilization. George Brown, leader of the Reform party, boomed from his Toronto newspaper, *The Globe*, in 1856: "Let the merchants of Toronto consider that if their city is ever to be made really great if it is ever to rise above the rank of a fifth rate American town – it must be by the development of the great British territory lying to the north and west." Was the prairie West with all its inhabitants to become an economic colony to the central provinces in general, and Toronto in particular?

When prairie Canada was sold by the Hudson's Bay Company to the newly-formed Dominion of Canada in 1869, it was done without even minimal consideration of existing Indian and Métis land claims in the region. Friction quickly followed.

Louis Riel's first Red River rebellion of 1869-70 led to the reluctant creation of the province of Manitoba by the Macdonald government in 1870. Control of public lands and natural resources within its approximately one hundred square mile area was reserved for Ottawa — which was not the case for any other existing province — because the Macdonald government wanted to determine itself precisely how the West would be developed. Although arguments still exist that federal control of prairie homesteading was necessary for a number of years if life was to be breathed successfully into national settlement and railway policies, the future was thus determined for both English- and French-speaking Métis. Central Canadians had essentially ignored their aspirations and needs by making a farce of their provincehood.

Social humiliation for the Métis, who in fact constituted about three quarters of Red River's 12,000 residents, followed the birth of Manitoba. Degradation came primarily at the hands of those of Colonel Wolseley's disbanded soldiers who remained in Manitoba and who were openly contemptuous of anyone who was "French," "papist" or a "breed." The new province quickly became a boiling cauldron of animosity. A minority of Métis left for the more hospitable social climate of the western United States. Some left Manitoba to attempt to recreate their former lifestyle along the North Saskatchewan River near Prince Albert; most chose to remain on their farms in Manitoba or to establish new ones on land promised to the Métis.

Following the crushing of the North-West Rebellion in 1885, the Métis were completely routed as a people. Their homes were looted and burned, their cattle were stolen, and the people themselves were dispersed. Many sought entry into Indian bands on the basis of their Indian blood. Some migrated to northern Alberta. Their independent spirit was severely dampened.

The census records tell the story. In 1881, of the 56,500 people in the North-West Territories the overwhelming majority, 49,500, were either Indian or Métis. By 1901, of a total population in the region of 159,000 only 26,304 were listed as Indian or Métis. Many of the missing 23,000 Métis and Indians, concludes the Métis historian Don McLean, had simply "moved on, beyond the reach of the census takers, to the marginal bushlands at the fringe of the Arctic. Others fled to the U.S.A., while many who remained were reluctant to identify themselves as Métis, fearing reprisal and persecution."

In 1901, the highly-respected Father Lacombe and others developed a plan with the Laurier government to establish a Métis reserve in central Alberta. For various reasons, including Métis distrust of both Ottawa and the western branch of the Roman Catholic Church (many felt their church had sided with Macdonald against Riel in 1885), only eighty families were persuaded to move on to the reserve near St. Paul des Métis (later shortened to St. Paul) in northeastern Alberta. Against the wishes of a frail and aging Lacombe, the reserve was later disbanded and settlers from

Quebec first arrived to settle on it in 1908.

By the Depression year of 1930, the demoralization of a proud people was complete and their leadership was virtually dormant. Those who had succeeded in the transformed prairie order as farmers and entrepreneurs, concludes McLean, "were coming to be seen in the community as 'white men', not Métis."

Since 1945, the progress of the Métis people has been more positive. According to the 1986 census, there are today approximately 150,000 Canadians of Métis origin, about two thirds of whom live in Western Canada. Educational opportunities have improved, and Métis people have entered trades and professions in the West and some have found recognition outside their own region. Douglas Cardinal, for example, is the architect of the new Museum of Civilization in Ottawa. Blatantly racist interpretations of Canadian history are being revised. Métis community pride has revived to a considerable degree, and Métis associations have been rejuvenated in both Alberta and Saskatchewan.

Métis rights were entrenched at least in theory in the Canadian constitution, and leaders like Louis "Smokey" Bruyère, president of the Native Council of Canada, are being heard. Bruyère himself notes: "Just before his death, in 1885, Louis Riel predicted it would be three hundred years before the Métis took their rightful place in Canada. We've just passed year 100, and Métis are entrenched as an aboriginal people in the Canadian Constitution, the highest law of the land – not bad for starters." Much remains to be done, but a brighter Métis future is clearly indicated.

While the Métis children of Manitoba won a land grant of sorts from Macdonald, prairie Indians from the 1870's on were treated as wards of the federal government. Alexander Morris, who arranged the initial prairie treaties for the Macdonald government, revealed much when he said: "Let us have Christianity and civilization to leaven the masses of heathenism and paganism among the Indian tribes; let us have a wise and paternal government faithfully carrying out the provisions of our treaties. [Native people] are wards of Canada, let us do our duty by them." This policy would result in a considerable number of cultural, mental, and physical deaths for Western Indians over the decades.

The changing world of Indians on the Canadian prairies in the second half of the 19th century is caught well in the following description: "A typical Cree youth might have been hunting buffalo and raiding for horses in the 1860's just as his grandfather had done sixty years before; in the 1870's, he might have succumbed to the whiskey trade or been struck by an epidemic; almost certainly he would have been removed to a reserve and perhaps even taught the rudiments of agriculture. In the 1880's, some of his children might have been attending school, and he, having faced starvation for three or four years in succession, might have participated in the violence associated with the 1885 uprising. But nothing within his power could alter the circumstances of his life: the buffalo had disappeared, trains and fences and towns now dominated the plains, and the old ways had disappeared beyond recovery."

The white Canadian invasion of the western plains hit full stride after 1870. Just before that date there were 25-35,000 Indians, another 10,000 Métis and fewer than 2,000 whites on the Canadian prairies. A concerned Macdonald government, which held the constitutional responsibility for Indians and their lands, signed a number of treaties by the end of the 1870's with as much pomp and ceremony as individual circumstances permitted.

There were probably three major misrepresentations by the officials "negotiating" the treaties. First, they knew the value of the land to be ceded to the Crown whereas the Indians clearly did not. Second, the chiefs and bands had no legal or other knowledgeable advisors. Third, most of the Indians who signed could not really have understood the meaning of many treaty terms or their binding effect on future generations. They were simply swindled.

Prairie Reality

In the 1870's, prairie Indian bands had no choice but to sign treaties because the huge buffalo population, which at its peak had numbered 50-60 million throughout the North American plains, was annihilated between 1874 and 1879. Some token conservation measures were considered in Ottawa and by some of the territorial governments, but nothing worthwhile was done in time to regulate the massacre by the white and native hunters supplying the American hide trade. Indians, who for a century had relied on the buffalo for food, faced starvation in the 1880's. The Macdonald government did move more quickly to provide emergency rations to Indians, as Friesen points out, than it had to preserve the buffalo. "But," he goes on, "what is striking, in retrospect, is the government's apparent use of food rations as a means of coercing reluctant Indians into the treaties and, later, as a tool for controlling Indian diplomatic activity."

For example, three major Cree leaders, Big Bear, Piapot and Little Pine, sought to create adjoining reserves for their bands in which they might jointly maintain considerable autonomy. Ottawa's Indian Affairs Commissioner, Edgar Dewdney, first used food rations as a means of sending each of their bands to different locations on the prairies which were 300 miles apart. When a Cree revolt over the issues of local autonomy and larger reserves seemed imminent in 1883, Dewdney threatened ration cuts: 'submit or starve'. He abandoned this option only when Prime Minister Macdonald agreed to enlarge the Mounted Police and to amend the Indian Act to permit the arrest of any Indian present on another reserve without the permission of Indian Affairs officials.

When some young Crees and Assiniboines killed nine white men at Frog Lake in Central Saskatchewan during Riel's North-West Rebellion in 1885, Dewdney and Macdonald had the perfect opportunity to crush Cree efforts to win treaty revisions and a single large reserve. Chief Poundmaker of the Crees, who had not approved of the uprising and in fact had ordered his followers not to slaughter a contingent of Canadian soldiers who had attacked them at Cutknife Hill, soon found himself on trial for treason with eighty other Indians. His trial was a caricature of justice. George Denison, a police magistrate and observer of the proceedings, said that the chief was "convicted on evidence that, in any ordinary trial would have ensured his acquittal without the jury leaving the box...." Poundmaker died, broken in spirit, within four months of his release from Stoney Mountain penitentiary near Winnipeg. Centuries of Indian hegemony on the prairies died with him.

The loss of land, hunting and fishing rights, dignity, self-sufficiency and nationhood by Western Indians was both a regional and a national tragedy. In 1895, the Cree Chief Piapot, known for both his humour and his eloquence, put a common Indian view this way: "In order to become sole masters of our land they relegated us to small reservations as big as my hand and made us promises as long as my arm; but the next year the promises were shorter and got shorter every year until now they are the length of my finger, and they keep only half of that."

West of the Rockies, the pattern was similar although both coastal and interior Indians were largely undisturbed by outsiders until the late eighteenth century. British, Spanish and Russian explorers thereafter arrived by sea; fur traders came from the East to establish posts in the early nineteenth century. By the 1860's, British Columbia Indians had been severely weakened by European diseases, and those remaining were terrified of ending up on reserves. The British Columbia government nonetheless set aside reserves for them, although the issue of title would remain unresolved to the present day. Probably again because there was no need for settlement lands, no treaties were obtained by Ottawa from Indians anywhere in the province except in an extreme northern corner. Chief William of the William's Lake Indian band wrote to *The Victoria Daily Colonist* in 1880: "I am an Indian Chief and a Christian. 'Do unto others as you wish others should do unto you' is Christian doctrine. Is the white man a Christian? This is part of his creed — 'take all you want if it belongs to an Indian.' He has taken all our land and all the salmon and we have – nothing. He believes an Indian has a right to live if he can live on nothing at all...."

Indian Act

Few prairie Indians realized early on that the aboriginal rights recognized in the solemn treaties signed with Her Majesty the Queen were subject to the Indian Act of the Canadian Parliament,

136

passed in 1876 and still in full force today. As Harold Cardinal, the former President of the Indian Association of Alberta, puts it, "They never understood that the agents who came among them came, not because of the treaties they had signed, but because there had been a piece of legislation called the Indian Act...legislation totally separate, totally remote from the whole treaty-making process."

The Indian Act mandated the federal Indian Affairs Department to control virtually every aspect of Indian life, including economic development, municipal and provincial government matters, politics, land use and education. Cardinal notes that the only power chiefs and councils possess under the Act which does not first require them to seek permission from the Indian agent is controlling weeds on reserves. The legislation purports to protect and encourage Indians, but in fact affords no respect whatsoever for their culture, religion or traditional way of life.

The policy behind the Indian Act was based on two misconceptions: first, Indians were regarded as incapable of managing their own affairs, a view which led to a perceived need for paternalism; second, the values, culture and lifestyles of native peoples were looked upon as inferior to those of the white society. Such views, notes law professor Peter Cumming, "resulted in the virtual destruction of the Indian people. They have been deprived, unlike any other group of Canadians, of the opportunity of learning by self-experience and initiative. They have been placed in the proverbial 1984 welfare state with consequential destruction of pride and ultimately self-identity."

The manner of federal government control and administration of reserve lands is virtually unchanged from that adopted in 1876 when the Indian Act became law. The provisions of the legislation do not allow for aboriginal self-government and self-management. "Today Indian legislation generally rests on the principle that the aborigines are to be kept in a condition of tutelage and treated as wards or children of the state," said the 1876 document of the Department of the Interior. Georges Erasmus, President of the Assembly of First Nations, believes such attitudes towards the native peoples still prevail in the 1980's and views his people as ''wards of the government with no real ability to influence their communities.''

Native War Records

The contribution of Indians and Natives in both World Wars is of considerable interest. Between 3,500 and 4,000 Indians from a total of 11,500 eligible for service across the country enlisted voluntarily in the Canadian Expeditionary Force during World War I. This constituted a 35% enlistment rate and was at least equal to the ratio of the non-Indian population. Native people also raised approximately $44,000 by the end of the first World War to donate to various war relief funds.

The Indians who volunteered paid a significant price in terms of the killed, wounded and sick. Many of them were decorated for conspicuous bravery. Alberta historian James Dempsey writes: ''In summary, the contributions of Indians in the military aspect of the war effort were comparable to that of other Canadians. The major difference was that Indians were not required or expected to serve, but they did so with gallantry and valor.''

Returning Treaty Indian veterans did not receive the same assistance as other soldiers. Their lot had not improved and their contribution was soon forgotten. Fred Gaffen in his work on the native peoples' role in both World Wars, *Forgotten Soldiers*, describes the problems many Indians faced in obtaining land grants under the Soldier Settlement Act of 1919. He concluded: ''only half a dozen grants of free land under the Soldier Settlement Act were given to Indian veterans of the Great War on the Prairies off the reserves.'' Out of 25,000 soldier settlers to whom land loans were granted, only 224 were Indian soldiers, most of them from Ontario, with their locations on the reserves. Indian veterans on reserves in need of help were to be treated like other Indians on reserves rather than as veterans and were not eligible for War Veterans Allowance. It was not until 1936 that this policy was modified and the Indian veterans on reserves received the same benefits as others. After 1918, the hope of the better future for which they had fought faded away for many Native veterans. Dempsey puts it, ''The hopes of the Indians not only did not materialize, but in fact their economic status decreased from what it had been before the war. As a result, the era of the 1920's has been noted as a time of marked decline for the Indians, economically, numerically and politically.''

When World War II began, Canadians of aboriginal origin again responded well. Approximately 3,000 treaty Indians enlisted along with many Métis and non-status Indians. Those who survived and returned were again treated with contempt. Louis Bruyère writes: ''One of Canada's greatest shames has to be how aboriginal veterans were presented medals and decorations via the back doors of legions by the same comrades they fought with. The laws and cultural ignorance of the day made it impossible for aboriginal veterans to sit in taverns and bars with their non-aboriginal buddies and reminisce about the war.''

The living conditions of Indian veterans and their families again deteriorated from what they had been before the war. Bruyère: ''The families of those Indian men who had to give up their Indian status in order to join the Canadian armed forces and were killed in battle faced new odds because they lost the support systems of the reserves. Wives and children with little or no marketable skills were forced to turn to the welfare system for survival and today you can witness the results. Many of the grandchildren of these people are also on welfare because they had no other role model to imitate or follow.'' In such circumstances, the demonstrated patriotism among natives from Western Canada and elsewhere borders on the astonishing.

A report prepared by Indian Affairs officials and published in 1980 documented the story of Indian conditions during the previous ten to twenty years. Life expectancy was on average 10 years less than that of the national population. Indian death rates were 2 to 4 times the national average. The number of deaths due to suicide was almost 3 times the national rate. The report concluded that the major causes of Indian deaths were illnesses associated with poor housing and living conditions. In the 1980's the native unemployment rate in some regions reaches 90%. Many of Canada's 700,000 aboriginal people live amid alcoholism, unemployment, despair and suicide.

Recent Trends

The 1960's and 1970's witnessed a reawakening Indian consciousness, a rebirth of native pride, a rediscovery of Indian culture and traditions, and a growing desire of native peoples to redefine their place in Confederation. Indians who astonishingly until 1960 were not even allowed to vote in federal elections (unless they relinquished their legal Indian status) sought to reaffirm their right to self-determination. Indian leaders emerged who forcefully expressed their desire to gain equality with other Canadians and at the same time to maintain their heritage.

Since 1977, aboriginal groups have actively sought recognition of their "inherent right to self-government," a right they exercised before Europeans arrived in North America and which many believe has never been extinguished. Claims that political structures were unknown to native people prior to contact with Europeans ignore the fact that most First Nations have complex forms of government that go back centuries.

As religion was an integral part of the aboriginal life, their governments were operated according to spiritual values. Government was often conducted on the basis of traditions modified with pragmatic innovations. The Potlatch, for example, was a West Coast system for calling assemblies. Through ceremonies, songs, dances and speeches, new leaders were installed in office. Ottawa chose to outlaw the Potlatch, and attendance at Potlatch functions was prohibited by law as late as 1951. People who lived according to Potlatch had to practise their religious beliefs clandestinely and were forced to live under a system of government imposed on them.

The House of Commons Special Committee on Indian Self-Government in its 1983 report emphasized the value of the understanding it had gained during the hearings. "All Canadians," it said, "would benefit from similar information so that their understanding of their relationship to the Indian First Nations could be extended. In this way, the popular view of Indians could be corrected. They would learn that Indians were not pagan and uncultured, but peoples who moved from free, self-sustaining First Nations to a state of dependency and social disorganization as the result of a hundred years of nearly total government control." The special committees made 58 recommendations. The first was that the federal government should establish a new relationship with the Indian First Nations, and that an essential element of this relationship must be Indian self-government.

Meech Lake

A fourth and final First Ministers' Constitutional Conference held in March 1987 in Ottawa focussed on the self-government issue, but failed to produce an amendment to the Canadian constitution. No further meetings are planned, and the prospects of amending the constitution to accommodate aboriginal self-government in the near future are poor.

The 1987 Meech Lake Constitutional Accord is seen by native leaders as having a negative impact on aboriginal peoples. "Aboriginal peoples are left out of any realistic chance of being included in the future constitutional order.... It ransoms our long term future for the short run gains of eleven First Ministers," says Louis Bruyère. Aboriginal leaders have put forward several proposals addressing their concerns which might be accommodated within the framework of the Meech Lake Accord. Hope persists among the native leaders that public pressure on the federal and provincial governments will eventually bring about native self-government.

Northerners, native and white, generally share with natives the sense of being left out by the Meech Lake Accord because they see opportunities for provincehood in the two Territories virtually eliminated. The creation of new provinces in the future requires the unanimous consent of all provinces. "This requirement effectively denies the Yukon's hope of future provincehood and is unacceptable to Northerners," says the Yukon government leader Tony Penikett.

The fallback position for the Dene, asserts Erasmus, is provincial status for the North because only above the 60th parallel are aboriginal peoples sufficiently numerous to be able to influence their own governments. Otherwise the vast North will remain a storehouse for the future resource needs of Southern Canadians.

But how will all ten provincial governments agree to provide status as required by the Meech Lake Accord? The accord, Erasmus goes on, ''has made it impossible for us to become provinces.'' The only other option for Northerners, an attempt to renew the constitutional negotiations, seems equally unlikely to be productive.

In Fort Simpson N.W.T. late in 1987, Pope John Paul II called for more self-government for natives and for a new round of talks so that aboriginal rights may finally be entrenched in the Canadian constitution. He reaffirmed for native peoples the need for a ''just and equitable degree of self-governing with a land base and adequate resources necessary for the development of a viable economy for present and future generations.'' In reply to a question, he said that Canadian natives ''don't have it good,'' adding that the opportunity to call for the re-opening of the constitutional talks and a just and equitable land-claims agreement were important reasons for his trip.

Northern Blues

An estimated 10,000 Indians and Métis and 17,000 Inuit share 1.2 million square miles with 20,000 whites in the Northwest Territories. In the much smaller Yukon territory, there are currently about 3000 Indians and Métis and 19,000 whites. Both territories are essentially still colonies of Ottawa, and many of the same practices which troubled Western Canadians earlier are still carried out as a matter of habit north of the sixtieth parallel.

One major native grievance is the continuing attack on hunting and trapping, the traditional way of life and source of livelihood, by animal rights groups in metropolitan Canada. Trapping in fact remains one of the major economic activities over approximately two-thirds of the land area of Canada.

There are many other grievances, one being the relocation during World War II of many Yukon natives from their hunting camps into towns – some forcibly – by our federal government. The same thing happened in the Northwest Territories during the 1950's. Effective control of native lives by whites is especially frustrating because there are not enough town jobs in the North and many do not wish to move out of the North.

An important mix of language and aboriginal title issues recently arose east of Yellowknife where the Inuit, representing more than 95 percent of the permanent residents of the vast Eastern Arctic, contend their traditional language of Inuktitut must be entrenched in any land-claim settlement under the Canadian Constitution. The Inuit negotiators are determined that their language, which holds, for example, twenty words for the different types of snow, does not disappear like so many other aboriginal languages because of anglicization. Ottawa's negotiators have until now refused to consider this, contending in effect that to concede a constitutional language right here would somehow require Ottawa to concede the same to languages spoken by new Canadians in Southern Canada. The Inuit's persuasive counter is that without constitutional protection the same pressures could result in the same consequences as have appeared over the decades for minority official languages in various provinces. If Ottawa recognizes Inuktitut as an official language in work places, schools and courts only within the land claims area along with English and French, it would also assist more Inuit to find jobs locally. An important language ball is clearly in Ottawa's court following its recent success in signing a historic agreement with the Dene and Métis of Northern Canada.

Native land claims have emerged in recent years as the focus of the North-South dispute partly because many northern natives see land, in the language of Northerner René Lamothe, as "Mother because she gives life, because she is the provider, the protector, the comforter.... We cannot stand on her with integrity and respect and claim to love the life she gives and allow her to be ravaged." The Edmonton academic Gurston Dacks judges that most northern natives believe a favourable settlement of their land claims would give them within Canada "a meaningful control over the many features of their lives that influence their self-definitions and their collective life as a people."

In the western half of the present Northwest Territories, the Dene and Inuit co-existed with Europeans for many years. No treaties were entered for a long period, most likely because no one in Ottawa thought there was any land in the region worth controlling. Indeed, as Georges Erasmus points out, Treaty No. 8 was made applicable to part of northern British Columbia and part of the territory north of 60 degrees only after the Klondike Gold discovery in 1896, so that Ottawa could open a right of way for thousands of panhandlers streaming north to Dawson City. Only in 1921-22 after oil was discovered at Norman Wells, he adds, was Treaty 11 negotiated with the Dene, presumably so that southern access for oil exploration could be enhanced.

Erasmus, a Dene himself, stresses that aboriginal peoples across the North as well as in Southern Canada had considerable experience with treaties long before the European version arrived. Peace and friendship treaties were common, as were others providing for an exchange of hunting privileges. What was different about the Canadian treaties for aboriginals, says Erasmus, was that the Canadian treaty negotiators, unlike native ones, ''could look you in the eye and lie. What made it even worse was that they could do so in front of their own holy men who often observed the discussions.'' The Northerners thought Treaty 8 and Treaty 11 were peace and friendship treaties of the earlier type.

Only in the late 1960's, when roads within the Treaty 11 land area began to appear, did younger Dene began to question their elders' view that there was little more than peace and friendship involved. Some elders, trusting in the oral version, simply did not believe the written version of Treaty 11 when it was read to them. Very hard feelings resulted in some communities when it became clear that Dene land title might have been surrendered. When the move to build the Mackenzie Valley Pipeline began in the 1970's, other northern peoples realized that without reserves or other land bases their futures were gravely threatened. They pushed hard for comprehensive settlements of their claims to win the possibility of economic self-sufficiency through resource royalties.

In the native view, ten years of negotiations ended badly in March 1987, when the federal cabinet indicated that the settlement would consist not of land and royalties but of a cash payment over a 20-year period. That meant only perpetual poverty to many northern natives.

The essential legal demand of the northern aboriginal peoples, including the Métis Association of the N.W.T., the Dene Nation, the Inuit Tapirisat and the Committee for Original Peoples Entitlement (COPE), is that particular areas of the North should be designated as governmental units. Those governments should then be delegated responsibility for some matters of importance to their native residents. The organizations argue that native people enjoy rights to lands occupied by them since time immemorial and that accordingly ''the customary law of native people [must] be protected and recognized.''

Some observers believe that, if a reasonable accommodation of native views is not recognized quickly by Southern Canadians, Northern Canada could become a new centre of major separatist activity.

A significant breakthrough in longstanding northern land claims was reached in September, 1988, when Prime Minister Brian Mulroney and representatives of 15,000 Dene and Métis signed an agreement-in-principle. The agreement provides the natives of the Mackenzie River Valley with ownership of 10,000 square kilometres, surface rights to an additional 170,000, and a $500 million settlement in cash. The agreement, which took 15 years to achieve, is welcome. It represents a large step forward in resolving northern land claims even though some critical areas remain to be settled, particularly those dealing with aboriginal rights and self-government. A pattern for future settlements with other northern native groups has been established, and the way is open to settle Canada's account with our aboriginal peoples honourably.

EIGHT

Louis Riel
Patriot without a Country

A GOVERNMENT OF CANADA hanged Louis Riel 103 years ago, but many Canadians will still not let him die. The man who during a turbulent life was founder of a province, member of the Parliament of Canada, an outlaw, an exile, and a victim of the hangman has remained the storm centre of Canadian politics. He continues to capture imaginations and controversies in a way no other Canadian figure has done.

The transformation of the founder of Manitoba from a regional agitator and national traitor to a major Western Canadian hero in our popular mind has taken much of a century. For a long while, Canadian historians because of partisanship or for other reasons ignored the details of his life. Even the *Makers of Canada* collection of biographies published in 1905-1908 did not include him. Today, as the Winnipeg historian J.M. Bumsted points out, "he is the only major Canadian whose papers have been collected and published with the full panoply of scholarly apparatus developed for figures like Thomas Jefferson, George Washington, Benjamin Franklin and John Adams...." To Canada's Native people, Riel has come to symbolize their aspiration for a fuller share in our national life, "What Canadians do not understand is that Louis Riel is a Father of Canadian Confederation.... He intuitively sensed the future for Canada and wanted to guarantee a place for Métis people in that future. The fact that he was betrayed and martyred for his efforts only guarantees the fact that today he is hailed by his people as a freedom fighter of the highest order...,'' says Louis Bruyère. This sketch will make a case that Riel's statues should stand not only near the legislature buildings in Winnipeg and Regina, as they now do, but in prominent places in all four western and northern capitals, and in Ottawa itself.

At the age of 14, the young Louis, who was in fact of seven-eighths white ancestry, followed his father's footsteps to Montreal to study for the priesthood. The Catholic Bishop of St. Boniface, Alexandre Taché, was so impressed by his academic ability and religious ardour during his elementary schooling that he had persuaded the wife of a later Lieutenant Governor of Québec to pay what the Riel family could not afford.

During the next decade at the Sulpician seminary, Louis proved a serious and indeed brilliant student. His father's death hit him so hard that afterwards he avoided other students, faltered and missed classes. In the final year of the seminary he abandoned his religious studies and spent a little over a year in Montreal working for a brief time as a student-at-law. In 1867 he went to St. Paul, Minnesota, before he finally decided to return to Red River a year later.

His first act of leadership occurred in the fall of 1869 well before the vast Rupert's Land was formally transferred from the Hudson's Bay Company to the government of Canada. William McDougall, Prime Minister John A. Macdonald's Minister of Public Works, had ordered a survey to be done on the mile-square system of the Americans to accommodate new settlers from Ontario. The Quebec land system, already working well for the Métis in Red River, had provided each settler with a small river frontage and, in recognition of the water shortage problem, with a "hay privilege" as well, going back from the river for two miles. Understandably, the Métis were greatly disturbed when McDougall's agent, Colonel John S. Dennis, began his American system and doubtless illegal surveys in their community. When a survey crew began work on the hay pasture of André Nault, a

French Canadian, Riel in company with a group of unarmed Métis appeared on the scene and declared that the territory south of the Assiniboine belonged to the people of Red River and not to Canada, and that the Métis would not allow the survey to proceed any further. His argument was that the Canadian government "had no right to make surveys on the Territory without the express permission of the people of the Settlement." That ended the surveying for the time being and established Riel at only 25 years of age as the new Métis leader of Red River.

Within days of the Nault incident, William McDougall was appointed by Sir John as the Lieutenant Governor of Rupert's Land. The Prime Minister's ignorance of the West was again evident; the Red River Métis seethed. The governor-designate soon reached Minnesota by train and proceeded north to Pembina. There he received a note signed by Riel as secretary of the National Committee of the Métis of Red River ordering him not to enter the territory of the North-West without "special permission" of the Committee. McDougall impetuously drove two miles north to a local Hudson's Bay post, but quickly obeyed an order delivered by Ambroise Lépine, a giant of 6'3" in height, on behalf of Riel's Committee to return to the American side of the international boundary.

In fact, McDougall's mission was one of mismanaged conquest meeting Métis resistance, not rebellion or insurrection. Until Queen Victoria consented to the transfer, which was not finally done until June, 1870, the only legal authority for the region was that of the Hudson's Bay Company, but it had, in Howard's words, "signed away its authority and its embittered agents had virtually ceased to govern.... The new government which McDougall was attempting to impose and against which the Métis 'rebelled' did not exist either, and the 'Governor' had no more right in the country than any private citizen. He was not even entitled, at the moment, to the courtesies due a visiting dignitary, because he was no longer a member of the Canadian Cabinet."

On the same day that McDougall was ordered out of Rupert's Land, Riel formally succeeded John Bruce as leader of the New

Nation and with 120 followers seized Fort Garry. He did this to obtain control of its muskets and cannon, explaining to the protesting Hudson's Bay Company officials, who were confined to quarters, that he wanted to prevent bloodshed and guard the fort against danger.

Riel then turned his attention to establishing both order and democracy. The English-speaking parishes were invited to elect twelve representatives to meet with his equal-sized council of French-speaking Métis. Both groups cooperated. The first convention met in mid-November, 1869. It produced a bill of rights which in effect demanded full provincial status. Its specifics included the right to elect a legislature, a free homestead law, treaties with Indians, use of French and English as official languages, respect for all rights present before the transfer of sovereignty, and fair representation in the Parliament of Canada. None of the people in the heterogeneous community could argue that their interests were not protected.

In the meantime, McDougall remained fuming with his wagons and entourage near Pembina. The prime minister in Ottawa soon learned from Queen Victoria that she hoped the Métis would present their grievances to her governor general in the new country. Macdonald, for once prudent about the West, advised caution to McDougall, but the self-professed democrat without any authority from anyone drafted out of his own imagination a proclamation dated December 1, 1869, announcing in the Queen's name the completion of the transfer to Canadian sovereignty and himself the governor of the North West Territory of Canada – "an act," in the words of W.L. Morton, "at once rash and completely illegal."

Copies of the proclamation quickly appeared on walls at Fort Garry at McDougall's direction. Knowing from his spies in McDougall's party that Queen Victoria had made no such proclamation, Riel immediately denounced it as fraudulent. In one of the most comical scenes in our entire national history, McDougall on the same day as he issued his bogus proclamation took a party of seven men north a few miles over the border and in a snowy gale read it to the stars and north wind before rushing back to Pembina. The gesture, as Howard wrote, "convulsed America, horrified Ottawa and ruined him forever in the West." He compounded matters the next day by issuing yet another illegal order authorizing the surveyor Col. J.S. Dennis, "Lieutenant and Conservator of the Peace" in Rupert's Land, to organize and arm a force sufficient to disperse the armed men in the settlement "unlawfully assembled and disturbing the public peace." Dennis, invited in effect to begin a civil war, managed to occupy lower Fort Garry, twenty miles north of Winnipeg, but his campaign soon collapsed and Riel's government continued. The Prime Minister later repudiated everything the pair had done and wrote in a self-revealing note to a friend, "The two together have done their utmost to destroy our chance of an amicable settlement with these wild people."

Riel doubtless knew from the start that his little colony could not maintain independence from both Canada and a hovering United States with unconcealed continental ambitions. On December 8, 1869 after successfully arresting 45 armed Canadians who had occupied the home of Dr. John Schultz in Red River, Riel opted to negotiate with Ottawa rather than Washington despite various inducements offered by the Americans to do so. His declaration of that day said many things, but the effect of it was that the Provisional Government established in Rupert's Land the previous month was the only lawful authority in the region and it now "wished to enter into such negotiations with the Canadian Government as may be favourable for the good government and prosperity of this people." In 60 days, Riel had driven McDougall permanently out of the West. The latter's lieutenant, Dennis, had been unable to ignite a civil war and Riel's List of Rights and Declarations had provided the necessary ingredients for the successful resistance to a crude conquest attempt. No one at Red River had been robbed or attacked. Ottawa, moreover, had decided to send three commissioners west to negotiate the terms of entry into Confederation.

The commissioners were led by Donald Smith, manager of the Hudson's Bay Company's Montreal district and husband of a Métis woman. Fully a thousand people from the Red River's scattered settlements of approximately twelve thousand attended a mid-January open field meeting to consider Ottawa's case. After two days of five-hour meetings in temperatures of 20 below zero, Riel, as president of the Provisional Government of Rupert's Land, moved that a convention of forty (half elected by the Scots and English, half by the French) consider Smith's proposals. The North-West die was clearly already cast in favour of Canada and against the American hopes for annexation of the region, but it would be a long while indeed before Riel got much credit in Central Canada, or among its politicians and historians, for choosing Canada.

At the convention, Riel attempted to include in a new bill of rights a demand that the region be admitted to Canada as a full province rather than a territory. This was rejected by the English-speaking delegates who were supported by three French-speaking ones. His Provisional Government, however, later made this request at his insistence and it is on this basis that his place in history as Manitoba's founder was established. Smith approved the new bill of rights in principle.

In a particularly astute move, Riel then won full legal status for his Provisional Government by persuading the convention to reestablish his government on the basis that the delegates to Ottawa would need official status. Riel was elected president of its assembly, or council, elected on February 9, 1870. Three delegates were chosen to go to Ottawa.

The ultimate cause of most of Riel's problems, the execution of Thomas Scott by his government, occurred only days after his installation as president. The basic facts are well known. In hindsight, it was really the only error committed by the young and inexperienced leader of an infant nation. Yet, for Riel thereafter, in W.L. Morton's words, "there was to be no peace in the North-West he loved. No peace anywhere but the forlorn peace of exile and the final peace of the gibbet at Regina." Few now recall that Riel prevented 600 well-armed and mounted Métis from destroying an unmounted and lightly-armed group of several hundred settlers, mostly from Portage La Prairie, who attempted to free the remaining prisoners from the earlier seizure at Schultz's home. As the prospects of a confrontation heightened, the remaining 24 prisoners signed peace oaths and were released. Most of the settlers from Ontario then dispersed, but about 50 who did not were arrested and jailed for two days, including Major C.W. Boulton. Riel wisely granted mercy to Boulton, the leader of the short-lived uprising, after the mother of John Sutherland, one of two dead victims of the affair, pleaded with him to do so.

Thomas Scott, hot-headed and aggressive, was not a popular figure in Red River. Donald Smith himself called Scott "a rash, thoughtless man whom none cared to have anything to do with." Scott, who interpreted Riel's clemency in Boulton's case as timidity, deliberately antagonized and insulted guards at every opportunity. "The Métis are a pack of cowards. They will not dare to shoot me," he shouted defiantly. In any case, Scott, who had been arrested for being part of Boulton's uprising, was convicted of insubordination while in custody by an ad hoc court-martial and shot by a Métis firing squad on March 1, 1870. He was the only individual killed by the Métis during the 10 anxious and dangerous months they controlled Rupert's Land, and the execution was doubtless carried out partly to prevent others from challenging the new government. As Riel later put it, "If there was a single act of severity, one must not lose sight of the long course of moderate conduct which gives us the right to say that we sought to disarm, rather than fight, the lawless strangers who were making war against us." Years later, just before dying on a scaffold, he told his priest, "I swear as I am about to appear before God that the shooting of Scott was not a crime. It was a political necessity.... I commanded the shooting, believing it necessary to save the lives of hundreds of others."

Unfortunately for Riel, his nemesis John Schultz had already escaped and would travel from town to town in Ontario haranguing anyone who would listen about the blood-thirsty Riel and the Métis. The Ontario government later offered a $5000 reward for the capture of its hero's murderer, even though the act had occurred outside both Ontario and the Dominion. "Scott and Riel," in Howard's words, "ceased to exist as men. They became symbols solely: Scott the Protestant, Riel the Catholic.... That was the picture: young, progressive, dedicated Protestantism destroyed by entrenched, superstitious, corrupt Catholicism. It was a good sharp picture and it made for a foul and vulgar fight, whose repercussions echoed ominously throughout the next fifteen years.''

Scott's execution also prevented the granting of an amnesty by Macdonald's government for any "illegal" acts committed by anyone in Red River in 1869-70. The prime minister had in fact issued an amnesty proclamation, but it did not arrive until four days after Scott's death, and the prime minister took the view that it did not apply to those involved with Scott. The lack of an amnesty clearly prevented Riel from becoming either the first premier of Manitoba in 1870 or a leading member of Parliament from the province. Its consequences doubtless contributed to his subsequent mental breakdowns.

Two of the three delegates en route to Ottawa were briefly imprisoned by Ontario authorities for alleged complicity in Scott's murder. Macdonald would even protest that he never recognized Riel's Provisional Government, something flatly contradicted by both the record and the fact of the negotiations with its delegates. "The Right Honourable John A. Macdonald lied (excuse the word) like a trooper," an exasperated Archbishop Taché wrote subsequently.

On May 2nd, 1870 a bill called the Manitoba Bill, embodying most of the features of the Métis "List of Rights," was introduced and quickly passed. The historian G.F.G. Stanley recognized Riel as "the father of the province of Manitoba," conceding that the federal government would not willingly have granted provincial status to "the infant half-breed colony at the time of the transfer of the Territories to Canada, had it not been for Riel's protest.''

The legislative assembly of Rupert's Land heard the delegation's report when it returned from Ottawa and unanimously voted to accept the Manitoba Act and to enter Canada on the terms proposed. An ominous beginning occurred when Ottawa, once again grossly mismanaging events in the West, permitted Colonel Garnet Wolseley and his Red River Expedition of 1200 mostly Ontario and British troops to reach the new province before the new lieutenant governor, Adams Archibald, could arrive. Riel rejected the advice of those who wanted to fight, and insisted on welcoming Wolseley in peace. But his scouts subsequently indicated that the approaching expedition intended to deal with the rebels and Riel felt obliged to leave his new province for the U.S. for his own safety.

Wolseley paid off his exhausted troops after their incredibly arduous journey and publicly denounced the Métis as "banditti and cowards," despite Ottawa's clear order that the Provisional Government should remain in place until its governor arrived. The conduct of some of his men and those, like Schultz, who had slunk back into Red River, towards anyone involved in Scott's death was as outrageous as it should have been predictable in Ottawa. Two suspects were murdered. Another was bayoneted and left for dead. Riel's mother was terrorized at her home. Archibald, an honourable and fair administrator, received little help from Ottawa and reported to Macdonald a year later that many of the Métis "actually have been so beaten and outraged that they feel as if they were living in a state of slavery."

Macdonald's mishandlings of Manitoba continued virtually unabated. Only five of his first 85 appointments in the new province went to Métis. Archbishop Taché went to Ottawa to see about the amnesty for Riel and Ambroise Lépine. The prime minister produced $1000 in cash and indicated that he might be able to speed the amnesty up if both would leave the country for a year. Taché eventually did persuade both to leave with their families.

Riel returned briefly to Manitoba in the fall of 1872 to be nominated for Parliament, but withdrew in favour of George-Etienne Cartier who had been defeated 10 days earlier in Montreal East. After Cartier died a year later, Riel ran in the Provencher district as an independent candidate and won by a landslide in the general election of 1874. Still no amnesty had been granted.

When Riel appeared at the House of Commons in Ottawa to

claim his seat in late 1874, the new Manitoba attorney general, Henry Clarke, had already indicted him for Scott's murder. The question of how a Manitoba court could assert that it had jurisdiction over an incident happening before the province itself was created was essentially ignored. Mackenzie Bowell, the Grand Master of the Orange Lodge and future Conservative prime minister, moved for and won Riel's expulsion from the House. But the new Liberal government of Alexander Mackenzie, put into office in the "Pacific Scandal" election of 1874 by voters seeking to punish Macdonald, proclaimed an amnesty for Riel in April, 1875. Unfortunately for Riel, it was made conditional upon his exile for five years under an extraordinary Manitoba court order made against him a few months earlier. In effect the Manitoba court finding of "outlaw" against him amounted to a bizarre finding of guilt for the murder of Scott in Riel's absence. The order in the circumstances thus probably had no basis in law certainly none in justice — and should have been ignored by Mackenzie.

Following the federal election in 1878, Riel's arch-enemy John A. Macdonald was returned to power. In the interval after his expulsion from the House, Riel travelled widely in America and clearly suffered several bouts of mental illness. Much of the time he was penniless. In 1876, he was committed to a mental hospital near Quebec City for a period even though he was still banished from Canada. Even Howard his biographer and admirer was convinced that he showed "symptoms of paranoid schizophrenia." The Riel of 1884-85 was clearly not the perfectly rational leader of 1869-70, but bearing in mind what he had been through since, whose mind could have resisted better?

When he returned to the West in 1878, he found that the steamboats and Red River carts had gone overnight with the arrival of the railway. The buffalo were gone; the local Métis were discouraged, and felt threatened by the westward advance of an agricultural civilization. "These impulsive half-breeds...must be kept down by a strong hand until they are swamped by the influx of settlers," John A. MacDonald had written to Sir John

Rose in 1870. The process had begun.

Riel worried about his people, but resolved to move on to the freedom and older ways of Montana. He became a wood chopper, a trader and mediator between Indians or Métis and white Americans. In 1881, he married 21-year-old Marguerite Monet, the daughter of a buffalo hunter, to whom he was unfailingly considerate until his death. A son, Jean, was soon born and then Marie Angelique. Riel became an American citizen and was active in Republican politics. He also taught Blackfoot Indian boys at a mission school at St. Peters.

In early June 1884, Gabriel Dumont and other Métis from what is now northern Saskatchewan came to invite Riel to take charge of their campaign to seek redress from Ottawa for their grievances. Riel, who had long maintained a wish to help his people, agreed to go without any payment until September. He and his family loaded a cart and departed. Riel evidently told a Montana priest, before crossing into Canada: "I see a gallows on top of that hill, and I am swinging from it." The party pushed on to Batoche, a Métis settlement 40 miles southwest of Prince Albert.

Riel's speeches in the North-West were moderate, making such reasonable requests as free title for the Métis on existing land, provincial status for the region, and representation in the federal Parliament. In December, a petition drafted under the guidance of Riel was sent to Ottawa, proposing in addition to the above items, responsible government, provincial control of natural resources, and the building of a railway to Hudson's Bay to provide access to Europe for prairie products.

Macdonald, who had been for some time Minister of the Interior as well as Prime Minister, again demonstrated his lack of interest in the North-West by essentially ignoring the numerous memorials and petitions received from the region. After Riel arrived in the North-West, Macdonald's only response was to increase the number of Mounted Police in the Batoche district. Even the commanding NWMP officer at Fort Carlton, L.N.F. Crozier, urged Macdonald to survey the Métis land in the manner they preferred; had he done it, the North-West Rebellion might not have occurred. "Old Tomorrow," as the Western Indians had first named the prime minister, finally opted instead to appoint a commission to investigate Métis complaints; but the Métis had long since lost faith in his word and the North-West Rebellion broke out in late March of 1885.

The gross insensitivity of Macdonald and his government was clearly the major cause of the uprising. Not a few Canadian historians have recognized that the Métis rebellion, coming at precisely the right time, saved the federal government from political limbo and the CPR from bankruptcy. To Donald McLean, a Saskatchewan authority of the Métis, this was not a "fortunate coincidence" but a careful "design."

The CPR certainly received further public funding because of the role it played in crushing the Métis rebellion, and its transcontinental line was completed nine days before the execution of Louis Riel in Regina. William Van Horne, the CPR general manager, later was quoted as saying that "the CPR should erect a monument to Riel."

Riel's decision to establish a provisional government under the protection of the Métis cavalry was in retrospect both a tragedy and an act of folly. Rupert's Land in 1869 lacked a government; the North-West Territories in 1885 had both a government and an almost-completed railway capable of delivering Canadian troops in a matter of days, not months. Nonetheless, Riel called a mass meeting, formed a council and called his people to arms against the oncoming police. The support he had enjoyed among the Catholic clergy and whites vanished immediately. The tragic last stand of the Métis people was underway, although Riel and Dumont both knew in their hearts from the outset that they could not win a full-scale war.

The war for Western Canada's future was mercifully brief. Approximately three thousand troops were soon in the Territories and moving against fewer than 500 Métis soldiers. At Fish Creek, outnumbered six to one and later ten to one, Dumont's soldiers held off 400 white troops until they withdrew and were immobilized for two full weeks. Three battles had taken place and three times the Métis-Indian alliance had won; but only 200 sharpshooters remained as the North-West Field Force neared the final

LOUIS RIEL

encounter at Batoche. After a four-day battle, the Métis gave up, thus ending two months of combat. Riel surrendered to Middleton; Dumont fled to Montana.

Riel's conviction in Regina of high treason, for which at the time death was the only penalty, raises many questions. Did a territorial magistrate's court have jurisdiction to hear one of the most important trials in Canadian history? Could Riel as an American citizen be properly convicted in the particular circumstances under a British treason statute of 1352? Should the presiding judge, Hugh Richardson, as a member of the anti-Catholic Orange Order and a part-time magistrate serving only at the pleasure of the federal government, not have disqualified himself from the case? Why was the trial held in Regina and not in Winnipeg? Why were the six jurors selected all English-speaking Protestants who were thus obliged to depend on interpreters for much of the testimony? Why did Judge Richardson select the names of the 36 prospective jurors?

In his personal address in English to the jury, Riel spoke of conditions of the Prairie Métis and their various unanswered petitions to Ottawa, indicating that he felt God wanted him to make a better world for his people. He wished to be judged both sane and not guilty, he argued, because "I have acted reasonably and in self-defence while the government my accuser, being irresponsible, and consequently insane, cannot but have acted wrongly." Riel's team of defence lawyers from Quebec attempted from the outset to prove him insane in order to save his life. But the accused's stirring speech to the jury was so lucid overall that it undid him because the jurors could simply not accept that anyone insane could deliver such an address.

Riel's chief counsel, Charles Fitzpatrick, who later became chief justice of Canada, addressed the jury for two hours. He stressed that Riel had abandoned his security in the U.S. without asking for any payment in order to help his people in the North-West Territories and to seek redress from a stone-deaf government two thousand miles away. Would a sane man have declared war on the British Empire as Riel did? He ended by urging a

159

verdict of not guilty by reason of insanity. "I know that you shall not weave the cord that shall hang him and hang him high in the face of all the world, a poor confirmed lunatic; a victim, gentlemen, of oppression or the victim of fanaticism."

The judge's charge to the jury was anything but fair and balanced on the evidence heard, especially with respect to the all-important insanity issue, but neither the Manitoba Queen's Bench nor the Judicial Committee of the Privy Council in Britain would later order a new trial. After retiring for only an hour, the jury returned with a guilty verdict and a recommendation of mercy.

Riel thanked the jury for "clearing me of the stain of insanity" and spoke of being "hunted like an elk for fifteen years." He then asked for a commission to decide whether he was a murderer of Thomas Scott. One of his jurors, Edwin J. Brooks, answered this question only five decades later in a newspaper interview: "We tried Louis Riel for treason, but he was hanged for the murder of Thomas Scott." Richardson sentenced him to be hanged, showing in his remarks that his view of the case was identical with that of the prosecutors. A few days before the Riel trial, Richardson had acquitted Riel's white assistant, Will Jackson, of treason on grounds of insanity.

A flood of petitions and pleas for clemency soon reached Ottawa from many people at home and abroad. Macdonald's resolve only hardened as families, friends and the political parties throughout Canada split bitterly over the issue. In an interview, the 72-year-old Prime Minister stamped his foot and said what are possibly the most insensitive words ever uttered by a Canadian prime minister: "He shall hang though every dog in Quebec bark in his favour." He also tried to persuade a concerned governor general that "this North-West outbreak was a mere domestic trouble, and ought not to be elevated to the rank of a rebellion.... It never endangered the safety of the state." This was indeed an outrageous comment on an incident that his government had publicly characterized as a major rebellion, whose leader it prosecuted on a charge of high treason.

The governor general nonetheless prevailed on him to appoint a medical commission to determine whether Riel was still sane. If not, this would provide his government a sound reason to exercise the royal prerogative of mercy without disturbing the court verdict.

The prime minister shamelessly manipulated the commission in a gross abuse of his office, admonishing one commissioner to find Riel sane and seriously distorting the conclusion of the other commissioner that Riel was "not an accountable being." Both Queen Victoria and the President of the United States, Grover Cleveland, declined to interfere, the first because an adamant Macdonald indicated his government would brook no interference, the second evidently because his secretary of state and possibly the British ambassador counselled restraint. Clearly the decision not to show the same mercy to Riel as to the other convicted rebellion prisoners was based on political necessities. Macdonald balanced his reelection prospects in Ontario against those in Quebec and decided he could better afford to lose a few seats in Quebec than to have English Canada turn against him.

Riel died as he prayed, with courage and dignity. Somehow a final indignity was allowed by the federal authorities to its hired executioner, Jack Henderson, a friend of Thomas Scott and Riel's former prisoner. George Stanley describes the last moments of Riel in this grim account: "Near the enclosure behind which the Métis tragedy was drawing to a close, there stood various groups of people, talking and grumbling because they could not see the hanging. As the moment of the execution approached, there was silence. Then a dull heavy sound as of a body falling. 'The God damned son of a bitch is gone at last,' said one voice. 'Yes,' said another, 'the son of a bitch is gone for certain now.' There followed some heartless laughter. But it was thin and brittle."

Three weeks later, Riel's body was taken secretly home to St. Boniface from Regina. After remaining in his mother's home for two nights while hundreds of Métis filed past, it was moved to the cathedral in St. Boniface. Archbishop Taché conducted the requiem before a large crowd and one of Western Canada's greatest sons was buried nearby. On the brown granite tombstone are the words "Riel, 16 novembre 1885."

161

NINE

An International Community
The Peoples of the Region

"A MAN IS OF ALL SORTS OF BAGGAGE, the most difficult to be transported," wrote Scotland's Adam Smith in the 18th century. Yet, as history indicates, between 1880 and 1914, millions of people left their homelands in search of greater economic opportunity, freedom and peace. The migration from Europe to North America in that period has been described as "the mightiest movement of people in modern history." Western Canada became the destination of several million immigrants, not only from Europe but from other parts of the world, who were attracted by the promises of a better life in the "Last Best West." The result was a unique model of ethno-cultural cooperation without assimilation. As the years passed and the dust from arriving newcomers settled, and after often bitter experiences of adaptation, prejudice and discrimination, a truly international community has developed in the region.

The mosaic analogy is particularly apt for Western Canada because literally dozens of ethnic groups today resemble inlays of differing size, distribution and colour in a larger design. Their diversity of language, dress, culture and custom has created a kaleidoscope in our West and North. The term 'mosaic' itself was first applied to Canada by an American writer, Victoria Hayward, who wrote of our Prairies in 1922, "The New Canadians, representing many lands and widely separated sections of Old Europe, have contributed to the prairie provinces a variety in the way of Church architecture. Cupolas and domes distinctly Eastern, almost Turkish, startle one above the tops of Manitoba maples or the bush of the river banks.... Here and there in the corner of a wheat field, at the cross-section of a prairie highway, one sees, as in Quebec, the tall, uplifted Crucifix set up. It is indeed a mosaic of vast dimensions and great breadth, essayed of the Prairie."

Since the beginning of the twentieth century, Western Canada has continued to develop its culturally pluralistic, multi-political and multi-religious form. This is partly because no cultural community is numerically dominant; there are several large groups, including the English, German, Ukrainian, Scottish, Irish and French-Canadians. Members of every cultural community, including the larger ones, believe people are of equal worth and that all should have the freedom to choose their own life-style. A pattern of permissive differentiation, whether in religion, political ideology or language, instead of assimilation, emerged early in the West and set very firmly. More than in any other region of Canada, multiculturalism began as an acknowledged reality here and flourished as the decades went by.

The prairie population grew from about 400,000 in 1901 to 2.4 million by 1931. A passenger on a CPR train disembarking in Winnipeg in 1914 would encounter on Main Street languages and people from virtually every corner of the earth. As the historian Gerald Friesen points out, "almost half of all prairie residents at the start of the First World War had been born in another country, and the proportion was still one in three as late as 1931. Those who were British by 'origin' (a census term defined by the ancestral roots of a family's male line) had similarly declined to about 50% of the prairie total (of this group, half were English, one-quarter Scots) while the various Eastern European groups (Ukrainian, Austro-Hungarian, Polish and Russian) numbered about 20%, and Western Europeans (German, Dutch, French, including French Canadians) also numbered about 20%."

Five separate waves of immigrants swept over Western Canada. The first, resulting from the fur trade, created the French-and English-speaking Métis. The second, occurring during the final years of the nineteenth century after Confederation, consisted mainly of British Canadian families, although there were also Icelanders, Mennonites, Jews and others. The largest wave swept in between 1897 and 1913, bringing roughly equal numbers of settlers from other provinces of Canada, Britain, America and Continental Europe together with a few Chinese and Japanese. The fourth, arriving during the 1920's, was essentially an extension of the third in terms of points of origin. The fifth, persons arriving since World War II, included Europeans displaced by the war and, after 1962, immigrants from Asia and the Pacific Rim nations.

Clifford Sifton and his belief in the potential of the West deserve much credit for the diversity and vigour of the immigrants who came between 1897 and 1930. As immigration minister from 1896 to 1905, he spent large sums of public money attracting farmers from Europe, Britain and America. Although he personally believed in the assimilation of newcomers to Anglo-Canadian norms, no one can fault him for not casting his net to include farm communities virtually everywhere, most notably in Central and Eastern Europe. His successor as immigration minister, Edmonton's Frank Oliver, reduced recruiting in Europe and increased it in the United Kingdom. In consequence, more British immigrants came after 1905, including an astonishing 80,000 children from English slums whose passages were assisted by British charities. Robert Borden's Conservative government kept the immigration door open to unskilled English immigrants after 1911 but continued a Laurier regulation measure of 1908 which in practice excluded most Asians and Arabs. In 1925, Prime Minister Mackenzie King allowed the Canadian National and Canadian Pacific Railways again to recruit farmers in Central and Eastern Europe; as a result, almost 370,000 Europeans arrived in Canada during the following six years. Between 1931 and 1941, the immigration gates were all but closed to everyone as a reaction to the huge unemployment created by the Great Depression.

By the time of the 1986 national census, the population mix of the four western provinces was significantly different from that of Canada as a whole. In all three prairie provinces less than forty percent of the residents claim a single country of family origin from Britain or France. British Columbia is slightly over forty percent, whereas in Ontario and all four Atlantic provinces well over forty percent of the residents assert a single family origin from the British Isles. In three of them (Nova Scotia, Prince Edward Island and Newfoundland) that proportion is over sixty percent. In the profiles which follow, I will highlight the diversity of Western Canadians through glances at a number of ethno-cultural communities. The sketches feature some of those who have arrived relatively recently but are already making a major contribution to the West, along with groups of longer standing. All have had to meet in some measure the challenges of pioneering and all have responded in their own "Western" way.

More than seventy distinct ethno-cultural groups can now be identified in Western Canada. To tell their respective stories within a framework of one chapter is thus impossible. While attempting to provide an overview of the almost infinite variety of the region, I am forced to focus on only some representative groups which in my opinion reflect well the essence of the other Western Canadian communities today. The singular history of the Métis people in Western Canada was recorded in an earlier chapter. In addition to the Métis, those groups chosen for discussion here appear to me to capture the pioneering spirit of all the first westbound settlers who came, or are coming, to start their lives anew. The chapter concludes with a discussion of the role of bilingualism in a multicultural region.

Scandinavians

Our region is home to almost 80% of all Canadians who claim Scandinavian ancestry: 130,000 Westerners are descended entirely from Danes, Norwegians, Swedes, or Icelanders, while another 380,000 have some Scandinavian forebears. Most Canadian Westerners of Scandinavian origin came to the West as

American immigrants between 1893 and 1914, when nearly a hundred thousand moved to the Canadian Prairies. Many of them settled in fertile parts of central Alberta and Saskatchewan, where they became major players in the formation of the dairy industry. From the beginning, Anglo-Westerners viewed all Scandinavians as close cousins. This was encouraged by such familiar images as Shakespeare's Hamlet, Prince of Denmark. Relations between the historical monarchs of Norway and Scotland were so close that Scotland's Hebrides held the tombs of eight Norwegian kings. And Hans Christian Anderson's fairy tales were as dear to Anglo-Canadian children as to Scandinavian ones.

Scandinavians were among the first settlers who ventured into the North-West at the beginning of the nineteenth century. The earliest Norwegians were brought by Lord Selkirk in 1815 to build a portage for his Selkirk colony on the Red River. At the north end of Lake Winnipeg they established Norway House, which remains a commercial centre to this day. One Norwegian, Peter Dahl, stayed to homestead. During the mid-19th century, the Hudson's Bay Company continued to recruit boatmen from Norway, but the first large influx came later from the south. Between 1871 and 1895, 660,000 Swedes, 330,000 Norwegians and 160,000 Danes reached the United States. Most of them settled in the Midwest, although many had arrived first in Montreal by steamship.

When the price of American farmland later began to rise, the promise of free homesteads in the Canadian West brought many Scandinavians northwards. The first group were Swedes who settled near Minnedosa, Manitoba, and Stockholm, Saskatchewan, in the 1880's. Norwegians in turn founded Numedal in southern Manitoba, and New Norway, Camrose, Olds, Lacombe, Wetaskiwin, Sundre and other centres in Alberta in the mid-1890's. Calgary's first major industry, a sawmill run by a predominantly Norwegian crew, was founded in 1886. Another group of Norwegian fisherman founded Hagensborg in 1893 near Bella Coola on the British Columbia coast. Most Scandinavians settled in Saskatchewan during the early twentieth century. Their practical experience in the American Midwest proved an excellent training for success in the age of wheat.

Icelanders began to arrive in Manitoba in the last quarter of the nineteenth century from an island homeland where entire villages had been swept away by volcanoes. In 1875, a group of them chose to settle in Gimli ("paradise") on the shores of Lake Winnipeg for various reasons, including freedom from prairie grasshoppers, an easy waterway to Winnipeg, an abundance of fish in the lake and the availability of a large tract of land. The new settlement, with its own administration and Icelandic law, was called "New Iceland," and about 1,200 people moved there. They founded a school, churches and an Icelandic-language newspaper. A few years later, Governor General Lord Dufferin visited Gimli and in praising the Icelanders noted that each one of the new homes he had entered contained "a library of twenty or thirty volumes; and I am informed that there is scarcely a child amongst you who cannot read and write." In time, many Icelanders moved to Winnipeg; that city and the province of Manitoba remain the centre of their settlement in Canada. By 1986, still about half of all Icelandic Canadians continued to live in Manitoba, and Vancouver attracted a good portion of those who left.

The first Danes in Canada reached Hudson's Bay in 1619 when their ship captain, Jens Munck, was looking for the Northwest Passage to the Orient. His attempt to found New Denmark at what is now Churchill, Manitoba, expired when 61 crew members died of scurvy, although Munck and two others somehow managed to sail back to Denmark. At the beginning of the twentieth century, Danish settlers reached the Prairies in response to the call of Canadian Pacific Railway land agents and publicity in Denmark by the Canadian government. In 1903, Danish immigration from Nebraska began when two Danes, Jens and Henry Larsen, returned from the Canadian prairies to report rich forests and grazing lands. Danish settlers were equally successful on the Prairies and transposed from Denmark both their system of agricultural cooperation and training in Danish Folk High Schools. In the 1950's, a number of Danish professionals came to settle in Western Canadian cities. Difficulties arose in maintaining the Danish language and culture beyond the first generation because of the scattered nature of the Danish population, intermarriages with other cultural communities, and the fact that so many of them had begun in the United States to adapt to the North American way of life.

Swedish immigration to Central Canada began in the 1850's because of famines and land shortages in Sweden, but most immigrants soon left for the milder climate and readily available farmland in the United States. Later, many re-crossed the frontier, some to work as miners and lumberjacks and others to help build the Canadian Pacific Railway line westward. Upon the railway's completion in 1885, Winnipeg became the centre of Swedish immigration for all of Canada. By 1911, however, Alberta also had significant Swedish populations in Strathcona, Red Deer and Medicine Hat. Saskatchewan became the most popular western province for Swedes and by 1931 a quarter of all Swedes in Canada lived in the wheat province. With the outbreak of World War II, many prairie Swedes relocated to British Columbia to work in its war industries. Today 62,000 Canadians with Swedish origins live in British Columbia.

The Norwegian settlement in Western Canada was prompted by mounting debts and a lack of land in the American Midwest. The Canadian Prairies offered a second chance and many thousands moved to Alberta and Saskatchewan. In 1912, some of these moved to Alberta's Peace River district around Valhalla and were later joined by others from further south during the crop failure of the 1930's. Many Norwegian-Canadians on the Prairies remained in farming occupations until much of the prairie topsoil simply blew away in the 1930's. Many were then forced to move to other parts of Canada or to return to Norway. A number moved to the lower mainland of British Columbia, and by the 1986 census, British Columbia had 54,000 part-origin and 20,000 sole-origin Norwegian-Canadians, the highest number for any province in the country.

The Scandinavians of Western Canada adapted readily to their surroundings and quickly became part of rural and later urban Western Canada conditions. Today, they are still playing vital roles in the growth and development of the region.

South Asians

Western Canadian South Asians include people from India, Pakistan, Bangladesh, Sri Lanka and Afghanistan, but also many whose families were established, often for generations, in Africa and the Caribbean, though having South Asian roots. According to the 1986 census, Western Canada contains approximately 110,000 sole-origin South Asians and another 21,000 who claim part South Asian family beginnings.

The cultural, religious and linguistic backgrounds of these communities are probably even more diverse than the heritage of their fellow residents from Western and Eastern Europe. India alone has fifteen official languages and a hundred or so minor ones, several hundred million Hindus, three times more Muslims than there are Canadians, and millions of Sikhs and Christians.

Until the 1960's, few South Asians lived anywhere in Canada beyond British Columbia. The first to arrive in the lower mainland in 1904 were a group of self-reliant Sikhs from the Punjab in Northern India who had learned of the province from Indian soldiers passing through Canada on their way to the coronation of King Edward VII in Britain. Relying on the then well-established principle that immigration within the British Empire must be unimpeded, other Sikhs attempted to follow. Future prime minister William Lyon Mackenzie King, at that time deputy minister of labour, quickly devised a way to get around this: his 1908 order-in-council prescribed that any immigrant from India must reach Canada on a ''continuous voyage.'' Since there was at the time no direct steamship connection between Canada and India, Sikh immigration immediately ended.

In 1914, a wealthy British Columbia Sikh, Gurdit Singh, challenged the regulation by chartering the Komagata Maru to bring about 400 Sikhs and Muslim Punjabis to Canada. The ship was forbidden by Canadian officials to land in Vancouver and the passengers were forced to remain on board for two months while the lawyers argued that King's regulation violated both the Magna Carta and the British North America Act. This effort ultimately failed, and the arrival of a Canadian naval cruiser alongside compelled the would-be immigrants to return to India.

The measure would bar virtually all South Asians immigrants to Canada until it was rescinded in 1947.

In 1951, under pressure from newly-independent India, Pakistan and Ceylon, the Louis St Laurent cabinet agreed to some token immigration from each of the three countries. In 1967, under the government of Prime Minister Lester Pearson, the quota system was finally replaced by a point system which admitted newcomers on the basis of skills, education and economic criteria. In consequence, large numbers of South Asian teachers, professors, medical doctors and other professionals settled in major western cities during the 1960's and 1970's.

Strong family, religious and cultural practices remain a distinctive feature for South Asian Westerners regardless of their particular country of origin. Marriages often occur within the same community and partners of both sexes may come from the Indian subcontinent. Most marriages arranged by parents seem to prove remarkably durable and happy. Many South Asian young people in the West have adopted the general lifestyle of other urbanites, but also maintain their traditional culture and worship.

South Asians are the most varied of all ethno-cultural communities in the West. Many are first-generation Canadians and some worry with good reason that discrimination can deny them employment opportunities commensurate with their efforts and abilities. On the optimistic side, the passing of each year provides a larger proportion of South Asian Westerners who are long-term residents of the region. The immigration policies and practices which kept a talented community tiny for decades are now gone or going. The chain migration of family and friends is growing, and carries with it a range of positive consequences.

Scots
According to the 1986 census, almost 300,000 Westerners claimed Scotland as their only place of family origin and another 1.2 million persons included it as one of their origins. Scots are thus, along with the English, Germans, Ukrainians, French-Canadians and Irish, among the largest communities in the West. For the 1971 census, Statistics Canada ignored centuries of

171

distinct Scottish history to group them with the English, Irish and Welsh as "British." But Western Canadians of Scottish origin felt entitled to a separate treatment of their ethnicity, settlement and immigration, largely because of their history of antipathy toward England. True, Scotland finally disappeared as an independent nation in 1707, but few Scots altered their coolness toward London thereafter and many maintained close ties with Europe, most notably France.

In the eighteenth and nineteenth centuries, moreover, had not Scottish thinkers such as David Hume and Adam Smith completely reshaped English thought in economics, philosophy, and science? As the Manitoba historian, J.M. Bumsted, puts it, the "English might have had the political power, but Scots dominated the life of the mind." A major reason was the superiority of Scotland's educational institutions and the insistence of its reformers on achieving both a fully literate population and a curriculum which stressed contemporary needs. Scotland's most important gift to Western Canada and civilization as a whole was probably the concept of the "democratic intellect" based on ability rather than family financial resources.

Another Scottish gift to the world was hundreds of thousands of "surplus" people from both the Highlands and Lowlands of Scotland who helped to populate many corners of the world while romanticizing their former homeland. The first to reach Western Canada arrived in Red River in 1812 through Hudson Bay, under the sponsorship of Lord Selkirk, to lay the foundation of a new colony. It grew until by 1820 it was firmly rooted as the first farming settlement in the West. The Highland clearances at the end of the 18th century by absentee landlords, who concluded that cattle and sheep were more profitable than tenant farmers, produced thousands of immigrants for Canada. Crofters, whose homes had been burned to ensure their departure, responded particularly well to advertisements for free passage, free land on arrival and free provisions for a year.

Once in Central Canada, the Scots quickly established a reputation for mutual support in religion, politics, business and education, and earnestness and honesty in personal conduct. The

Scottish presence in the West has been lengthy and highly significant. Scots such as Alexander Mackenzie, Roderick Mackenzie, Simon Fraser and James Macleod tapped the West's fur resources, explored and mapped waterways, and established many forts and trading posts which later became permanent settlements. Approximately 240,000 Scots were among the newcomers who arrived in Canada during the first fifteen years of the 20th century. Another 200,000 came to Canada between 1919 and 1930; 147,000 more arrived between 1946 and 1960. Many came directly to farms and cities of the West; some stopped for a generation in Atlantic or Central Canada before moving to Western Canada. Once here, most western Scots gravitated to cities and non-agricultural employment. There has been a good deal of assimilation of Scots within the greater Western Canadian community. The use of Highland Gaelic has all but disappeared; memories of the "old country" have faded for all but the most recently arrived. On the other hand, most Scots in the West today still consider themselves to be a distinctive tile in the western mosaic. Among themselves, perhaps at the annual Robbie Burns suppers, some will even argue they have dominated the economic, cultural and political life of Western Canada. Others will quickly reply that Burns, that most revered of Scots, would mock such vain boasting!

Chinese

Immigration to the West was largely a movement from Europe through the ports of Eastern and Central Canada, but many people came through British Columbia from the nations of the Far East. Among these are numbered the Chinese, a group which has participated in the building of Western Canada since the mid-19th century.

Western Canada in 1986 had approximately 170,000 persons of solely Chinese origin and about 22,000 more of partly Chinese descent. Seven in ten single-origin Chinese Western Canadians live in British Columbia, and fully 100,000 of these reside in the Vancouver area. A little less than half of all Canadians of single

Chinese origin live in the four western provinces, the Yukon and Northwest Territories.

Chinese Canadians born outside Canada have come from many countries. The 1981 census shows that in this group 24% were born in Taiwan; 23% in China; 9% in Vietnam; 4% in Malaysia or Singapore; and 34% elsewhere, primarily Hong Kong. Eighty-seven percent of those born outside Canada entered Canada during the 1965-81 period and in recent years approximately 13,000 have entered Canada, many from Hong Kong, as entrepreneurs. The unemployment rate for both Chinese men and women was at the time of the 1981 census less than that for Canadian men and women as a whole. Considerably more Chinese Canadians (28%) than all Canadians (16%) have some university education.

Western Canadians of Chinese origin are part of the huge diaspora of more than eight million "overseas Chinese" who have prospered from South Asia to the Caribbean. As late as the sixteenth century, China had the highest standard of living on earth. During the eighteenth century, its population more than doubled, reaching 430 million by 1850. When Europeans forcibly opened China's markets in the 19th century, its cottage cloth industry was all but destroyed by machine-made foreign cloth. A migration of young men became necessary to help feed their closely-knit families who were left at home.

The first of these men from China came to British Columbia in 1858, lured by the Fraser River gold rush, and by 1860 approximately 4,000 of them lived in the lower mainland of the colony. Some mined, others sold vegetables or wood, or operated restaurants and laundries. The legal equality in the workplace of those who stayed after the gold rush was removed by the B.C. provincial legislature in 1878 when it unanimously resolved that persons of origin in China could no longer be hired on provincial public works – a rule which astonishingly remained in effect until after World War II. The franchise was denied to them in 1872.

Nonetheless, as many as 17,000 Chinese came to B.C. between 1881 and 1884 to assume a Herculean part in the completion of the Canadian Pacific rail line between the Fraser Canyon and

Vancouver. As the project neared completion, the B.C. provincial government encouraged them to leave the region through such measures as a $10 head tax on all Chinese, banning the removal of dead bodies back to China, denying Chinese the right to buy provincial Crown land, and prohibiting further immigration from China. Prime Minister Macdonald's government in Ottawa played its part by imposing a $50 head tax on all Chinese entering Canada after 1886. In 1900, Prime Minister Laurier raised the head tax to $100, and in 1904 to $500. In 1923, the government of Mackenzie King barred all Chinese immigration, and it did not begin again until the legislation was finally repealed in 1947.

The combination of legislated and other discrimination against the Chinese in British Columbia and better opportunities to establish small businesses elsewhere in Canada, by 1921 had caused an estimated 40% of the 40,000 Chinese then resident in Canada to move eastward, some as far as Newfoundland. Virtually every prairie town soon had a Chinese restaurant and laundry. The three prairie legislatures proved not immune to anti-Chinese propaganda seeping over the mountains. The Saskatchewan assembly disenfranchised Chinese as early as 1908, which meant in practice that they could not vote in federal elections either or join professions whose associations required members to be registered voters. The prairie fever here reached a sufficiently high temperature that the Saskatchewan and Manitoba governments, even before British Columbia's, barred Chinese restaurants from hiring white women out of a preposterous fear that they would be introduced to opium and sold into white slavery.

Between 1924 and 1946, only eight Chinese immigrants entered Canada because of Mackenzie King's Chinese exclusion law of 1923. Many of the Chinese men already resident in Canada thus aged without families in Canada. Ironically, events of World War II helped the Canadian Chinese cause because white Canadian sympathy for China grew markedly as a result of the Japanese aggression there. As the historians Jin Tan and Patricia Roy point out, "[During the war,] racial prejudice became unfashionable." The Vancouver Parks Board, for example, repealed its rule that Chinese persons could swim at a public pool only during a specified two-hour period once weekly. The legislature of Saskatchewan restored the franchise in 1944 and in 1945 British Columbia enfranchised everyone who had served in either World War, including the Chinese but not the Japanese. The public on the coast generally welcomed the repeal of Ottawa's Chinese Immigration Act in 1947.

In fact, many Chinese Westerners continued to face real difficulty in entering Canada after 1947. With the violent events accompanying the creation of the People's Republic of China in 1949, some quite understandably entered Canada illegally. In 1962, a federal amnesty was offered to illegal immigrants of "good sound character," and by the time the program ended in 1973 more than 12,000 had changed their status. Racial discrimination in immigration officially disappeared in 1967 when new regulations began to screen potential immigrants on a "point system" which reflected their prospective economic contribution to Canada. This put the Chinese on an equal footing with other immigrants. Between 1972 and 1978, almost 80% of our Chinese immigrants came from Hong Kong, most choosing to live in suburbs rather than in Chinatowns. The so-called boat people of 1979 and the early 1980's included Vietnamese, Laotians and Cambodians as well as Chinese, and among them, Tan and Roy note, "were urban professionals, both men and women, once-wealthy businessmen and persons of influence in their own countries as well as poor illiterate peasants and fisherfolk." The warm response by Western Canadians and Canadians generally contrasted markedly with that given to Chinese newcomers earlier.

Today, a large number of Western Canadians of Chinese origin are entrepreneurs and professionals. A majority of them are in sales, services and other white-collar work. Most of them think of themselves as Canadians first and Chinese second. Alone among all cultural groups in Canada, however, they know that their families were forced to pay an entry fee (1885-1923) and were effectively barred from immigration by legislation (1923-1947). Attitudes have finally changed throughout Canada and institutionalized racism is gone. No longer do whites expect them or anyone to be "assimilated." They can now preserve and celebrate their cultural identity and remain both Canadian and Chinese in whatever proportion they choose.

Ukrainians

The four western provinces hold 300,000, or approximately three quarters, of all Canadians who give their sole origin as Ukrainian and 370,000, or 68% of those who give it as one of their family origins. Most Westerners originating in Ukraine came in one of three waves. The largest by far was the 1891-1914 migration of farmers from Galicia and Bukovina, provinces in the Austro-Hungarian Empire, who sought to escape poverty, malnutrition, shrinking landholdings, primitive farming practices and growing indebtedness. Thousands of them took 160-acre homesteads in Western Canada on paying a $10 registration fee. Clifford Sifton was genuinely enthusiastic about immigrants from Ukraine, and most of the estimated 170,000 Ukrainians who came before World War I settled in the Canadian Prairies. By 1921, Manitoba had the largest Ukrainian population in Canada, followed by Saskatchewan and Alberta. The hardships were great: virgin land to break and frequently forests to cut by hand, a new language, few roads or local improvements, mammoth distances and farm isolation, mosquitoes in summer and bitter cold in winter, nonexistent or rare medical and social services. Immigrants from Ukraine were among the first settlers who broke the land and helped lay the foundation of the region's wealth. Therefore, they are one of our founding peoples, central to the West's beginnings.

The 1914-1918 period was complicated for Ukrainians in Western Canada because of prejudice and discrimination on the part of the dominant Anglo-Celtic population. The federal government enacted a number of measures to segregate and monitor the activities of immigrants from enemy countries. Public hostility and official sanctions were directed at Germans and Ukrainians, who were now considered "enemy aliens." The 1914 War Measures Act led to the internment in concentration camps of about 6,000 Austro-Hungarians, the overwhelming majority of whom were Ukrainians. As Vera Lysenko notes in *Men In Sheepskin Coats*, during World War I, "One repressive measure followed another, directed against bewildered Ukrainians. Thousands of harmless 'Galicians' were rounded up by the police and herded into concentration camps.... The slightest criticism on the part of a Ukrainian and he was dragged from home, factory or hotel and placed in an internment camp."

There were other forms of suppression. English-Ukrainian bilingual classrooms on the Prairies were abolished during the war. Some Ukrainian publications were censored or banned. Most outrageous was the Wartime Elections Act of 1917, which disenfranchised every enemy alien naturalized since 1902.

In 1918, an independent Ukrainian state was proclaimed; it survived only until 1920. In 1922, most Ukrainian territory was incorporated into the Soviet Union, with substantial segments of population falling under Polish, Czechoslovakian or Romanian rule.

Almost 68,000 persons came to Canada between the two world wars, most from Galicia and Bukovina as they had earlier. In contrast to the first wave of immigrants, the inter-war Ukrainians were better educated and more nationally conscious. This group had a much easier time in Western Canada because immigrant aid societies of the Ukrainian community already present assisted both financially and morally. Tragically, Ukrainians were dropped to a "non-preferred" status by Ottawa during the 1930's; this may have prevented the escape to Canada of at least some of the estimated seven million who were deliberately starved to death by Stalin during that period. Very few Ukrainians managed to reach this country until after World War II.

During the Great Depression, Ukrainians suffered at least as much as any other group in Canadian society. As jobs became scarce, discrimination against "foreigners" became a fearful reality. The western historian James Gray catches in his *Winter Years* what many non-Anglo-Saxon Westerners faced during the 1930's in addition to the Great Depression: "For them [Ukrainians, Poles and Jews] Winnipeg was far from being a city of

250,000 in which they too were free to search for work. As much as two-thirds of it was barred and bolted against them.... Anyone with a Ukrainian or Polish name had almost no chance of employment except rough manual labour. The oil companies, banks, mortgage companies, financial and stock brokers, and most retail and mercantile companies except the Hudson's Bay Company discriminated against all non-Anglo-Saxons. For the young Ukrainians and Poles there was a possible solution if they could beat the accent handicap. They could change their names. So they changed their names, sometimes formally and legally, but mostly informally and casually.''

During World War II, an estimated 40,000 Ukrainians, or more than ten percent of the entire community in Canada, enlisted in the Canadian armed forces despite the fact that one of our allies (the USSR) had oppressed their people for centuries. After the war, many thousands of Ukrainians who had been deported to labour farms, concentration camps or German factories in Western Europe simply refused to return to Ukraine, which was then entirely part of the Soviet Union. A tragic repatriation of many thousands was finally stopped, and the remaining refugees from Ukraine were granted "displaced person" status and resettled abroad. The Ukrainian Canadian Committee urged the King and St. Laurent governments to accept refugees. Between 1947 and 1953, approximately 34,000 Ukrainians came to Canada, many well-educated professionals.

A major problem for Ukrainians in Western Canada since World War II has been the declining use of their language. Between 1951 and 1971, the use of Ukrainian as a mother tongue in the 0-9 age group dropped from 61 to 21 percent. In the 10-19 group, the drop was even worse, from 85 to 30%. Finally, the community pushed successfully to have Ukrainian restored as a language of study in prairie schools. In Alberta this was achieved in 1959; in Manitoba, in 1961. By the 1970's, all three prairie provinces allowed Ukrainian as a language of instruction for up to half of the school day. The community also advocated a multicultural Canada to the Royal Commission on Bilingualism and Biculturalism in the early 1960's. By 1971, in large measure

179

because of pressure created by Western Canadians of a non-British, non-French background and led by the Ukrainian Canadian Committee, Canada became for the first time a nation with two official languages, but no official culture. A fuller recognition of the culturally diverse nature of Canada is still needed, argue Ukrainian Canadians, who as a group face the possibility of assimilation in Canada and russification in Ukraine. The Ukrainian Canadian Committee, a coalition dedicated to democratic principles, to promoting Ukrainian cultural goals in Canada and to supporting the aspirations of Ukrainians in the USSR, has led the successful campaign to ensure that their community is not assimilated in Canada.

During 1988, Ukrainian communities around the world are celebrating the Millennium of the official adoption of Christianity in Ukraine. In 988, Volodymyr, the Grand Prince of Kievan-Rus (modern day Ukraine) had the inhabitants of Kiev baptised, thus bringing his country into the Christian fold. A thousand years later, Christianity continues to enrich the lives of the people of Ukraine dispersed throughout the world. During the past 300 years, Ukraine lost its independence and there have been difficult periods of government repression in the Soviet Ukraine, but the Ukrainian Church still exists there, although clandestinely.

Having survived against all conceivable odds, Christianity would appear yet to sustain the hopes of the Ukrainian nation and to serve as a source of strength for millions of Ukrainians living abroad. Pope John Paul II observed in a letter to the late Ukrainian Catholic Cardinal Josyf Slipyi: "...When Ukrainian sons and daughters leave their own country, they remain always, even as immigrant settlers, bound with their church, which with its tradition, language and liturgy, is for them a spiritual legacy that continually refreshes and nurtures the soul."

Japanese

Of the 54,000 Canadians wholly or partly of Japanese origin, 31,000, or about 57%, lived in Western Canada at the time of the 1986 census. Many Japanese Canadians are found in the major western cities, with over 15,000 in Vancouver. This shows a significant dispersal, since in 1941 95% of Canada's 23,450 Japanese lived in British Columbia.

Immigration from Japan began in 1877, nine years after the Emperor Meiji ascended the Japanese throne. He actively encouraged trade and travel with the West. The first immigrant, Manzo Nagano, settled in British Columbia. By 1896, approximately 1,000 Japanese, mostly males, were working in British Columbia in fishing, mining, logging, railway construction and farming. By 1911, the community had grown to about 9,000.

Active discrimination against Japanese began in 1895 when the British Columbia legislature took away the vote from Japanese Canadians. They remained disenfranchised for over fifty years. In 1907, at Ottawa's insistence, the Japanese government agreed to limit the number of male immigrants to 400 per year. In the same year, a mob fired up by anti-Asian agitators who wanted to keep British Columbia white, attacked the Japanese and Chinese parts of Vancouver. In 1928, Japan agreed to reduce the flow of immigrants even further to 150 persons yearly. Japanese Canadians, whether immigrants called Issei or Canadian born called Nisei, were also excluded by provincial law from most professions, the provincial public service and teaching. The minimum wage law of the province authorized a substantially smaller wage for Asian Canadians.

British Columbia remained essentially a ghetto for Japanese Canadians throughout the 1920's and 1930's. Even those who had fought for Canada in World War I were denied the vote. Ottawa exacerbated the already poor conditions in the 1920's, as historian Ann Sunahara points out, "[by limiting] the number of fishing licences to Japanese Canadians, thus denying many Japanese Canadians their traditional livelihood. During the Great Depression, Japanese Canadians received only a fraction of the social assistance that white applicants received and medical facilities were segregated." Second-generation Japanese Canadians with university degrees found themselves unemployable on the coast except as store clerks within the Japanese community or as labourers in sawmills and pulp mills.

The meagre economic gains of Japanese Canadians, won through

40 years of hard labour, vanished swiftly after Japan's attack on Pearl Harbour in late 1941. Pushed by the scapegoat-seeking and profoundly racist Ian Mackenzie, British Columbia's representative in the Mackenzie King cabinet, the federal cabinet twelve weeks later ordered 20,881 Japanese Canadians removed from all locations within 160 kilometers of the Pacific coast. The pretext was "national security." The decision was opposed, as Sunahara puts it, "by Canada's senior military and police officers and by senior civil servants. The Royal Canadian Mounted Police, aware that Japanese Canadians were controlled from within by their own leaders, was confident that they presented no danger of sabotage. The military in Ottawa were equally confident, having long recognized the practical impossibility of an invasion of Canada's Pacific Coast. "

First, thousands of women and children, most born in Canada, were held in the barns of Vancouver's Pacific National Exhibition while the men were sent to road camps. Later, 12,000 were confined in detention camps in the British Columbia interior. Some kept their families together by volunteering to work as sugar beet labourers in Alberta and Manitoba. In 1943, the cabinet authorized the Custodian of Enemy Property to sell Japanese Canadian farms, homes and fishing boats for fire sale prices, to deduct a disposal fee, and retain from what was left whatever had been paid to the detainees to buy necessities in the camps. In the spring of 1945, the inmates of detention camps were offered a choice by Ottawa: immediate resettlement in Central Canada or repatriation to a then-starving Japan at an unspecified date. In despair, and to keep their poorly paying jobs in the detention camps, almost 7,000 Japanese Canadians over sixteen signed repatriation forms. With their 3,500 dependents they represented 43% of Canada's citizens of Japanese origin. In November 1945, well after Japan's surrender and six weeks after refusal by the House of Commons to give the Cabinet the authority to deport any resident of Canada, the King cabinet ordered the deportation of 10,000 Japanese Canadians. While lawyers argued the matter in the courts and the Canadian public strongly protested, 2,000 Japanese with an equal number of dependents despaired of reestablishing themselves in Canada and sailed for Japan. Another 4,700 chose resettlement east of Alberta. By 1947, when Ottawa finally withdrew the deportation threat, only about 6,800 Japanese Canadians were left in British Columbia. The social and career losses, humiliation and shame could never be removed. Only in 1949 were the remaining restrictions lifted from Japanese Canadians and full voting rights obtained.

Since the Second World War, Japanese Canadians have become Canada's third most highly educated and prosperous minority after the Jews and the Chinese. Their restraint, perseverance, hard work and educational achievements allowed the Canadian-born Nisei, in the 1950's, to win their rightful place in all fields of Western Canada society. Today they are notable in the professions, trade, businesses and the arts. In 1981, 20% of Japanese Canadians had some university education compared with only 16% of the Canadian population as a whole.

In 1988, after years of lobbying, Japanese Canadians won from the Mulroney government a long overdue apology on behalf of their fellow citizens and a compensation package for internment survivors. One of the worst periods in our national history had finally been addressed.

Jews

Approximately 35,000 of the 246,000 Canadians who indicated a solely Jewish origin in the 1986 census live in Western Canada. Virtually all of them live in larger cities, especially Vancouver and Winnipeg. Another 27,000 of part Jewish origin live in the West. As most demographers define Jewishness as essentially a religious identity, Canadian Jews should probably not be described as an ethno-cultural community at all. Fully a quarter of respondents to the 1961 national census giving Jewish as their religion refused to designate it as their cultural origin as well. On the other hand, most of the Jewish community across Canada today was formed by immigration between 1880 and 1930 of families from Eastern Europe who shared a common orthodox Jewish faith. Later immigrants also shared a fairly homogeneous cultural origin.

Jewish immigration to Western Canada before 1930, when the Great Depression all but ended immigration from anywhere, originated largely in the Pale of Settlement located on the western extremities of the Russian empire. It had been established in the late eighteenth century to prevent Polish and White Russian Jews from moving into the heartland of Russia. Punitive taxation, a system of permanent military conscription for Jewish sons, the sudden expulsion of Jews from Moscow, and the pogroms (attacks on Jewish persons and property) by officials of the Czar left approximately 100,000 Russian Jews homeless in the years 1881-82 alone. World War I and the 1917 Russian Revolution proved even more calamitous because most East European Jews then lived in the Pale at the centre of the German-Russian slaughter. As many as 250,000 Jewish civilians were killed or starved or froze to death between 1914 and 1918.

Between 1933 and 1939, anti-semitism in Ottawa's political and bureaucratic circles barred all but about 4,000 Jews from entering Canada from Hitler's Europe. Bernard Vigod, the historian, reminds us that Canada's performance here "compares most unfavourably with that of other countries in the Western Hemisphere." After 1948, a wave of displaced persons, including Jews who miraculously survived the Holocaust, were allowed into Canada. Nearly 7,000 Hungarian Jews arrived after the 1956 Hungarian uprising and another 8,000 have come from the Soviet Union. Thousands more came during the 1960's from Islamic countries.

In Western Canada, as Stuart Rosenberg points out in his book, *The Jewish Community in Canada*, "Western Jews in Saskatchewan, Alberta and British Columbia feel themselves to be part of a single, closely knit regional family. No matter where they go or how far from home they wander, these Western Canadian Jews always remain 'Westerners'.... Canadian Jews in the West usually do not suffer from problems of 'Jewish identity'."

Their settlement in the West began in 1883 when 1,300 attempted to farm at New Jerusalem near Moosomin, Saskatchewan.

It became a nightmare because of bad luck, poor organization and lack of farming experience by the participants. A devastating fire, drought and early frosts finally proved too much for the colony. Later settlements in Saskatchewan and Alberta, notably Hirsch, Edenbridge and Sonnenfeld, were successful, but by the 1920's most Jewish settlers had become tradesmen and store-keepers in cities and towns. Concern about maintaining their faith in isolated rural communities was another reason why most western Jews moved to larger centres.

In Western Canada today, as for the community at large, Jewish assimilation has fortunately not reached American levels. The influx of new Jewish immigrants since 1948, many of whom are actively religious, provided a new impetus to Jewish life. Vigod and many others, myself included, contend our English-French language duality has provided part of an ideological basis for our cultural heterogeneity which makes it perfectly healthy to wear one's ethno-cultural identity proudly. A network of educational, cultural, welfare, recreational, community service and religious institutions have provided strong support to the maintenance of Jewish identity even in smaller western centres. In addition, the Universalist notion of the 1950's and 1960's in which modernity implied being "universal" rather than culturally "parochial" has melted away. Finally, six million Jewish deaths in the Holocaust and the determination of Jews everywhere not to provide Hitler any posthumous victories, combined with the generally hostile treatment of Israel in the western media and academic circles since the 1970's, is a major impetus to solidarity among Western Canadian Jews.

A common misconception in Central Canada about Albertans since the advent of James Keegstra is that anti-Semites and other bigots are somehow more numerous in our region than elsewhere in Canada. A study by the Institute for Social Research at Toronto's York University published in April, 1988, indicates in fact that the lowest levels of anti-Semitic sentiment are found in prairie Canada and British Columbia.

True, the survey also indicates that unacceptable levels of prejudice of all kinds still exist across Canada, but Westerners are showing leadership in the need for tolerance and mutual respect. A 1987 study on anti-semitism by the B'nai Brith suggests an important reason for a national war on illiteracy: "The highest levels of prejudice are found among people who are, by some definition, illiterate."

English

Early contributions to the Western Canadian mosaic were made by the English, who since the time of the earliest European visits have formed a large proportion of the West's population. The 1986 census locates within Western Canada approximately 1.4 million persons who gave a single family origin as English. If Westerners claiming part English origin are included in the English group, it comes to another 1.7 million people. Almost three in seven Western Canadians therefore have a little, some, or solely English blood in their veins.

The first English contact with Canada was made through an Italian explorer, Giovanni Caboto, who was hired by authorities in London to find the Northwest Passage to the Orient. His discovery of Newfoundland's Grand Banks led to much further English exploration in North America. From the standpoint of Western Canada, Henry Hudson's discovery of Hudson Bay in 1610 was especially important. The incorporation of the Hudson's Bay Company in 1670 by Prince Rupert, a cousin of England's King Charles II, and others became another major catalyst. The travels of English explorers out of Hudson Bay included Samuel Hearne's voyage down the Coppermine River to the Arctic Ocean in 1771-72, Henry Kelsey's wanderings during 1690 across our prairies, and Anthony Henday's sighting of the Rockies in 1754. In the late 1770's, the English sea captain, James Cook, explored our western coastline. At Nootka Sound, he traded with Indians and claimed the region for England. George Vancouver, who had accompanied Cook, later returned with more English ships to chart the coast of what became British Columbia and to recapture English property taken earlier by the Spanish.

The influx of English loyalists into Eastern and Central Canada at the time of the American Revolution transformed a sparsely-populated Upper Canada (now Ontario) and Atlantic region into predominantly English communities. This new reality would encourage countless English newcomers to relocate to many parts of Canada, including the West. Between 1815 and 1855, almost a million British emigrants, many of whom were English, landed in British North America. Many of them, or their children, came west once the completion of the railway made homesteads on the Prairies accessible. Many others, fleeing a suffocating English class structure and limited economic opportunities, went directly from Liverpool or London to the "last, best West" in Canada. In 1906 alone, 65,000 mostly English immigrants arrived from Britain; by 1913, the figure had reached 113,000. After World War I, the English government itself assisted another 130,000 of its citizens to settle in Canada.

The English adjustment to frontier life in Western Canada was assisted by the common use of their language in the region, although Canadian usage was often very different from that at home. There were many other new things for the English pioneers to learn as well, such as using western tack for horses, ploughing straight furrows, and wearing denim instead of tweed. Western historian Gerald Friesen states: "Like members of other ethnic groups, the English tended to marry their own, to locate in boarding-houses run by their countrymen, to congregate in certain areas of the cities, and to support their own football teams, music halls, and fish and chip shops. One bastion of their community was the Church of England, the prairie branch of which was dominated by English immigrants after 1900.... They sponsored their own when openings came up in a mine or plant, and they dominated the hiring system in such companies as the T. Eaton Company department stores and the CPR shops. "

The English immigrants had a major impact on the West, especially in our cities, where they erected many of the buildings and houses. Their influence on western politics and trade unions was also important because they came from so many walks of life. Their weight was especially felt in Canada's strong role in both world wars. Howard Palmer's comment about the English

187

newcomers in Alberta is probably equally true for all four western provinces. The English presence, he notes, was "evident in the creation of a skilled labour force in the urban areas before World War I, and in the early strength of labour unions and socialist parties in the cities, and mining settlements.... The British influence also contributed to the numerical and social prominence of the Anglican, Presbyterian and Methodist churches and to the imported class distinctions which some tried to introduce in a city like Calgary before World War I. "

In the post-World War II period, more English immigrants, including many war brides, came to Western Canada. In 1957 alone, 75,546 English immigrants arrived in Canada; in our centennial year, more than 43,000, although the numbers have fallen off greatly since. The major English contributions to Western Canada include the common law and court systems used in all four provinces and both northern territories and our system of parliamentary democracy. The Red Cross, Boy Scout and Girl Guide movements all came from England. English influence remains important in many facets of Western Canadian life, from industry and government to commerce, the professions and the performing arts.

Arabs

In 1986, approximately a seventh of the 100,000 Canadians giving their single or partial family origin as the Arabian Peninsula lived in Western Canada. Alberta ranked third after Ontario and Quebec as their favoured province.

The first Arab immigrant, Abraham Bounadere, reached Montreal in 1882; virtually all those who followed him before World War I came from Syria and what is now Lebanon. Arab immigration in effect stopped altogether in 1908 when the government of Wilfrid Laurier, seeking to terminate immigration from China and Japan, ordered that all newcomers from "Asia" must have at least $200 on arrival in Canada. In an act of blatant bureaucratic racism, immigration officials extended the measure so as to include immigrants arriving from the then mostly destitute Arab world. In 1913, the superintendent of immigration, rebuffing a campaign to establish that Arab nations were not Asian, cited unfavourable comments about Syrians from *Strangers Within Our Gates*, an astonishingly racist book by the Winnipeg clergyman and superintendent of All Peoples Mission Church, and future CCF national leader, James S. Woodsworth, as a reason neither to change the offensive order-in-council nor to alter his bizarre interpretation of it.

There was little improvement in the prospects for Arabs seeking to come to Canada until Prime Ministers John Diefenbaker in 1962 and Lester Pearson in 1967 reformed our immigration policy. A trickle of less than a thousand Arab immigrants arriving between 1911 and 1961 grew to a flood of many thousands thereafter. Most came from Egypt, but smaller numbers came from Lebanon, Morocco, Syria, Jordan, Tunisia and other Arab countries.

The first decade of the twentieth century established the Arab communities in Western Canada. Winnipeg and Edmonton were the most popular population centres, but small groups settled in Vancouver, Calgary and Saskatoon. Others homesteaded near Saskatoon and Swift Current in Saskatchewan, Lac la Biche in Alberta, and in Manitoba. Arab-Canadian institutions were usually founded in larger cities. An exception was Lac La Biche, where the success of a hundred Arab families in fur trading and mink ranching allowed the building of an impressive mosque which continues to astonish visitors. The Al-Rashid Mosque, built in Edmonton in 1938, was the first mosque built in Canada.

Despite early immigration barriers, Canada is now a preferred country of immigration for Arabs. More recent waves of immigrants have included both Muslims and Christians from various lands. Most are highly-educated and skilled. They have achieved prominence in virtually all occupational fields in Western Canada. Preservation of culture and language remains very important for Arab Westerners because many in the community hold strongly to religion and traditional heritage. The earlier assimilation of some young Arabs to more homogeneous Western Canadian values appears to have been offset by a recent large wave of Lebanese immigrants who prefer more traditional linguistic and cultural values.

Baha Abu-Laban, a University of Alberta sociology professor and author of a book on Arabs in Canada, *An Olive Branch on the Family Tree*, concludes: ''Arab Canadians have contributed significantly to the development of this country; this is as much true of the early peddlers as of the skilled labourers, business people, professionals and semi-professionals of today. The names of Arab Canadians who have achieved prominence in their respective occupations are to be found in virtually all fields. In return, Canada has contributed toward the realization of what was a dream for many Arab Canadians of their immigrant forebears: economic well-being and financial security.'' Western Canadians of Arab origins must now ensure that the olive branch remains an important feature of the regional family tree.

Poles

The Polish presence in the West, although originally not great in number or conspicuous in character, dates back to when the region was being opened. There were Poles in Lord Selkirk's expeditions to Manitoba in 1815 and 1817 to protect Red River settlers. Edwin Brokowski became editor and owner of *The Manitoba Gazette* in Winnipeg in the 1870's; Karol Horecki conducted geographical studies in the Rocky Mountains at the Peace River watershed and prepared, in the years 1870-1880, the technical documentation of the Peace River region for the CPR.

Today, approximately 83,000 Canadians declaring Poland to be their only place of origin live in Western Canada. This is a little less than forty percent of sole-origin Polish Canadians, whereas about half of all Canadians claiming part Polish origin live in the West. Combining the two groups of Poles produces some impressive numbers in major western cities: Vancouver has 36,000, Edmonton 43,000, Calgary 24,000, Regina 10,000, Saskatoon 10,000, and Winnipeg 46,000.

At one time Poland, in union with Lithuania, was a major Central European power. During the Renaissance, Poland's most glorious period, the persecution of religious minorities so prevalent in other European nations was largely absent. For example, when Jews were persecuted in Western Europe and were driven out of Spain, Portugal, England and the German principalities, they found shelter in Poland. By the late 1700's, however, a combination of aggression by close neighbours and various internal problems led to a series of partitions of Poland. These events resulted in considerable emigration. Ottawa's Dominion Lands Act of 1872, which made easier the founding of prairie homesteads, at first attracted only a few Poles to Western Canada. Only at the turn of the century did Clifford Sifton's recruitment in Europe attract large numbers of them. An estimated 115,000 Polish settlers came to Canada between 1896 and 1918, mostly from the Austria-dominated province of Galicia. Most of these came west.

Following World War I and the formation of the Polish republic, which established a consulate in Winnipeg, more Polish farmers began to arrive in Western Canada. By 1931, there were 145,000 Poles spread across the nation. Their immigration slowed considerably during the Depression and the Second World War. Only 800 Poles came between 1940 and 1945, mostly engineers and technicians. Afterwards Polish immigration exploded. In 1946, 4,500 Polish ex-servicemen who had fought with the Allies came to Canada under a special order-in-council, and 36,500 displaced Poles were also admitted. Another 14,000 came later, either as normal immigrants or as visitors who were allowed to remain in Canada as immigrants. Many of this group were highly educated, but nonetheless encountered traces of the earlier prejudice against Central Europeans in parts of Canada, including the West.

Between 1953 and 1971, approximately 55,000 Poles came to Canada, many having first moved to the United Kingdom and Western Europe. The Communist regime in Poland in power since 1945 banned emigration until 1956, when a new government allowed the sponsoring of relatives. Polish Canadians were very proud when in 1981 Poland became the first communist country with a free trade union movement (now outlawed). Canadians have become acutely aware that the Poles have shown great political courage fighting a totalitarian regime for their civil rights. A large number of Poles, estimated at 5,036 persons, came to Canada during the period of Solidarity between 1980 and late 1981, and some 33,500 by the end of 1987. Most of these were both highly trained and convinced democrats.

Roman Catholic and other churches helped many Poles in Western Canada to adjust to their new surroundings. Indeed, the earliest families arriving organized themselves around the church. The Oblate fathers founded a number of Polish churches in Western Canada. Later, Polish Westerners formed other cultural, social and economic organizations. Community halls in every major western centre were completed through levies or members' dances and picnics. Polish credit unions were established across Canada. Much emphasis was also given by Polish parishes to maintaining the language of the motherland among the children of immigrants. Polish history, folk songs, dances and customs were also taught in parish schools. Scouting became a major youth activity and other youth clubs were also founded. Polish ex-service men and women have also ensured that veterans' organizations serving both sexes have become important parts of community life.

It would appear that the present cohesion of Western Canadian Poles will ensure a vibrant future. Their community possesses an abundance of intellectual and historical resources to resist assimilation even if fewer and fewer of them live outside our major metropolitan centres. As ever before, the Canadians of Polish descent are vitally interested in maintaining their cultural heritage in their new homeland and passing it on to both the younger generation and other Canadians. Westerners of Polish descent have contributed greatly to the West's prosperity and cultural heritage, first through the toil and sacrifice of the pioneers who helped to conquer the wilderness, clear the land and establish communities, and later through the efforts and achievements of those working in fields such as technology, law, medicine, education and the arts.

Germans

In the 1986 census, 556,000 residents of the four western

provinces reported only a German origin and another 805,000 indicated Germany figured in their origins. On a single-origin basis, they are thus second only to the English as the largest ethno-cultural group in all four western provinces. Most of them, like German-Canadians generally, immigrated from areas other than Germany itself; from Estonia in the north to the Black Sea in the south, from Alsace on the west to the Caspian Sea on the east. The Austro-Hungarian and Russian empires together provided to Western Canada a wide diversity in German-speaking settlers: Protestants and Roman Catholics, Mennonites and Hutterites, city dwellers and farmers, High and Low German-speaking. This diversity, combined with world political events, appears to have been a major obstacle to establishing a more cohesive German identity across Canada.

The first German-speaking settlers were known to live in the West as early as the 1820's at Red River; however, it was not until the 1870's that a significant wave of German-speaking immigrants flowed into the Canadian West. Between 1874 and 1880, approximately 7,000 Mennonites from Southern Russia were allotted two exclusive tracts of land in southern Manitoba. The growing pan-Slav nationalism of the czars drove them to Western Canada and they would long remain aloof from the godlessness and materialism they found on the Prairies. Villages, not homesteads, became their unit of farm production. The Mennonites prospered, but in 1916 some of them, refusing to accept a Manitoba school measure which made it compulsory for instruction to take place in English, left for Mexico and Paraguay. Their vacated land was in turn taken up by a new wave of Mennonites fleeing the civil war in the Soviet Ukraine. Eventually, as Gerald Friesen notes, their "village agricultural systems and the separate school were things of the past; the language and the faith remained."

In the period from 1880 to 1910, numerous German-speaking immigrants, most fleeing the growing shortage of land in Europe, joined the westward flood and became especially popular as newcomers to the West. By 1914, approximately 35,000 had settled in Manitoba. In Saskatchewan, the number of German

193

residents ballooned from less than 5,000 in 1901 to more than 100,000 in 1911. In British Columbia, the first large-scale German immigration began with the Fraser Valley gold rush in 1858. Few made fortunes in either that gold rush or the later one in the Cariboo Mountains, but most stayed to become successful grocers, farmers, craftsmen, shopkeepers and brewers. By 1911, the German population of British Columbia was about 12,000. Immigration from Germany itself fell sharply between the outbreak of World War I and 1927, when Germany was re-admitted to a "favoured nation" status, but between 1919 and 1935 about 100,000 German-speaking immigrants arrived from the Soviet Union, Poland, Austria, Czechoslovakia and Germany. Most were farmers who settled on the Prairies.

The First World War marked the end of the first phase of German immigration and the beginning of a period of anti-German sentiment. The reversal in public opinion across Canada about Canadian Germans during World War I was astonishing in both its severity and its speed. A highly-praised community of residents suddenly faced both official and unofficial discrimination. German Canadians lost jobs in the early years of the war. There was also abuse, sometimes physical, at the hands of returned soldiers. More than 8,000 German Canadians and Austro-Hungarians were eventually detained at internment camps located on the Prairies, and in British Columbia and northwestern Ontario. Most were released by 1916 when manpower became short. By 1921 many German-speaking Canadians were even reluctant to admit their German origin. For example, the number of Manitobans indicating a German origin in 1921 had declined by an astonishing 43% since 1911; in British Columbia the percentage drop over the same period was 38%.

In the late 1930's, there was a pitifully small flow of about 5,000 Jewish refugees from Nazi Germany into Canada. A group of 1,000 Sudeten Social Democrats reached Canada from Czechoslovakia in 1939, many settling on abandoned farms in northern Saskatchewan and on uncleared land in north-eastern British Columbia. Adolf Hitler and his Third Reich in fact repelled the vast majority of the German population in Western Canada, as elsewhere in Canada, despite the best efforts of a pro-Hitler German Consul in Winnipeg. Only a small group of recent German immigrants in the West, who were shaken by the stresses of the Depression, were attracted to the Reich. Most of the community remained loyal to their adopted country and many volunteered in the Allied cause during World War II. The community's financial support for the Allied war effort equalled that of other ethno-cultural communities. Most of the 800 German-Canadians interned at the start of the war had been released by 1941. The wartime hostility to German-Canadians was in fact considerably less than during World War I.

At the end of World War II, numerous German-speaking refugees from Romania, Yugoslavia and Austria-Hungary came to Canada, many to the West. When the ban on immigration of German nationals, in force from 1939 to 1950, was finally lifted their numbers increased dramatically. Between 1951 and 1960, an estimated 250,000 German immigrants reached Canada as a whole. By the time of the 1971 census, persons of German origin had become the second largest ethno-cultural group in British Columbia, Alberta and Saskatchewan. In 1981, almost 95% of those of German origin indicated that English was their daily language.

Canadians of German origin have contributed greatly to all facets of Western Canadian life. For example, few Canadians in the West or elsewhere realize that it was the early German settlers who introduced to Canada the endearing tradition of the lighted Christmas tree. Agriculture, science, business, the arts, politics and the professions have felt the positive impact of the German-Canadian presence.

French and Western Bilingualism

It is often forgotten that French was used in much of Western Canada for most of two centuries. The French and French Canadians were the second founding cultural groups of Western Canada, after the aboriginal peoples: in the 1700's explorers, traders, and canoeists made French the first European language to be spoken on the Canadian Prairies. At Fort Edmonton, so many

Hudson's Bay Company employees were French Canadians and Métis that French was the most commonly spoken language there until as late as the mid-1800's. French communities were established and flourished throughout north-central Alberta, in southern Saskatchewan and in British Columbia. In 1818, French Canadians founded St. Boniface, which is now part of metropolitan Winnipeg, and it remains the major focus of French language and culture in the West.

For various reasons, however, most French-speaking Quebecers with wanderlust just could not be persuaded to move west in large numbers. Some preferred the proximity of Quebec's own northern frontier on the Canadian shield; others opted for jobs in the factories and mills of nearby New England. By 1900, more than a million French Canadians were living in America. Railway fares to the West were higher for people from Quebec than for newcomers from Europe, who got special rates, and many Quebecers were also discouraged by reports about Louis Riel's problems in 1869-70, the acrimonious debates about his amnesty, and the 1885 North-West Rebellion.

Nor was the reported treatment of the French language and Roman Catholicism in the West encouraging. In the North-West Territories Act of 1875, the Canadian Parliament allowed for the use of French in the legislative council and courts, and authorized the right to organize Roman Catholic schools in which French could be the language of instruction. In 1890, the Manitoba legislature, by then dominated by English-speaking Protestants, eliminated both the language and Catholic school rights of its French-speaking minority, restoring them partly in 1897 only to abolish them again in 1916. In 1892, the Assembly of the North-West Territories voted to make English its sole language and later in the same year ordered that French could henceforth be used only in the first two or three years of school for children who spoke no other language. The thousands of Protestant Ontarians arriving in the West after 1890 were for the most part convinced that the region must be made "British."

The perceived lack of congeniality in the West to French-speaking Canadians resulted in there being only 23,000 of them living throughout the Prairies by 1901. The U.S. census of 1900 reported that one-third of all French Canadians on the continent lived south of the Canadian border. One of the great "ifs" of our national history is this: had French Canadian migration gone to Western Canada instead of the United States, might some of our historical language and cultural difficulties never have arisen? In Western Canada, English as a common linguistic currency became ascendant; by the end of the First World War, legislation and official policy throughout the region had severely suppressed the use of French in official and school spheres. By 1916, there were only 25,000 Albertans of French origin in a total provincial population of about half a million. Newcomers to the West from everywhere, including Quebec, were told bluntly that English was the only language of the region. The strong bilingual origins of Western Canada were thus forgotten by many and never known by many newcomers to the region.

By the 1971 national census, more than forty ethno-cultural communities were identified in the four western provinces. The mother tongue of 79.4% of Westerners in 1986 was English, for two percent it was French, and 14.4% of Western Canadians, or approximately a million persons, spoke a mother tongue other than the two official languages.

Long-stilled language tensions reignited throughout the West during the late 1960's and 1970's as residents became isolated from Central Canada on a range of issues. This was accompanied by a growing conviction that the Trudeau government was preoccupied with Quebec and was ignoring legitimate concerns in the West. The election of the separatist Parti Québecois to office in Quebec City in late 1976 fostered even greater attention in Ottawa circles to Quebecers.

The implementation of federal official bilingualism following Prime Minister Lester Pearson's Royal Commission on Bilingualism and Biculturalism (a title which itself bothered many Westerners) in fact awakened Western Canada to its own cultural distinctiveness. How were we to weave official bilingualism into the vibrant multicultural reality present throughout the region?

An essentially bicultural federal thrust seemed to collide with western reality.

The notion of two founding peoples never found much support among Westerners. Official bilingualism was seen by some as special treatment afforded by Ottawa to an important linguistic community that was, nonetheless, neither as numerous as nor more concentrated than, say, those of Ukrainian, German, or Scandinavian origin. How could one enhance French language rights within the region on any but a national unity basis? The bilingualism issue in essence was, and remains, a matter of reconciling national obligations with a distinctive regional demography.

Too little effort was made by Ottawa during the 1970's to explain the rationale or political necessity for the Official Languages Act. A good deal of insensitivity by Ottawa officials was demonstrated towards the multicultural character of the West; official bilingualism came to be perceived by many as a policy of, by, and for the benefit of "eastern elites."

"When you call the public affairs branch of the federal transport department in Edmonton," an Albertan told me recently, "the telephone is answered in both languages. When I did the same thing in Montreal, the response was in French only." The widespread awareness in the West that Quebec is now officially unilingual at the provincial level makes such occurrences of federal insensitivity even more annoying to Western Canadians.

The recently passed amendments to the Official Languages Act (Bill C-72) were characterized by some as an anti-western measure because more federal management positions, including some in the West itself, appeared likely to pass out of reach for all but the less than ten percent of Westerners who are functionally bilingual in the two favoured languages. No longer, they argued, would as many of the best qualified candidates for federal positions be able to take language training once in a job because the pool of bilingual people (almost always from outside Western Canada) was now large enough to reduce in practice the number of appointments of unilingual people to bilingual posts.

It should be emphasized that many cultural communities in the

West do not feel the Meech Lake accord fully recognizes our multicultural reality. Ihor Broda, a Westerner and vice-president of the Ukrainian Canadian Committee, articulated the concerns of many Western Canadians to the Special Joint Committee of Parliament on the 1987 Constitutional Accord: ''We believe that our constitution must reflect the reality of Canada as it is today. [A] major weakness of the accord is its failure to recognize the fact that Canada is both a multicultural and officially bilingual society.... In our view, it is inaccurate to describe Canada just in terms of the two predominant languages spoken.''

David Bai, a prairies vice-chairman of the Canadian Multiculturalism Council and one of the authors of the recently-enacted federal Multiculturalism Act, sees cultural pluralism which includes regional and cultural diversity as the West's true identity. In the absence of greater heritage language rights for all under the Charter of Rights, he believes official bilingualism in practice promotes biculturalism, which is contrary to the intent of both the Charter of Rights and Freedoms and the principles of multiculturalism. ''If we are truly a nation which has two official languages,'' Bai argues, ''yet accepts the principles of a multilingual, multiracial, multicultural society, then we must introduce a Multicultural Act along with an amended Citizenship Act to properly translate the policy mandate as stated by this and former governments.''

I agree with Bai that this is ultimately the best way to have the two official languages accepted across the West. The debate sparked by the Saskatchewan and Alberta government language announcements and Bill C-72 has obviously renewed language tensions in the West, at least temporarily. Not a few Westerners challenged the need for extending the Official Languages Act in the region; weary francophone communities in the two prairie provinces protested the repeal of Section 110 of the North-West Territories Act requiring statutes to be translated into French. Francophones in Western Canada would also appear to be anxious to have more say than they do now in the way official bilingualism is implemented by Ottawa in the West.

In my view, federal official bilingualism is essential to our survival as one nation, although I understand completely the anxiety of people who feel pressured by the stupidities of those who administer it. Possibly none of these was worse than the recent attempt to reclassify the court registrar's position in Vancouver as a bilingual one. Bilingualism will win general acceptance ultimately on its own merits, but attitude cannot be legislated.

In 1981, Stanley Roberts, a former president of the Canada West Foundation, noted, "It is clear that an interesting contradiction has developed [in the West]: western alienation is increasing while bilingual resistance is decreasing." Following a comprehensive survey of western public opinion, the Foundation concluded during October, 1980, that 53% of those surveyed were in favour of entrenching language rights in the constitution of Canada.

Eight years later, a majority of Canadians in every region appears to support official bilingualism at the federal level. "Our province," says a western educator, "has two competing language visions: those who send their children to French schools and believe in official bilingualism, versus those who want their offspring to speak Ukrainian, Mandarin, or whatever, as well as English." Some in both camps believe official bilingualism is the rock on which multilingualism is also built: remove it, and the political will to nurture languages other than English will be lost. Overall, official bilingualism at the national level as an essential national policy is probably questioned less and less in the West. The large enrolment in French immersion schools in the four provinces reflects this movement.

After three generations of language neglect, western francophone communities are finally receiving better support. In Alberta, French immersion schools were allowed by 1976, and by 1979, forty percent of Alberta children whose mother tongue was French were receiving instruction in either bilingual or immersion schools. The Charter of Rights in effect since 1982 guarantees francophones everywhere "where the number of those children so warrants" the right to attend publicly-supported French schools. Since 1970, most French-speaking Westerners have been able to receive all daily programming from Radio-Canada's television network in Montreal. Today, with the amendments to the Official Languages Act passed recently by the Mulroney government, the prospect of achieving the same rights for French-speaking Westerners as have long existed for English-speaking Quebecers is a good deal brighter.

Westerners generally now understand better what happened to our region's bilingual origins, and French, which was an important part of earlier western history, is being rewoven into the regional tapestry. Given time, intelligence and sensitivity, western attitudes will move further. Extended federal and provincial services to francophone communities across the West will be better accepted by a tolerant population if there is also ample support given to the teaching of other languages. Greater language sensitivity also remains necessary for real success because many Westerners distrust policies imposed on them by legislators or officials in Ottawa.

Westerners, while determined to preserve cultural heritages and our host of languages, are moving to provide a unique western dimension to the concept of an officially bilingual nation within a multicultural environment.

A Concluding Comment

The ethno-cultural profiles in this chapter are a mere sketch of Western Canada's singular mix of diverse peoples. They are brief of necessity, and thus do not fully reflect any group's experience of settlement in the West or integration into the society, religion, work, language, politics, culture and community life of the region. All of these aspects are of great importance to understanding how the various peoples settling the West shaped our society and how, in turn, they were affected by complex processes of integration and assimilation. Western Canada's present mosaic should ensure the survival of ethnic cultures while each group is integrated rather than assimilated into a larger society. "Unity in diversity" acquired new dimensions when applied to western realities.

201

Social theorists researching problems of ethnicity have identified three major benefits of ethnic group survival for the society. First, ethnic group participation is essential to individual satisfaction and self-development. Second, cultural pluralism is an essential freedom. It favours a social climate in which cultural distinctiveness does not restrict social participation. Third, the preservation of ethnic groups benefits the society as a whole because each culture has a valuable contribution to make to that society. The interaction of diverse groups based on the principles of equality and mutual respect can be a creative and enriching social experience: each group affects the others, yet each maintains its distinct identity.

Western Canada meandered a long way before it awoke to appreciate the benefits of ethno-cultural survival and began to promote multiculturalism actively, not so much as a government policy but as a fact of life.

In the past, some groups struggled for survival as distinct groups in the face of a strong pressure to assimilate within a dominant Anglo-Canadian culture, and also strove for acceptance both as a group and as individuals — often a painful and uphill battle. History shows that most communities succeeded in maintaining their identity and stamping it upon the character of their new homeland. Today, ethno-cultural groups represented by various multicultural organizations and individuals face even more complex challenges with all their subtle and dynamic forces.

Concerned individuals realize that the future they face will depend on the conscious desire to survive as a distinct group and on the dedicated work of many individuals within each group. They closely follow the policies of both the federal and provincial governments on multiculturalism, education, human rights and immigration, analysing the impact on the future of their respective groups. A large part of their activities today is directed to integration of individuals and the transmission of aspects of their culture to the society, rather than to the preservation of traditional culture as such. Their work concentrates on making their communities fully realize and appreciate the cultural heritage each group carries, reflected in a historic memory of their pioneering contribution to the development of our region. Virtually all communities agree with a thought of Peter Savaryn, a Ukrainian Canadian and former chancellor of the University of Alberta, that our federal government must treat "all minorities and regions equally and justly." He goes on: "The inter-pollination of cultures will make Canada great."

TEN

Grant MacEwan
Ongoing Legend

AUTHOR OF 32 BOOKS, master livestock judge, lieutenant governor of Alberta, historian of Western Canada, mayor of Calgary, agricultural scientist and husbandry professor, broadcaster and public speaker extraordinaire, conservationist, leader of the Alberta Liberal Party, outdoorsman and hiker — Grant MacEwan remains an institution in his adopted province of Alberta. The list of his accomplishments, moreover, is incomplete without mention of his more than 2,500 newspaper columns, 5,000 speeches and 1,000 broadcasts, as well as uncounted magazine articles and contributions to scholarly, technical, and popular publications.

As one of countless examples of the MacEwan phenomenon, in early 1986 he was invited to participate in events at Grant MacEwan Community College in Edmonton. Rising at perhaps 5 AM at his home in Calgary, he boarded a Greyhound bus for the four-hour trip to the provincial capital. There he visited the several campuses of the college for "Grant MacEwan Day" and was dropped off at the Edmonton public library to do some research. Declining to be put up by the college overnight at the local YMCA (where he invariably stays to protest the self-indulgence of people on travel expense accounts), he changed his clothes in the library's public washroom and was picked up there to attend an elegant college dinner as guest speaker. He spoke for

20-25 minutes without notes on the subject of public service and Tommy Douglas (who had recently died) and was then driven back to the bus depot to catch the late bus for home, doubtless arriving well after midnight. He was 83 at the time.

MacEwan would probably be surprised to learn that anyone would make something out of such a day. From all recent indications, he continues to live at the same pace, chopping wood for his fireplace, riding barely broken horses, building log cabins and hiking or walking long distances. He credits his constitution and undiminished stamina to his grandparents, so this brief account of the life of an extraordinary Western Canadian begins with his forebears.

George MacEwan left the highlands of Scotland in 1857 and settled in Guelph where, as a youth of 12, he first earned his living as a blacksmith before becoming an engineer with a sewing company for 40 years. His wife, Annie Cowan, whom he met in Canada, was also from Scotland. Their oldest son, Alexander, was determined to be a cowboy, so no one was surprised in 1889 when at eighteen he boarded a westbound train of the recently-completed Canadian Pacific Railway. He was bound for the American West, but fortunately for Canada his small savings gave out as the train pulled into Brandon, Manitoba. His first job as a farm hand near Brandon paid twenty dollars a month plus room and board; he stayed four years. When a homestead became available nearby, he invested his savings in a deposit and with a team of horses managed to break the entire quarter section the first summer. Within two years he had done so well financially he was able to return to Guelph for a visit with his parents.

Bertha Grant of Pictou County, Nova Scotia, moved to Brandon at about this time and entered the first nursing class at Brandon General Hospital. Her brother James, who farmed near Alex, was particularly impressed with the care his bachelor neighbour took of his Clydesdale horses. One day as the team was passing, James rushed out to invite the driver in to meet his sister. They were married in an auspicious month, January, 1900; Grant was born in the summer of 1902 and his brother, George, in 1907.

It was a near-perfect rural setting: two tightly knit families, rolling land, good wheat crops, excellent neighbours, hard work, Brandon and its fall fair within view, and countless outdoor experiences. Bertha MacEwan was a strong Presbyterian and the church was important in Grant's early years. There were barn dances, ball games and picnics, but next to Christmas the annual Sunday school picnic was clearly the most important day in the year for the MacEwan family.

The years between 1900 and the outbreak of World War I were truly golden for the prairie West. The region was then most important to Canada as a whole; the master switch of national progress appeared to many, both in and outside the West, to lie for once in our national history somewhere on the Prairies. The family farm became the dominant institution, as more than half the inhabitants of the Prairies lived either on farms or in agricultural centres like Brandon. Free land offered a fresh start to anyone willing to work hard. The region was afforded full-blown utopian status by author Charles W. Gordon, the Winnipeg church minister who wrote under the name Ralph Connor. His books glorifying western communities sold over five million copies.

By 1908, Alex had earned enough to retire at the age of 37. He had no intention of putting his feet up for the rest of his life, but, as his elder son would himself demonstrate many times, change was good for people. The farm and its contents were sold at a public auction. Soon afterwards, Bertha took her two young boys by train to Nova Scotia to visit her parents. Grant would note years later that his "mother was so clannish I thought I was a Nova Scotian." His biographer, Rusty Macdonald, believes that except for frugality, which clearly came from his father's side, the personal qualities of the Grant side of the family tended to dominate in young Grant MacEwan.

The family move to "The Wheat City" of Brandon almost bankrupted Alex. His venture into the making and selling of fire extinguishers thrived only as long as the city's building boom in wooden structures, which lasted until the outbreak of war in 1914. Unfortunately, his profits from it went mostly into buying lots around Brandon, and they became unmarketable almost overnight when speculators from London and Paris took their investments home as the war loomed. The opening of the Panama Canal in 1914 was also a heavy blow to confidence in both Brandon and Winnipeg because goods going to B.C., Alberta and Saskatchewan no longer had to go by rail through Brandon and Winnipeg. Economic conditions deteriorated quickly for the business community with the outbreak of war: freight rates rose, employees became hard to find and wages climbed. On the land, however, wheat rose in price, and horse, cattle and sheep sales soared. Alex was delighted when he managed to trade his Brandon lots for what was represented as a good working farm at Margo, Saskatchewan, 400 miles to the northwest.

Grant and his father reached their new home by train. "To our horror," Grant put it, "the fences were down, the home was a shambles and uninhabitable, the horses didn't exist, the land was not ready for crop – nothing was as represented." They reloaded their animals and equipment on a rail car and journeyed on to Melfort, 50 miles east of Prince Albert, where years earlier Alex had bought an unbroken section of land which he knew to contain rich black soil. Bertha and George arrived and the family began the endless work of building a new farm again. Despite some crop losses and a resultant shortage of money, the farm soon began to provide a good living. The excellent 1918 crop brought $6,000 into the family coffers, but in 1919, hail, rust, late rains and early snow decimated most of it. Better ones would come later and the family persisted with characteristic determination.

Later on, Grant, allowing himself a rare personal note in his writing, would sketch a loving portrait of his father in his first book on early western pioneers, *Sodbusters*. The chapter, "Another Unknown," dedicated to his father, honours "that host of pioneers whose names as individuals will never appear on the pages of history": "The editor of 'Who's Who' never heard of this one. Here was a Sodbuster who never won a sweepstake for wheat. He never won a championship for bulls and he never won an election. He won a homestead and a lifetime sentence tending his soil and fighting weeds and growing food to nourish human bodies.... But he is typical of an army of brave men who congregated with him on the frontier in the '80's.... I said I wasn't going to identify this Sodbuster. I've almost changed my mind. I'll tell this much about him. He gave me my first spanking.''

In 1921, Grant, then 18, resolved to study at Ontario Agricultural College in Guelph and worked his rail passage down as a herdsman to a load of Toronto-bound cattle. Alex's parting comment was: ''Well, there he goes to that Eastern college – and he'll come back a damned fool.'' The fool-designate plunged into campus life, attempting everything available on campus before returning to Melfort for the summer. The next year he did so well, he resolved to enter the degree course, selling nursery stock to cover his expenses. By his third year, he had become completely independent of his family. When his brother, George, died tragically of spinal meningitis, Grant rushed home to comfort his parents. When his OAC studies were later completed, he returned to Melfort where he judged cattle and generally distinguished himself in the community before working for the election of a successful Liberal candidate in the 1926 federal election. He looked after the farm and 100 head of cattle for his parents who had not had a vacation since 1915. One day in Regina, he met William Rutherford, dean of agriculture at the University of Saskatchewan, who suggested he do graduate work at Iowa State College. On finishing there, he accepted an assistant professorship in animal husbandry at the University of Saskatchewan from Dean Rutherford.

MacEwan's period in Saskatoon was a happy one. He judged cattle and horses at countless fairs around the province. He was an interesting and popular lecturer for the students, inspiring them with the importance and dignity of agriculture. In the year he was offered a junior professorship, he bought two quarter sections of land. Fortunately, neither his position nor his salary suffered during the depression and drought of the 1930's. He became an elder in Knox United Church. During 1930, he also met Phyllis Cline, a primary school teacher and his future wife, at a Halloween masquerade party. Their five-year courtship ended in marriage in 1935. Ever frugal, the bridegroom somehow persuaded her to do most of the honeymoon trip to the West Coast on a bus. On returning to Saskatoon, he continued his busy life to such an extent that his bride once counted forty nights in succession in which he was away on community service.

The year 1937 was beyond doubt the cruelest of the "Dirty Thirties" for most Prairie Canadians, including Grant as manager of a university farm. He noted that no rain came to the Saskatoon area when needed with the result that "from 1000 acres of crop we did not harvest a bushel of grain." Noticing that desperate cattle could survive on the Russian thistle weed, he researched the matter and then used radio and newspapers to publicize this phenomenon throughout the province. The next year, under the influence of the historian, A.S. Morton, he began a love affair with western history which would last the rest of his life. He also gave his first speech on western history in Moose Jaw when directed by his dairyman host to speak on any subject but cows or dairying. In 1942, when CBC radio invited him to do four broadcasts, he chose to talk about notable pioneers of the West. Due to the series' popularity, it was extended into 1944. The sketches were later published as *Sodbusters*, which became the first of numerous books by Western Canada's most prolific popular historian. The MacEwans' only child, Heather, was born in 1939.

When war was declared by Britain in 1939, Grant was slightly overage and did not enlist. He had no desire to kill anyone and genuinely felt that his greatest value would be through research in livestock feeding, breeding and production. He served on a number of food production committees. In 1941, he published *Breeds of Farm Livestock in Canada*, the first book of its kind. During the war, he also sold his two parcels of Saskatchewan land in favour of a section of land on the Highwood river in the foothills southwest of Calgary and another half section at Priddis, closer to Calgary, with the secret intention of becoming a full-time writer in Alberta later on. His aging parents sold their own model farm and moved to White Rock, B.C.

In 1942, he was elected as the unpaid president of the struggling Saskatoon Exhibition and brought to it new life and an unexpected profit. Having twice declined to run for the Liberal party, during 1944 he met John Bracken, the new national leader of the newly-named Progressive Conservative party, and found that they agreed on agriculture policy and pay-as-you-go spending, but after two weeks of reflection decided not to run. The CCF was quickly gaining ground at the time, and soundly defeated the Liberals in the 1944 election. After the provincial Liberal rout, much pressure was put on MacEwan, who was now known from one end of the province to the other, to run for the leadership of the provincial Liberal party. In fact the weight was so great that for once he turned tail and ran to a Saskatoon hospital for some elective surgery while the leadership convention began without him.

In 1945, to the shock of some colleagues, MacEwan was appointed a director of the Royal Bank. At about this time, his thoroughly outward-looking attitude toward the wider community also ran afoul of a suddenly inward-looking trend among staff at the university. As president of the Saskatoon Kiwanis club, he was at a speaking engagement in Winnipeg when the president of the University of Manitoba offered him the leadership of its College of Agriculture. He accepted immediately, thus ending 18 years of service to Saskatchewan. Saskatoon's *Western Producer* newspaper said that he was "widely known as a colourful, able educator and extension man." The B.C. farm journal, *Country Life*, noting that the new dean was the ablest and best known judge of cattle and horses, said editorially that he "has rendered far more service to the primary producers of Canada than will ever be known or recompensed. His life is devoted to the welfare of others and he pays no attention to the sacrifices of time and energy he has to make."

From the start, MacEwan insisted that he had accepted the new challenge because he wanted to reorient the College of Agriculture toward the entire farm community of the province. He was soon riding his palomino mare in the freshman parade, the only faculty member at the university to participate. He quickly improved the morale of the dispirited college staff by persuading them to work as a team. The curriculum was modernized and flexibility was created to allow students who lacked the normal academic requirements to be "admitted for reason." He and his wife, neither very socially minded, personally paid for yearly parties for staff and their families. In his first year in office alone, he ventured into the wider community for functions on 124 occasions. He also attempted without much success to bridge a longstanding gap between the college and the provincial agriculture department and to encourage farmers to contact the college directly if the department could not help them. When the Red River flood of 1950 submerged about one quarter of Winnipeg, forcing a hundred thousand people to be evacuated, MacEwan boated out to the university and helped get the panic-stricken pigs, cattle and sheep to safety.

In 1948, the dean turned down an offer by the new Manitoba premier, Douglas Campbell, to join his coalition government as minister of agriculture. Three years later, the Brandon Liberal Association invited him to run in a federal by-election made necessary by the death of the Liberal incumbent. He hesitated. Phyllis clearly wanted no part of it, judging that the inevitable criticism, reduction in income, family relocation to Brandon and loss of kindred staff and students at the university were simply too high a price to pay. Grant was attracted by the hints he received from Prime Minister Louis St. Laurent that a cabinet post awaited him. He accepted the nomination. In the meantime, the university's Board of Governors held a special meeting to pass a resolution directing that if he accepted the nomination he must immediately resign his deanship. MacEwan was hurt by this reaction, noting later that "with the taint of politics on my character, I could never return to the university. A father may take back a prodigal son, and the church will accept a backsliding sinner but for a proud University, a politician would be forever an outcast."

MacEwan lost to the Progressive Conservative candidate, Walter Dinsdale, by 8371 votes to 11,124. Post-mortems on what was supposed to be an easy Liberal victory were many. Some voters obviously regarded MacEwan as a Saskatchewan man parachuted in after a 37-year absence from Brandon and resented the implication that no one from Brandon was fit to be elected. Brandon had a strong Liberal tradition and the party was clearly over-confident about its star candidate's prospects. Dinsdale and his family were popular and highly-respected Brandonites; he was a native son who not only had not left the community but had won the Distinguished Flying Cross for his work with the RCAF in World War II. The Liberal government in fact lost all five by-elections held that day; its grain marketing policies had made it particularly unpopular on the Prairies. MacEwan went to Dinsdale's committee room on election night to congratulate him, but afterwards was clearly concerned that, approaching fifty, he was now neither dean, MP, professor nor even someone with a job.

In what became the worst period of his life, the ex-candidate began a year-long search for a position. He was too late for the vacant post of managing director of the Calgary Exhibition and Stampede which greatly appealed to him. He became briefly the agriculture editor of *The Western Producer*, a weekly farm newspaper published in Saskatoon. Shortly after this, he accepted the position in Calgary as general manager of the Council of the Western Section of the Canadian Beef Producers. A relative, Wesley Nelson, noted pithily, "the defeat at Brandon was the best thing that ever happened to Grant... it sent him back to the province where he had really always belonged."

Things were by no means completely smooth for the MacEwans in Alberta. The polio epidemic which swept the Prairies in the summer of 1952 hit Calgary at about the same time as they did; that and the hot weather caused them to take Heather, then aged thirteen, to their cabin at Priddis. His regular pieces in *The Canadian Cattleman*, which he enjoyed doing, were terminated when a new editor took over in late 1953. The fiercely independent western cattlemen balked at increasing their association's funding of MacEwan's public relations campaign; he decided to ease himself out of the Beef Council work within two or three years.

At about this point, the Civic Government Association asked

him to run for Calgary City Council in the 1953 election. Though still worried about his Brandon debacle, MacEwan ran and received the second highest number of votes cast in the city. He found life on city council to be anything but tranquil, musing later on, "The alderman failing to attend all meetings will be scored for carelessness; if he attends avidly every call, he is a climber who is out to become mayor! If he accepts all invitations to parties and receptions, he must be a 'booze- hound' and if he fails to attend he's a 'kill- joy'. If he votes against spending, he's a 'tightwad'; if he supports big spending, he's the reason for high taxes. If he supports salary increases for aldermen, he's 'money hungry' and if he votes against them, he's 'putting on a show'."

Soon he was invited by some Liberals to contest the six-seat constituency of Calgary in the 1955 provincial election. After an aggressive campaign by all parties, he was elected as one of six MLAs representing the city. Despite some criticism, he opted to hold both his council and legislative assembly seats as the law entitled him to do. As one of 15 Liberals facing Premier Ernest Manning's 37 Social Credit MLAs, he spoke out on a number of issues, some of them advanced for the time in their environmental concern, such as the need to plant more trees around the province and to update surveys on soil erosion and wildlife. His reintroduction to partisan politics was abrupt. On one occasion, when his car broke down, he was obliged to hitch a ride with a farmer hauling a load of pigs. The driver, on learning that his passenger sat as a Liberal MLA, replied, "If I had known you were a Liberal, the only place you'd get in this truck would be back there with the other swine."

He continued to commute between Calgary and Edmonton and managed in 1957 to publish a book, *Eye Opener Bob*, about Calgary's immortal editor Bob Edwards. The next year came *Fifty Mighty Men*, character sketches of Western Canadians. His pattern of producing one book a year was set. Topping the polls in the 1957 civic election in Calgary, he commented that "politics is like jail: once in, it is not easy to get out." When the Liberal leader, Harper Prowse, resigned in 1958, MacEwan threw his hat in the ring and was elected on the second ballot. A year later,

however, a general election landslide for Premier Manning reduced the Liberals from 15 seats to one. Their leader was also
defeated and promptly resigned; he felt even worse than after the
Brandon loss because this time his party had lost with him. A few
years later, he abandoned his party affiliation altogether, noting
that he found party discipline both objectionable and an obstacle
to finding solutions. "If I ever ran again," he went on, "I'm
afraid it would have to be as an independent. "

The next political opportunity was as mayor of Calgary. Only
90 days after the provincial election disaster, MacEwan was re-
elected as a Calgary alderman with the largest vote in the city. He
also began a weekly column which ran for twenty years, mostly
on the subject of conservation, in *The Calgary Herald*, and one
on farm matters which was carried in fifty western weekly papers
in all four provinces and the Northwest Territories. When Mayor
Harry Hays resigned to enter federal politics in 1963, MacEwan
was elected by the other aldermen to complete the term. He won
the next election by 13,000 votes over a popular opponent, Art
Smith, and was an honest, economy-minded and competent chief
executive until 1965 when he declined to seek re-election. On one
representative occasion, he was running to city hall with his brief
case in the early morning when a police vehicle pulled up beside
him. "Two rookie police constables," as Macdonald puts it,
"seeing a tall suspicious character carrying a stuffed old brief
case running at a fast clip through early morning gloom, questioned him: where was he going? To work. Where did he work?
At City Hall. A flashlight shone in his face for a moment and then
two embarrassed constables apologized to their mayor and offered to drive him the rest of the way."

In late 1965, while speaking to young students about Western
Canada at the school where Heather taught, MacEwan got word
that he was Alberta's new lieutenant governor. From the start, he
stubbornly insisted that his private and public personalities must
remain the same. He continued to rise early to jog a mile or two,
to breakfast on porridge, and to refuse to ride in the back seat of
the vice-regal car. On one occasion, he asked his chauffeur,

Henry Weber, to stop while he helped two teenagers push a minibus out of a ditch. When the MacEwans hosted parties, no liquor was served. When he spoke to someone, that person had his total attention, with no attempt to look over a shoulder to see who else was present. When a cleaning woman arrived with her equipment at his office late one night ill, he asked Henry to drive her home and cleaned the office himself. He led numerous walkathons across the province to raise money for worthy causes.

In late 1967, the University of Calgary awarded him an honorary doctorate. In his convocation address, he referred to the naturalist religion which had developed out of his early Presbyterian faith, partly as a result of discussions with Chief Walking Buffalo of the Stoney Indian tribe. Its essence was harmony with nature and all other living creations of God. He had become a vegetarian in about 1956, which, as his biographer Macdonald notes, was ''a space-age step for a man who had spent a good part of his life instructing in the proper raising of livestock for slaughter.''

He wrote down his creed:

I believe instinctively in a God for whom I am prepared to search.

I believe it is an offence against the God of Nature for me to accept any hand-me-down, man-defined religion or creed without the test of reason.

I believe no man dead or alive knows more or knew more about God than I can know by searching.

I believe that the God of Nature must be without prejudice, with exactly the same concern for all His children, and that the human invokes no more, no less, of fatherly love than the beaver or sparrow.

I believe I am an integral part of the environment and, as a good subject, I must establish an enduring relationship with my surroundings. My dependence upon the land is fundamental. I believe destructive waste and greedy exploitation are sins.

I believe the biggest challenge is in being a helper rather than a destroyer of the treasures in Nature's storehouse, a conserver, a husbandman and partner in caring for the Vineyard....

I am prepared to stand before my Maker, the Ruler of the entire Universe, with no other plea than that I have tried to leave things in His Vineyard better than I found them.

When the moment came, he agreed at 68 years of age to serve another term as lieutenant governor. In the first, he had written five books in addition to attending to his numerous other duties. In the second, he built a log cabin near Sundre using only natural materials, with the purpose of leaving it to posterity as an example of the homesteads which covered the Prairies when he was born in 1902. He continued to write the history which has made Western Canada come alive for many. His motivation was stated clearly in his introduction to *Between the Red and the Rockies*: "The conversion of half a nation from wilderness to an enterprising agricultural community in a single generation is without parallel." His goal was to provide "entertaining, academic and cultural values."

As one of our few western writers born in the region, where his early impressions and outlook were formed and set, MacEwan writes about Western Canada out of his own experience. "He is a truly Western Canadian writer," wrote his biographer Macdonald, "When he writes, he does not look over his shoulder toward Eastern Canadian publishers, critics, reviewers. Nor does he look toward New York and Hollywood or seek to impress colleagues as many other 'western' writers do. "

Thousands of Albertans turned out to wish the vice-regal couple farewell as their second term ended in June, 1974. A book containing an estimated half million names of well-wishers was presented. At the legislature grounds Premier Peter Lougheed described the guest of honour as the most versatile man ever to call Alberta home. The government then presented him with a luxurious car. The next day, he went to the car dealer and exchanged it for a smaller model that would both use less gas and look less gaudy, seeing to it that the difference in prices went to the Alberta treasury.

ELEVEN

Making a Western Living
A Strategy for Diversification

SOME VISITORS to the Calgary Olympics apparently expected to confirm that Albertans are for the most part either cowboys or oil wildcatters. In fact the 1986 national census indicates that only about 100,000 persons in a work force of 1.2 million in Alberta are employed in basic agriculture and oilfield work: less than ten percent. Contrary to another common myth, only 29,000 British Columbians work directly in forestry or logging in an active work population of 1.4 million persons. In Saskatchewan, which is still occasionally thought of in terms of wheat alone, only 88,310 of a 500,000-person work force are involved directly in the primary sector of agriculture. In Manitoba, the most diversified western economy, the largest single industry grouping is currently ''manufacturing,'' with 66,000 persons in a work force of 542,000. Over two-thirds of all Westerners today are in service occupations and these are increasingly of a professional nature.

The Historical Perspective
During the ''frontier period'' between 1870 and 1900, the major source of economic development in the West was the relocation process itself. Furs were no longer the dominant export by 1870, but even though a little export grain left Manitoba during the 1870's, wheat was not yet an important regional staple on the Prairies. In British Columbia, gold had quickly

219

petered out and the age of forest products had not yet come. In such circumstances, expanding Canada's frontiers massively beyond the St. Lawrence valley was a brilliant and courageous policy regardless of whether Sir John A. Macdonald's dominant motive was to use the settlement process as an engine of growth for Central Canada or to develop the potential of the West.

From the beginning, Ottawa policy-makers saw grain exports and ranching in prairie Canada and mining in British Columbia as the major future economic activities of our region. In an era when agriculture was the dominant occupation of Canadians everywhere, western development along these lines was seen as essential both in attracting immigrants to Canada, and in eventually providing the exports which would allow Canada to continue to attract the investments from Britain and elsewhere which had helped to develop both Atlantic and Central Canada before Confederation.

Some large subsidies were provided by Ottawa for the opening of the West, including the free homesteads modelled on the earlier American experience and publicity spread throughout the continent of Europe. Cash subsidies paid to the Canadian Pacific Railway for completing its continental line were alone so large by the standards of the day that they pushed the debt charges of our new country to a third of total revenues by the early 1890's. High protective tariffs which began in 1879 to maximize the benefits of frontier settlement to eastern businesses were a key feature of the package of policies which became known as the National Policy, which endured essentially unchanged until the Great Depression in 1930. In practice, there was little western growth anywhere until 1898 because the combination of declining wheat prices and high rail transportation costs in the West discouraged most immigrants from homesteading. As late as 1891, less than two percent of the world's wheat production came from Western Canada.

Several factors moved dramatically in the West's favour after 1898. The region's population more than tripled between 1891 and 1911, during what became known as the Laurier boom. Other developments included a drop in the cost of moving grain to

Europe, advancements in dry-farming techniques, the closing of the American homestead frontier, and the economic pressures on farmers in various European countries which caused many to emigrate to Western Canada. In response to western political pressure, the Laurier government agreed to build two new continental rail lines, and these provided a boost to western coal mining and construction. Urban centres sprang up to serve adjacent farm communities. Saskatoon – which did not even exist in 1891 – had a population of 12,000 by 1911, and Winnipeg, with 25,000 people in 1891, had become the third largest city in Canada by 1911 with 130,000 people. Vancouver reached a population of 100,000 by 1911 although it was founded only in 1886. Economic growth on the coast occurred mainly in the forest, fishing and mining sectors and, interestingly, 70% of British Columbia's forest products during these years were sold to the booming construction industry on the Canadian prairies.

Before 1911, few Westerners anywhere questioned the dominant role afforded to wheat farmers by Ottawa through such initiatives as the Crow's Nest freight rate even if in practice they retarded diversification of the prairie economy. In grain marketing, for example, Parliament enacted before World War I a number of measures to redistribute grain profits from the railways, large grain elevator companies and other middlemen, but did little to diversify the regional economy. As the economic historian Doug Owram puts it, the adjustments made in favour of the West by the Laurier government before 1911 "could be made only within the general framework of the National Policy. When the government did attempt in 1911 to modify the National Policy by means of a reciprocity agreement with the United States, it was defeated by a combination of economic self-interest emanating from manufacturing circles in Ontario and nationalistic concern about American influence over Canada.''

The 1911 election – which ended with the two parties changing places, the Conservatives winning 134 seats to the Liberals' 85 produced a divided West on the matter of trade with our southern neighbour, something which even Westerners frequently forget today.

The combination of investments being repatriated to Britain in anticipation of the outbreak of World War I, falling wheat prices, and rising freight costs caused a recession throughout Western Canada between 1912 and 1915. The weakened farm sector soon created collapsing real estate prices and growing unemployment in western cities and towns, but a boom in the region returned with the fresh demand for food, metals and timber during World War I. Thousands of new prairie farms were established between 1916 and 1921, and another period of long-term western prosperity seemed assured.

The clouds on the horizon were those over the two new transcontinental railways, the Grand Trunk Pacific and Canadian Northern, both of which were teetering on the edge of bankruptcy. In desperation, the Robert Borden government finally nationalized them in 1918. From that day until the present, prairie farmers have sought not rail expansion, but maintenance of the branch-line system already in place.

An economic bust in the West followed Armistice Day. Unemployment in British Columbia soared to more than 14%. Deep-seated western complaints against Ottawa resulted in 64 seats for the Progressive Party in the 1921 federal election, 39 from Western Canada, on the basis of the need for a New National Policy largely written by the Canadian Council on Agriculture. The movement's short-lived electoral success demonstrated that Westerners, particularly farmers, did not feel they were being treated justly in Confederation.

The regional population of the West grew from 598,000 in 1900 to nearly three million by the end of the 1920's. Agriculture accounted in 1927-29 for 55% of the net value of production for the four western provinces. British Columbia received almost 80% of its net production value from primary resources and agriculture, forestry, fish and furs. Even in Manitoba, many of the manufacturing and service jobs were dependent on a healthy primary sector. In short, the region's dependence on a few primary resources was becoming ominous.

The West led the rest of Canada into the worst depression in

222

modern history. Wheat prices had been dropping since 1926 and the amount of unsold Canadian wheat reached 91 million bushels in 1928. No. 1 Northern wheat, worth $1.51 a bushel in 1925, collapsed to as low as 34 cents in 1933. Drought, hail, grasshoppers and diseases ruined millions of acres of prairie throughout the thirties. Realized net farm income dropped from $363 million in 1928 to an astonishing minus $10.7 million three years later. Many western farmers had taken on large loans to expand their production during the 1920's, and even keeping their farms became difficult for many of them.

Collapses in the farm sector were quickly followed by many elsewhere in the West; the provincial governments themselves were near bankruptcy from relief payments. Generally speaking, the less reliant a district was on wheat the less it suffered. British Columbia's economic position actually improved relative to the rest of Canada and its per capita income remained in the top two of all provinces throughout the 1930's. Saskatchewan, on the other hand, the most populous and wealthy western province during the 1920's, became the poorest in the 1930's and out-migration grew sharply.

Many thousands of western families were completely ruined by the twin calamities of the economy and the climate. The impact of this tragedy was exacerbated by the long-cherished western view that our region was the central economic fly-wheel for the entire country, as it had been since 1900, and considerable bitterness evolved toward whatever or whomever had allowed western ruination. New political parties and solutions sprang up. Relief costs for the government of Saskatchewan had, by 1937, reached $62 million, more than the total revenues of the province.

Prime Minister King appointed the Rowell-Sirois Commission in 1937 to examine the situation, and it quickly became a lightning rod for western discontent. The briefs of all four western governments displayed an amazing similarity of concern. Oppressive national policies were seen as aggravating large regional differences in standards of living. The rail freight rates, natural resource control and the protectionist tariffs were cited as evidence of deliberate unfairness created by Ottawa. One of the more bizarre responses by the King government was to raise tariffs in order to protect a sagging domestic market, but in the late 1930's the vulnerability of a western economy dependent on a few export products, primarily wheat, led Western Canada for the first time to talk seriously about the need for diversification. No real consensus was reached on how to achieve it, but even the discussion of it showed how desperate Westerners had become.

The return of adequate rains and wartime prosperity in the West masked some changes from earlier patterns. For decades, regional prosperity had depended on the state of the western agricultural sector, but a new and expanded manufacturing base in Central Canada became the driving force of the post-war national economy. Agriculture was by the mid-1950's clearly no longer capable of providing general prosperity to Westerners for various reasons, including U.S. farm export subsidies which cut into traditional Canadian markets. More than 200,000 prairie farm families left the land between 1936 and 1961. In the mid-1950's, increasing numbers of Westerners began to urge Ottawa to divert industrial development from Central Canada in the interest of regional justice. Others, accepting the staples theory, called for the processing and upgrading of all primary products in the region. Manufacturing, much of it related to the primary products of forestry, fishing and mining, began so quickly in British Columbia that by 1951 more than 70,000 British Columbians were employed in that sector.

Alberta's population grew slowly until oil was discovered at Leduc and Redwater in 1947. By 1961, the oil and gas boom had almost doubled Alberta's population to well over a million. Capital flooded in with the new residents, and the general prosperity allowed the provincial government to build a good infrastructure of schools, roads, and hospitals. By 1960 in Alberta the mining sector, which included oil and gas, was well ahead of agriculture in terms of its contribution to the provincial economy. Saskatchewan's dependence on wheat continued until the late 1950's only because it lacked an alternative. A potash, uranium and oil production boom hit the province in the mid-1960's and by 1966 a series of wheat and other sales to China saw Saskatchewan farmers regain for the first time since the 1920's the leading economic growth in the country. Manitoba's mix of agriculture and manufacturing provided stability in the 1950's, but at the price of a decline in both output per capita income and the province's share of the national population. During the 1960's, Western Canada was briskly dividing into two "have" and two "have-not" provinces.

Urbanization in all four provinces, which occurred at somewhat different rates and intervals, had a very significant effect on the regional economy. British Columbia was more urban than rural as early as 1931. Manitoba was 64 percent urban by the mid-fifties, and Alberta became more urban than rural sometime between 1951 and 1956. Saskatchewan did not become predominantly urban until the 1960's. The creation of new service jobs in all four provinces closely paralleled this process.

In the early 1970's, the marketable oil and gas in three of the four western provinces allowed the region to reassert itself as the motor of national prosperity. As Doug Owram stresses, "the concept of growth is, however, deeply imbedded within the western tradition." The subsidy created by Ottawa for consumers of oil after 1973 was seen by many Westerners as an attempt to deflect western prosperity to Central Canada. The conflict was again clear: maximizing western potential for the western region versus using western resources for Central Canada's purposes. Westerners insisted the presence of natural resources must bring a high degree of related processing in our region.

The Regional Economy Today

The western and northern economies today still depend heavily on natural resources, and we are as sensitive about them as other Canadians are about language issues. Many of us are still actively involved in the exploitation of resources or in their transportation, marketing or distribution. Even more of us in the service sectors depend on resources for part of our livelihoods.

The governments of all four western provinces are aggressively seeking a greater role in the international economy. British Columbia has opened five new offices abroad; Alberta has five;

Saskatchewan, four. The governments of Manitoba and Sas-katchewan each arrange about 25 overseas trade, investment or tourisms missions yearly, British Columbia about 40. Alberta sponsors 100 to 120 trade, 85 investment, and 100 tourism missions per year. This, as the American professor Earl Fry points out, constitutes a far more vigorous effort than that made by any of the thirteen western states.

Much of the impetus for such efforts comes from the recent realization of a long-time Western Canadian fear: that all of our economic pillars could fall at the same time. The international prices for oil, grain, potash, coal and uranium all collapsed during 1986. British Columbia's forest products faced a continuing threat from new American duties, similar to those threatened earlier against our softwood lumber and imposed on our shakes and shingles. The 1982 recession on the Prairies had lingered on into 1985 and both Alberta and Saskatchewan were hit very hard again when the bottom fell out of world oil prices in November, 1985. In 1986, an estimated 40,000 Alberta and Saskatchewan oil workers lost their jobs. Prices for grain had already dropped significantly because of the ongoing subsidy battle between the treasuries of the United States and the European Community. The non-stop rain and severe frost roughly halved the expected Saskatchewan wheat crop during 1986. The fact that Manitoba's more diversified economy did better than the other three western ones during the year only confirmed the widespread western conviction that it was necessary to diversify.

Figures released by Statistics Canada earlier this year con-firmed that the 1982 national recession has still not ended in parts of Western and Atlantic Canada. The limp state of much of the western economy since then also ended the westward shift of population as so many resource industries in the region were hit with falling prices and markets.

Interprovincial migration, a noteworthy feature of Canadian life, holds particular significance in the four western provinces, as both the level and direction of interprovincial migration tend to relate to regional economic conditions. According to the 1986 census, the westward shift of population of the 1970's – a direct consequence of the Alberta resource boom – ended in the early 1980's when falling oil prices brought about economic stagnation and Ontario replaced Alberta as the preferred destination. Between 1981 and 1986, more than 70,000 Albertans had moved to Ontario. The net loss of population for Alberta due to interprovincial movements equalled 30,000 people, for Manitoba 1,550 and Saskatchewan almost 3,000. Only British Columbia experienced a small gain of some 10,000 people. The serious demographic problems created for Western Canada between 1981 and 1986 are clear. According to studies, interprovincial migration tends to consist of younger, skilled and energetic persons. Emigration from any region reduces local employment and the standard of living whereas newcomers usually add to both. As Atlantic Canadians know so well, inter-regional out-migration reduces productivity and results in higher taxes for a shrinking population in order to maintain public expenditures from a reduced tax base. Because a smaller population decreases local demand for goods and services, some estimate that for every five persons who leave a region two additional jobs will also be lost.

A Western Strategy

Contrary to the view that the major economic assets of Western Canada are wheat, rocks, trees, oil, and so on, the evidence is overwhelming that our real strength is the nature and quality of our approximately seven million residents. Our economic models should be Switzerland, West Germany and Japan. Each has achieved a high general standard of living and relatively full employment by producing a range of high-quality finished products which are exported with real marketing skill and first-class service to customers. All three populations know that success today depends on intelligence, quality control and technology and act accordingly.

Economic life in all four western provinces has historically depended heavily on natural resources: fish, fur, wheat, beef, forest products, coal, oil, gas and minerals. Each still plays an important role in one or more parts of our region. A boom in one resource often carries many of us forward on its wave, just as a subsequent bust leaves many of us beached. Booming and busting have been too long the economic lot of Western Canadians.

There is a strong consensus in the West that we must build boldly on our comparative economic advantages by strengthening and adding new components to our natural resource and other existing sectors.

A more efficient management of our natural resources could bring large gains in terms of jobs with high pay to Western Canada. A recent study by the Institute for Research on Public Policy says that Western Canadians, as owners of their resources, by pursuing some aggressive reforms could receive substantially more economic value from that sector. Six resource industries, nickel in Manitoba, potash and uranium in Saskatchewan, hydroelectricity in British Columbia and Manitoba, the forest industry in British Columbia, and the Pacific salmon fishery, were examined. Grouping their conclusions around maximization of resource rents, distribution of these rents, and political markets, the study concluded: "Despite the problems associated with resource-based economies, the comparative advantages that Western Canada currently enjoys in staples and the potential gains from improved management are so great that policy-makers should be more concerned with rational resource management. For reasons of efficiency and equity, governments must give priority to the collection of resource rents. Efficient rent collection and rational resource policy is admittedly a demanding task, fraught with decisions made under uncertainty and political bargaining. But abandoning the task assures a less desirable future for all concerned."

Diversification

The goal of economic diversification should be to equip Western Canadians to compete more effectively in the emerging global economy and to minimize regional unemployment and instability without harming long-term job growth and average job earnings. A paper in 1985 prepared for the Economic Council of Canada by economists Harry Postner and Leslie Wesa, based on a study of the period 1970-83, concluded that a reallocation of manufacturing and services in the four western provinces could meet these three criteria. In the case of Manitoba, for example, the study concluded that some employment redistribution to sectors such as transportation/communications/utilities, trade, finance/insurance/real estate, food and beverages, printing and publishing, clothing, electrical and chemical products would be "winners." Other sectors with relative instability included mining, construction and commercial services. Machinery- and transportation-equipment manufacturing industries were seen as "losers" in an optimal diversification scenario for Manitoba. There appear to be considerable similarities here for Saskatchewan, Alberta and British Columbia. The oil sector in Alberta is not one which can be reduced because its long-term employment growth rate and average earnings are the highest in the province.

The study, noting in passing that the four western provinces are less diversified than the central provinces, concluded that the four provinces could, in the long term, reduce their employment instability as follows: British Columbia – 24%, Alberta – 17%, Saskatchewan – almost 30%, and Manitoba – 22%. In British Columbia, for example, more and further processing of forest resources would be useful both in providing diversification and reducing economic instability.

The diversification strategy for the West should therefore operate closely with the four provincial governments to invest both significant funds and a robust political will of a long-term kind in a number of directions of economic policy. I intend to outline only some of the possible directions the western economy could follow with the main central challenge to all of them: building on existing strengths.

Tax Reform

Western Canadians are certainly in favour – as is everyone – of a simpler and fairer system which would significantly increase the take-home pay of individuals through a better balance among the three major elements of the federal tax system — personal, corporate and sales tax.

It is patently unacceptable that, as was true in 1983 for example, 64 companies which each earned profits of more than $25 million paid no corporate tax whatsoever. Small businesses, which have created most of the new jobs across the country in recent years, paid taxes for 1982 at almost double the rate of businesses with assets of more than $25 million. As a result of tax concessions mostly to large businesses, the share of the income tax burden paid by companies slumped from 50% to 25% between 1950 and 1985, while the share paid by individuals and families increased correspondingly from 50% to 75%.

The administration of the federal sales tax has resulted in large distortions of economic decision-making and badly needs reform. Ours is evidently the only developed country whose tax system favours foreign producers at the expense of domestic ones. We impose a sales tax on exports which averages about one percent, whereas imports are currently taxed at roughly one-third less than comparable domestic goods. Major change is clearly needed here. There appears, however, to be considerable opposition in Western Canada to any business transfer tax applicable to services and food. For example, a tax on transportation services would reduce both the competitiveness of many of our exports and add significantly to the cost of consumer goods trucked or sent by rail from Central Canada.

Western Canada will benefit, in my judgement, if tax reforms
— remove the biases which currently favour industrial sectors over service work;
— relax the definition of what constitutes research and development for income tax purposes and provide to small firms the same tax incentives for R & D as large manufacturers now enjoy;
— provide incentives for investments in human resources, which are to the service sector what capital goods are to manufacturing, possibly through a tax credit for adding employees; and,
— create strong disincentives to mergers of companies above a certain size, on the premise that these usually lead to lay-offs, an undue concentration of ownership, and inefficiencies. (On the subject of efficiency it may be noted that there are disturbing

indications that only 3 or 4 percent of Canadian small businesses grow rapidly, compared with 12 to 15 percent in the U.S.A.)

Agriculture

Unfortunately, agriculture in the final years of the century is declining in its contribution to western output. There were approximately 174,000 farms in the four western provinces in 1982, contributing about 5.2% of the overall regional output and involving less than 8% of Western Canada's total population. The dropping number of full-time western farmers because of low grain prices, drought, cash-flow and credit-related problems represents a very serious problem for the region. Western farm families have been forced by events to earn much of their income from sources away from their farms. In British Columbia, outside earnings were as high as 80% during 1980.

A major reason for this, as the Edmonton economists Terrence and Michele Velman point out, is our ongoing cheap-food policy, under which Canadians generally spent in 1982 only 16.3% of disposable income on food. Growth, in short, depends largely on foreign markets for grains, oil seeds, and red meats. As recently as 1982-83, wheat alone comprised about three quarters of our grain and oil seeds exports but the prospects for wheat are important and problematic. The governments of both China and the U.S.S.R. have indicated they will reduce wheat imports in the years ahead. The continuing obscene grain price-war between the United States and the European Community is also causing severe problems for Canada in some of the sixty nations to which we currently sell grain.

The best longer term hope for our grains and oil seeds lies in better penetration of new and existing markets, especially the newly industrialized countries of the Pacific Rim, but new strategies, like the development of agricultural byproducts such as ethanol, are clearly required for western agriculture. Expanded research into the growth of non-traditional wheat types would help us to market better in developing nations, which prefer lower quality wheats and those appropriate for popular products such as noodles. Many studies indicate that agricultural research spending repays itself rapidly, and the Western Diversification Office (WDO) should allocate considerably more funds for research of this nature. WDO funds should also be directed towards helping to restore the soil quality in various parts of the Prairies.

Something is clearly wrong when the Natural Sciences and Engineering Research Council has to inform researchers – as it did in 1987 – that, because of budget cuts, "new applications will not be accepted" in the research areas of energy, food-agriculture and oceans. Basic food and agricultural research needs more funding, not less, and the WDO must do something really substantial here for the West.

As was suggested in a study by the Canada West Foundation, horticulture (including flowers, fruits and vegetables in greenhouses; plant and tree nurseries; vegetable seed products) offers major potential. Careful WDO investment should also encourage such products as berries (notably strawberries), sod, purebred livestock, horses for recreation, rabbits for meat, and goats for milk and meat.

There are policy initiatives beyond those already suggested for western agriculture which would assist growth. Virtually every related study indicates that agricultural research brings very high returns, yet both the federal and western provincial governments' contributions to it are inadequate. More research on key matters such as the best production strategy for dry land agriculture in Western Canada, higher-yielding wheat and barley varieties, the indicated change in consumer preferences for red meat and the relative merits of intensive versus less intensive production methods are required. The Velmans contend that improving "the skills, abilities and management capacities of farm families in western agriculture should be emphasized as of the highest priority in any long run growth strategy for the agricultural sector.... More attention must be given to soil and water conservation, and production systems which are ecologically sustainable in the long run must be developed." On water management, they call for "alternatives including the introduction of pricing for water and the reform of water rights systems."

Aside from the very serious reality of drought in large parts of

Saskatchewan and Alberta, the livestock industry is enjoying good prices and sales. The economics of the industry are changing and, as the Calgary economist William Kerr has pointed out, markets in the United States and the Pacific Rim, especially Japan, rather than the Canadian market, will provide most future growth. Between 1976 and late 1984, the western beef industry showed no real growth and in fact was characterized by low prices, ranch bankruptcies and a shrunken western slaughter industry. Livestock processing still ranked as the largest manufacturing industry during 1984 by volume of sales in both Saskatchewan and Manitoba, and was second only to oil refining in Alberta.

For the Prairies as a whole, livestock processing is the largest manufacturing employer, has the biggest payroll and is a major consumer of fuel and electricity. It is also a major value-adding industry, using local cereals, but it has considerable excess capacity. Canadian beef suppliers could do more to develop markets in California. The shortfall in the California beef requirement is so large that if Western Canada could supply even 10% of it, as Kerr points out, "this would equal a 22% increase in Alberta production." Much of the shortfall is now supplied from east of Omaha but transportation costs from Calgary are about three percent cheaper than the rates from Omaha to San Francisco.

In Japan, quotas and very high tariffs still restrict the entry of foreign beef, but a liberalization of these practices could offer enormous opportunities for western beef. A reason for Canada's accounting for less than one percent of Japanese beef imports as recently as four years ago is that our beef is too lean for Japanese tastes and fails to meet their difficult cutting specifications. Other growing markets of the Pacific Rim require a cheaper grass-fed product than is now produced in Western Canada. The grain-fed lean and young beef preferred by Canadians is simply not sought after in the Pacific Rim, and Westerners should address this problem quickly.

Some funding should be directed towards better equipping people in our meat industry with training and knowledge of selected foreign markets, and toward helping to modernize the processing side of the industry at some locations in Western Canada.

The Western Grain Transportation Act's current method of payment of the Crow Benefit directly to the railways retards diversification in western agriculture because returns to grain producers are higher by about $23 per tonne if they commit their products to export markets. Westerners who wish to diversify into livestock feeding and processing, high carbohydrate crops such as sweet sorghum, canola crushing, adding value to grain, and so on, thus lose much of our comparative regional advantage. The current payment method has a negative impact on the development of a domestic market for feed grains and additional investments in plants and technology for western meat packing and processing.

Western grain producers should be able to choose to have the Crow Benefit paid directly to them on an experimental basis: this would provide a major incentive to our value-adding agricultural industries. There might be a different view on this issue in each of the prairie provinces, so it would seem reasonable to permit all producers to decide by referendum how they wished the payment to be made. Precedents such as medicare and the Quebec Pension Plan already exist for tailoring programs differently for different provinces.

Forestry

The major recommendation of the 1984 study by the Economic Council of Canada on western forestry was that the "stock of mature timber in British Columbia be harvested at a faster rate than present policies permit, as soon as (and whenever) market conditions make it profitable to do so, and that this be done with full provision for environmental protection." A number of knowledgeable Westerners have criticized both the analysis and the conclusion. H.V. Lewis, an economist with the British Columbia Ministry of Forests, pointed out that British Columbia timber harvests "have followed United States housing starts with reasonable accuracy over the past decade or more, particularly if the effect of the exchange rates is taken into account.'' He added that a substantial increase in British Columbia's timber harvests would make future harvest reductions much more probable with a range of consequences for cities and regions dependent on forest products. If its analysis was dismissed, the Council at least drew attention to a range of choices in forest policy.

Most forests in the West are owned by their provincial governments which either contract with private firms to manage them or do so through provincial forest services. David Haley of UBC's Forestry faculty contends that in the first model there are inadequate incentives for efficient long-term management of the resource, and in the second the tendency is increasingly for forests to be seen as ''public utilities'' rather than as businesses producing an essential raw material for an important industrial sector which must sell the bulk of its product in increasingly competitive world markets. Haley argues that transferring title would result in more efficiently-managed timber production.

World timber consumption is expected to increase by about 50% over the next three decades, but before Canadians can expect to benefit from the estimated 300,000 new jobs the industry could create over the next twenty years, many of them in Western Canada, further major improvements in forest management are required. The distinguished British Columbia forester, Les Reid, estimates that 25,000 new jobs can be created in forest renewal alone, an additional 75,000 through the increased manufacturing of wood products resulting from better harvests.

In close collaboration with the ministers responsible for forests in the four western provinces, the WDO should include the following initiatives:

— further encouragement to harvesting energy from forest biomass, which could provide an economic boost to our forest industries and help Canada to become a world leader in biomass energy technology;

— additional federal support to our western forestry schools (located at the Universities of British Columbia and Alberta);

— the recruitment to public and private forestry service of more scientists, policy analysts and economists; and

– substantially more federal funding for western forest renewal through renewed Forest Resource Development Agreements with all four provincial governments.

Manufacturing

The economist Douglas North argued three decades ago that four types of manufacturing can locate successfully in peripheral regions: material-oriented industries; equipment manufacturers for extractive industries; industries producing consumer goods for local markets; and footloose activities in which transportation costs do not influence location. Meat and fish packing, flour-making, and petrochemicals are examples of material-based manufacturing in Western Canada which exist because of the degree of reduction in the bulk or weight of a primary product. Oil and gas machinery manufacturers in Alberta and transportation-equipment producers in Manitoba are instances of makers of equipment for regional extractive industries. Dairy and bakery products, construction materials, furniture, commercial printing and such products are examples of local consumer goods manufacturers which have located in our larger western regional centres. The growth of biotechnological centres in Saskatoon and other technology centres in Western Canada appears to offer the best hope for footloose future-oriented manufacturing jobs in Western Canada. More effort is clearly needed to develop more footloose industries in all four western provinces.

In particular, as the geographer Neil Seifried has pointed out, if Alberta is to diversify industrially, its manufacturing output must become less oriented to its dominant oil and gas sector than it was during the 1967 to the 1970 period, and more oriented to external markets. Manitoba manufacturing over the same period, particularly its clothing, transportation equipment and electrical products, was focussing more successfully — from a diversification standpoint – on markets external to the region, including Ontario, Quebec and the United States.

The 1984 Economic Council of Canada development scenario for the West asserted that manufacturing cannot contribute much

236

to the regional economy because our manufacturing base is too small. A 1985 study by Winnipeg economists Norman Cameron, James Dean and Walter Good was far less pessimistic. Examining 49 clothing and 44 transportation equipment firms in Manitoba on the basis of the volatile years between 1970 and 1984, they concluded that manufacturing is not robust enough to drag the rest of the western economy along after it. On the other hand, a rising western population would create large enough regional markets to allow manufacturing to become cost-competitive with manufactured products from outside the region or Canada itself. In both clothing and transportation equipment, a substantial reduction in western imports has resulted; Cameron, Dean and Good believe that textiles and clothing should be added to printing and publishing, metal fabrication, wood industries and furniture and fixtures as sectors with particularly good western prospects. Among the factors which they consider favour additional manufacturing in Winnipeg are an entrepreneurial pool, good employee productivity, local receptiveness to business and industry, an efficient transportation system for raw materials and finished products, and favourable local taxes. This would appear to be equally true of many other urban centres across Western Canada.

There are advantages for some other traditional manufacturing operations which might locate themselves profitably in our region as well. The WDO could be a major catalyst here by targeting some high unemployment areas in the West for enterprise zones similar to the Enterprise Cape Breton model, which provides a package of incentives for new manufacturing operations locating in Cape Breton. It can also be helpful in providing marketing information and assistance about foreign markets for threshold exporters. Domestic opportunities for western firms should be helped by initiatives to ensure that full information is provided to them about federal government procurement and tendering practices. Elemental fair national play requires that both federal government and national institutions, public and private and including the chartered banks, must in future ensure that their procurement and other activities each year reflect the reality of the country. Much improvement in regional equality is needed for both Western and Atlantic Canadians.

Oil Sands, Coal and Natural Gas

A paper presented to provincial energy ministers in 1986 estimated that without new sources of supply Canada will require imports to meet one-quarter of its light crude oil needs by 1990 and more than half by 2000. It seems to me to follow that Western Canada should aim to become the technological world leader for oil sands energy development. A new mined oil sands project at Fort McMurray to start in 1996 and an upgrader in Lloydminster to start in 1993, recently announced amid much controversy as to its economic viability, could become important components of a prairie manufacturing base in the overall national interest.

The private sector is understandably reluctant to undertake such projects because of the uncertainty of price, but might go ahead if Ottawa negotiated a guaranteed price for a fixed volume of the product. The difference between the negotiated price and the world price would become either a loss or a gain according to the package negotiated between the successful consortium and the various governments involved. Security of future supply is so critical that the risk appears warranted. The U.S., for example, now has a strategic oil reserve of about 515 million barrels, which at $20 (U.S.) per barrel represents a $10 billion investment in oil security without including carrying charges on the investment.

Ottawa must also recognize that the oil sands sector badly needs help in other spheres. For example, new oil sand extraction technologies appear to hold real promise for efficiency and reduction of water and air pollution when compared to the hot-water processes now used by Syncrude and Suncor at Fort McMurray. Imaginative new research and development programs funded by Ottawa should assist the more promising of these technologies with a view to enhancing existing western strengths. World leadership, with all its spin-offs in terms of exports of services, should be the goal.

Western Canada's coal reserves are virtually limitless, and available data indicates that its liquefaction for fuel becomes economically viable in the $25 (U.S.) price range. At present there are more than 20 promising methods on the horizon. Ottawa should select for research funding perhaps ten not already being funded by provincial governments. After a period, the two levels of government might together choose the two or three most promising for further development. Ottawa should also support research on new technologies for co-processing coal with bitumen/heavy oil.

Major new markets for Western Canada's coal now appear to exist in Western Europe. One recent estimate is that Europeans might fairly soon absorb up to ten million tonnes of Western Canadian coal yearly, shipped through Port Churchill by rail from northern Alberta and B.C. Again, Ottawa should seek to become a catalyst.

Substantial growth for gas exports from Western Canada was predicted in a late 1986 study by the National Energy Board. If, however, the Board does not permit exports beyond 1991, as is a possibility, a cost-benefit analysis by the Alberta Research Council predicts a virtual calamity for exploration and development in this important western industry. It estimates that the present value of a no-export policy after 1991 for Canadian consumers, because of resulting lower prices, would be $8.8 billion between 1988 and 2003, but the net present loss to Alberta producers alone would be $25.3 billion, making a net loss to the economies and governments of the western provinces of $18.3 billion over the period. Given the indications of large quantities of gas still to be found within the western provinces, it is surely in the general national interest to continue exports beyond 1991. Ottawa or WDO might usefully address this issue, if only by funding further research on the employment and other costs to the West of alternative gas export policies.

High Technology

A major comparative advantage of Western Canada lies in biomass (energy, forest, agricultural) and it is probably in that large area that our best technology prospects lie. WDO can help us to seek world leadership in a series of carefully chosen niches here, just as Northern Telecom did in telecommunications. It will have to fund part of the necessary research and development, just as Canadian Bell Telephone users paid for a good deal of the research which led to Northern Telecom's success.

A study done for the governments of the four western provinces in 1986 by the Science Directorate of the Organization for Economic Cooperation and Development (OECD) assessed our general strengths and needs. It concluded that Westerners are well equipped for a knowledge-intensive economy for many reasons: regional pride; our strong desire to prove that we are an intellectual frontier of Canada; a host of universities, community colleges and technical schools; entrepreneurial dynamism; high quality technologies already available; and a multicultural population. More is needed, however, to link technology to the Western Canadian economies and to enrich existing industries, such as our natural resource and agricultural sectors, with new technologies. Among the recommendations of the OECD study to Ottawa, which could play an important role through WDO, are the following:

— The share of federal government R & D expenditures (both intramural and extramural) going to the western provinces over the 1981-85 period has been stable at about 22%. On a population basis, Western Canada is entitled to 30% of such spending. (Given our economic instability, we probably should have more than that during the next decade.)

— There is need for Ottawa to follow Saskatchewan in establishing a "single window" for programs to help with technology development, marketing, regional development and export development.

— All governments should cooperate fully on priorities and joint goals in such key areas as micro-electronics, telecommunications, and biotechnology and whenever possible relate high technology to our natural resource sectors.

— The federal government should expand western programs to enrich traditional industries through a better diffusion and adoption of new technologies, and become more activist in policies for technology transfers into the western provinces.

Some specific recommendations by the OECD to the federal government should probably be included in WDO budgeting. For example, funds should be provided for programs and support in recruiting top leaders for infrastructure projects, provided they relate to the technological strengths of each province and are supported by a network of entrepreneurs, industrially experienced academics and private capital markets.

Through added human and financial resources, the capability of federal ministries and agencies to contribute to liaison with regional R & D and innovation should be improved, and there should be better use of federally-sponsored facilities to meet provincial needs. While there are excellent centres in the West, they need to better network among themselves and with corresponding provincial organizations.

Similarly, joint initiatives by the federal and provincial governments on international programs, as recommended by the OECD study, might also become part of the WDO:

— commissioning of ''competitive analyses'' in areas of technology which are commonly the focus of provincial plans for knowledge-intensive economies;

— exchanges of researchers and scientists with foreign countries;

— commercialization of new technologies introduced in the western provinces by mobilization of the scientific and commercial networks and programs for international technology transfer.

Transportation and Tourism

Because of our small population, large distances and dependence on foreign trade, transportation remains very important to Western Canada. The WDO might well take a careful look at whether new VIA rolling stock would allow it to achieve better economies as similar ones appear to have done for AMTRAK in the U.S. Would our regional tourism industry benefit significantly? Again, why do we have no facility for manufacturing trucks when so many of them are sold into the four western provinces? Given the importance of electricity to Manitoba and British Columbia, WDA should do everything feasible to ensure that Western Canadians are actively involved in the world of future industries promised by superconductivity for power systems, electronics, transportation and science.

Tourism is already important to all four western economies and could be much more so. For example, in the summer of 1986, Canadians spent more than $800 million (out of a total of $2 billion) on overnight pleasure travel in the four western provinces.

In Alberta alone, tourism is a $2 billion-a-year industry employing about 85,000 people. About 30,000 people in each of Saskatchewan and Manitoba and some 120,000 British Columbians work in tourism-related industries.

Experts say Western Canada's tourism industry could be doubled with proper marketing, staff training and resort development. A number of new and intelligent programs to raise the appeal of the four western provinces as a world-class tourism destination, including more public education, could also help us draw many more visitors from other regions of Canada and abroad.

Services

Services are both the largest and most rapidly-growing sector of the four provincial economies. Can they be a major engine of economic growth? In its ''Western Transition'' report the Economic Council made a number of recommendations with that objective. All current anti-service biases in federal government programs providing assistance to businesses should be ended, and there should be encouragement to the export of western consultant services to Pacific Rim and developing nations generally. Specifically, in my view, the Canadian International Development Agency contracts should be awarded with a much greater determination to assist Western Canadian consultants to achieve the world-class successes already obtained abroad by Montreal-based consulting engineers. The Small Business Loans Act should ensure that services are not discriminated against and that the minimum loan is not of an amount which is unattractive to most new service businesses.

I have offered a long list of measures that are appropriate for a

Western Economic Diversification Strategy. Admittedly priorities will have to be tailored according to the financial cloth made available. Some proposals will no doubt have to be postponed. Diversification appears to be an old theme in the economic aspirations of Western Canada. It is time these aspirations materialized and took realistic shape. We need to act boldly and with vision if Western Canada is to enjoy the future that its potential offers.

Canada-U.S. Free Trade Agreement

Canada's entire trade relations with the U.S. have been at centre stage for three years. The battle lines were drawn as pro- and anti-free trade forces prepared for a major electoral confrontation in 1988, and the rhetoric has been reminiscent of the 1911 national election campaign. Some Ontarians, including their premier, have attempted to scuttle the Canada-U.S. free trade initiative from the outset even though from many indications their province has the most to gain from free trade. The province that now relies on the U.S. market for more than 90% of its exports has the most to lose if no free trade agreement is reached, because the alternative to free trade is not the status quo but growing U.S. protectionism.

In the West, the free trade agreement (FTA) is seen by many as a way to reduce the colonialism created by national governments over decades at the expense of western resources. Ontario, long the main beneficiary of western resources, has become the focus of much western anger and frustration. Recent statements by the western premiers and other Westerners suggest that if the Peterson government continues its stand on the FTA major regional conflicts will arise. It is no coincidence that most of the people in the West who say the NEP was good for the region, now say that the FTA is bad for us.

I firmly believe implementing the proposed FTA is in the best interests of both our region and all other parts of Canada. As a Western Canadian, I share with millions of those in the West and other regions a broader vision of trade that carries the opportunity for benefits to all Canadians.

The way in which many Westerners view free trade is based on a long-standing history of neglect by, and mistrust of, successive federal governments which have often seemed to our region to be of, by and for Central Canada alone. Some of us talk often about "nationalizing" Ottawa. Such questions as who has the power over the natural resources of our region, who can tax them and on what basis, who will transport them, how they will be transported, and who will pay, all remain vital questions with major implications to more than seven million Western and Northern Canadians.

The West's raw materials became the basis for what has been described as a classic example of mercantilism. The primary business of the West is still too much the production of staples which often continue to be exported from the region in a raw or semi-finished state to Central Canada, where products are then finished and exported back to the West. This is partly because capital development was and is controlled primarily by our five major banks, whose head offices are in either Montreal or Toronto. A resource-based economy will always be vulnerable to the capriciousness of external markets. But it is a source of profound concern in the West that these difficulties should be compounded by a host of discriminatory federal policies which sought to maintain the position of the West as a quasi-colonial resource producer rather than asserting its development as a manufacturing and services sector. Northern Ontarians, non-metropolitan Quebecers and Atlantic Canadians have a similar complaint.

Some examples of federal neglect and discrimination against the West were discussed in the chapters on alienation, and illustrate the scope of the problem. Most recent economic growth has occurred in Central Canada. Between late 1984 and the end of 1987, an estimated 902,000 jobs had been created in Canada. Almost 670,000 of these (73%) were in Ontario and Quebec.

National unemployment in March 1988 fell to 7.8%, but the levels in many western cities were higher. Saskatoon had a 12.1% unemployment rate, Edmonton 10.1% and Victoria 12.3%. And in May 1988 when Ontario and Toronto enjoyed 4.9 and 3.2%

unemployment rates respectively, British Columbia's and Victoria's rates remained high at 10.4% and 9.8%.

Tariffs on imported goods initially aided the industrialization of Central Canada and in so doing have provided jobs and profits there. That is all very well, but high tariffs mean that Western Canadians still pay significantly higher prices for manufactured goods without receiving a proportional amount of the jobs and the profits. The Canada West Foundation estimates that in the last twenty years, the net cost to the West of tariffs on U.S. goods alone is over $5.7 billion, whereas Ontario during the same period gained $6.8 billion from tariff protection on U.S. goods. The net loss to Western Canada of our national tariff system was $51 per person, whereas Central Canada gained $31 per person.

With western prices already inflated by discriminatory transportation policies, it seems unfair to many Westerners that after 100 years they should still be subsidizing Central Canada's manufacturing sector.

In Canada,twenty-seven percent of our GNP is directly related to exports, one of the highest rates in the world. One in three Canadian jobs depend, in some degree, upon trade. An estimated 2 to 2.5 million of our fellow citizens depend on exports of goods and services to the U.S. for their livelihoods. This means that there are approximately as many Canadians as there are men, women and children in the four Atlantic provinces combined who would be out of work if the U.S. market closed tomorrow. Even without a free trade deal, the West today sends 65% of its exports to the U.S., and Canada as a whole exports even more. As of 1988, a total of 77% of all products sold outside of Canada will be sold in the U.S.

One recent poll indicates that 49% of all Canadians support free trade. Thirty-four percent are opposed, and 17% are undecided. The agreement is in the interests of most ordinary Canadians in all regions and can benefit a great number of Westerners in such fields as lumber (which employed 87,400 Westerners in 1986), fish products ($90 million worth of these exports were sent south of the border from the West in 1985) and energy (which is currently a $15 billion a year industry with the U.S.). Western Canada also hopes to gain indirectly through the free trade agreement. With American banks being allowed to set up shop in Canada, the grip of our five major banks will, it is hoped, be weakened a little allowing for fresh, new investments and loans throughout the West.

In 1988, Canada expected to top the big seven OECD countries with business investment expected to rise by 17%. (In the U.S. and Japan, by comparison, 10% is expected.) This unprecedented increase in capital spending is partly fuelled by the prospect of Canada's free trade agreement with the U.S.

Canada West Foundation Perspective

A Western Canadian perspective on the FTA is well articulated in a report published by the Canada West Foundation early in 1988, *Evaluating The Fine Print: The Free Trade Agreement and Western Canada*. It concludes that for every 100 working individuals in Western Canada, 83 will notice little or no change if the FTA proceeds because the agreement will have minimal effect on them. Two Westerners out of the hundred are in industries on which assistance programs should focus, and fifteen work in sectors that will benefit from greater security in their present American markets (to which two-thirds of western exports of services and goods are now sold). In fact, the fifteen percent are in industries which produce about one quarter of our gross regional output so the effect of the agreement should be to protect existing jobs and create new ones in our most dynamic industries. Western consumers will be big winners because they "will benefit from reduced prices and greater variety with the elimination of tariffs, which are essentially extra taxes, on North American goods." Every western family is expected by the CWF study to save about $1000 yearly from phased-out tariffs once the FTA is fully implemented.

The report sets out the probable effects of the FTA in Western Canada by sectors. Those positively affected, which currently employ 514,000 people, are divided into three groups: enhanced exports (241,000 persons), moderate benefits (93,000), and greater export security (178,000). Those in which the export position will be enhanced include saw mills, meat packing, livestock, metal fabrication, petroleum and coal, electrical power, machinery, non-metallic minerals and chemicals. The second group includes transportation equipment and business services. The industries which should obtain more security of export access for their products from the agreement include oil, gas, minerals, pulp, newsprint, kraft papers, steel and non-ferrous metals. The sectors negatively affected (employing 59,500 persons) include printing, food processing, poultry products, soft drinks, furniture and tobacco. The rest (2.8 million jobs) will experience little or no effect from the agreement because their products or services are ''non-tradeable'' (most services), exempt from the terms of the FTA (cultural industries), local-market oriented, protected by unique arrangements (telephone services) or because, in some cases, no clear consensus has emerged as to the impact of the FTA.

Agriculture is a sector which the Canada West Foundation sees as being affected only marginally by the agreement. Tariffs on farm products will be reduced to zero by 1998, but Canadian marketing boards will in practice keep imports in supply-managed products to a small share of Canadian consumption. Western livestock producers are seen as big winners because the FTA will both exempt them from the U.S. meat import laws and exclude our beef and pork from the American meat inspections which now cause costly delays. The FTA will remove import restrictions on barley and oats: a two-way trade already close to $90 million, with Canada being a net exporter of feed barley and oats. Significant changes for grains are unlikely because the present import licensing will remain in force even if grain export subsidies by the two nations ever become equal. At present, U.S. wheat is subsidized at an estimated $50 per tonne more than Canadian wheat. The value of the bilateral grain trade, moreover, is today only one-tenth the value of cross-border trade in livestock. On balance, the Canada West Foundation judges that the FTA will maintain the status quo in agriculture: Canadians will export beef, pork and fish products; Americans will export fruits, vegetables and miscellaneous food products.

In regard to Canadian energy exports, the CWF concludes that the FTA assures secure market access of several species, and non-discriminatory access for the U.S. to Canadian energy supplies. Neither country will be able to restrict energy exports or imports except in times of short supply or in the case of national security for defence purposes. Oil, natural gas and electricity producers in Western Canada strongly support the FTA, and the Alberta petro-chemical industry is expected to benefit substantially as well. It is anticipated that the western mining industry will do further smelting and refining in the region with the elimination of all metal and mineral tariffs.

The western forestry sector views the FTA as essential to maintaining present export levels to America, thus increasing the stability of a volatile industry. True, the FTA does not affect the agreement under which a 15 percent export tax was placed on our softwood lumber exports, but overall it will create a better trade environment and diminish the threat of American countervail actions on other forestry products in the future.

Our transportation equipment, communication and computer equipment sectors expect to benefit from tariff-free access to the U.S. Construction, oilfield, woodworking, paper and other spe-cialty machinery made in Western Canada will have enhanced export opportunities. The world-class telecommunications equip-ment industry in Western Canada will benefit from the removal of the present 8.5 percent U.S. duty. In food processing, meat packing, which is still the largest sector in the West, will gain from the elimination of tariff and inspection barriers under the FTA. The removal of existing high U.S. tariffs on processed oilseeds will assist our oilseed mills. Business services, espe-cially consulting, engineering, architectural and computer serv-ices, will grow because business services will obtain indirect em-ployment benefits from better access to and security for primary and manufactured products sold to the U.S.; several business services will thus gain directly from exports of services to the U.S. market.

On the down side, the CWF analysis concedes that about

60,000 jobs, representing 1.8% of the Western Canadian labour force, are in industries which, it is expected, will experience a negative impact from the FTA. British Columbia's Okanagan Valley wine industry is the biggest loser because of the proposed elimination of markups and tariffs which discriminate against California wines; assistance should be provided to British Columbia growers and processors, as Ottawa has promised. Another 10,000 western jobs are in fruit, vegetable, poultry and other processor businesses which will face some negative effects from the FTA. In the short term, all western food processors now sheltered by tariffs will probably encounter greater adverse consequences than other food products. Western makers of doors, windows, and fine papers will be hurt by the phase-out of protective tariffs. Another 1,000 jobs in western commercial printing firms are likely to be affected when larger contracts become more accessible to U.S. competition under the FTA. Finally, an estimated 3,000 to 4,000 jobs in the western furniture-making sector could be lost because the present 15 percent tariff will be phased out over five years.

Provincial Winners

British Columbia's economy should benefit very significantly because B.C. sectors which expect a positive impact account for 18 percent of provincial output (and 185,000 jobs) whereas those expected to lose amount to only 2.4%. The softwood lumber, shakes and shingles, and pulp and paper industries on which British Columbians are especially dependent for the creation and maintenance of jobs will all benefit from the increased export security created by the FTA, says the Canada West Foundation. Increased investment, production and employment will also result for the B.C. industries connected with natural gas, lead, zinc, aluminum, and other metals. The CWF feels that new capital investment in British Columbia from Japan, Hong Kong and other Pacific Rim countries seeking tariff-free access to the U.S. will have ''a major bearing on the magnitude of economic gains for British Columbia under the FTA.''

The positive impact of the FTA on Alberta is expected to be the highest of any western province. More than 165,000 present jobholders, mostly in energy-related industries, are expected to benefit, whereas only about 16,500 can expect worse conditions. Part of this is due to the fact that 75 percent of Alberta's exports go to the U.S., more than those of any other western province.

Saskatchewan will be the least affected western province because sectors benefitting from the FTA account for only 20% of provincial output and those to be adversely affected amount to only one percent. Put another way, only 41% of the province's exports during 1986 went south, the lowest share of all ten Canadian provinces. On the other hand, the U.S. takes about two-thirds of Saskatchewan's non-grain exports and its products which are exported to the U.S., such as uranium and potash, are highly vulnerable to protectionist measures. Overall, the Canada West Foundation report estimates that approximately 85 of every hundred job-holders in the province will be minimally affected by the FTA.

In Manitoba, 48,000 jobs are in sectors expected to benefit from more secure access to the American market compared with 13,800 in industries likely to receive a negative effect. Fifty-five percent of the province's exports during 1986 went to the U.S. The considerable diversification already present in the Manitoba economy will allow an easier adjustment to freer trade than for the other western provinces. Natural-resource-dependent communities in the province should reduce their vulnerability to U.S. protectionist measures as a consequence of the agreement.

In summary, the free trade agreement is expected by the Canada West Foundation to have numerous positive consequences for the entire Western economy. Significant net gains in employment are anticipated for the region as a whole and for all the regions within the four provinces. For the number of communities and sectors negatively affected, adjustment programs should focus on persons in the forms of employment affected. In order to generate more jobs and investment in sectors materially helped by the greater export opportunities afforded by the FTA, encouragement should be provided to seek new export opportunities. The spin-off in new jobs from increased exports to the U.S.

should be felt mainly in the service sector across the West, which now accounts for 78% of our employment and 71% of our regional output.

John W. Dafoe, the legendary editor of *The Winnipeg Free Press*, speaking as a prairie Liberal in 1911, caught very well the essence of freer trade: ''Reciprocity means prosperity to every section of Canada. It means increased population; more trade; larger traffic for our railways; higher values for every foot of land in Canada; enlarged orders for our factories; bigger cities — in short an advance all along the line.''

These sorts of advances will be welcomed in the West, and they are long overdue. More diversified trade is something we all want, especially in Western Canada, given our ties with the Pacific Rim. It is hoped that a bilateral agreement with our neighbour will kick-start all of us to begin looking more aggressively for opportunities everywhere in the world.

Western Canada's past and present disenchantment is based on both economic and philosophical grounds. The classic elements of Western discontent formed the fabric of its political life and were the greatest impediment to the development of its full potential: the concentration of economic and political power in Central Canada, the lack of an effective regional banking system, the disadvantage to western consumers resulting from protective tariffs on imported goods, the lack of a national freight rate policy that permits western goods to compete in eastern markets, inequality in federal procurement and development funds, and the lack of a comprehensive development policy at the federal level which would lead to decentralization and equitable distribution of economic opportunity.

There are no one-shot remedies for the ongoing economic grievances of Western Canada. The status quo, however, is no longer acceptable, and as long as Western Canada remains a thinly populated economic hinterland within both the Canadian and North American market economies, there is little likelihood that our economic woes will completely disappear, or that the economic friction between the West and the national government will ever be altogether eliminated.

What the West needs is the broad, bold vision of a New National Policy that will encompass fresh economic initiatives, some of which I have outlined here. Central to all of them must be a principle of fairness and equality of opportunity for the part of Canada that worked so hard to strengthen central regions at the expense of its own unrealized potential. For too long, the benefits of the 'Old' National Policy flowed to Central Canada, and the costs to the West.

All Westerners should endeavour to see that our potential in human and material resources is developed into the real wealth and prosperity that have eluded us for most of our history. Only a greater degree of political power commensurate with the West's new economic strength will establish our region for the first time as an equal partner in Confederation.

TWELVE

Whither Reform
The West in Canada's Future

*E*ARLIER THIS YEAR, I flew from Ottawa to Edmonton with a senior official from one of the larger federal departments. We had gone to university together, so I showed her a speech I was to give later that day entitled "The West in Confederation." It focussed in part on the dismal record of the federal procurement of services and products in the four western provinces. She came by later to say that while essentially she agreed with me about the injustice, there was nothing to be done about it.

"Why not?" I asked.

On further reflection, she recalled that an earlier minister of her own department had not only insisted that all purchases for the ministry be done on a regionally fair basis, but had actually made it happen.

In short, with enough political will at the top, present habits can be changed. All ministers and crown corporations, if directed by their political masters to begin making regional fairness an important part of their mandates, could achieve as much.

In my view – to paraphrase the late Frank Scott – a rendezvous to force Canada's national institutions to fairly represent all regions will become the most important issue of national unity in the 1990's. If, for example, government members continue the long-established practice on second reading of bills in the House of uttering speeches prepared by unelected officials, public respect for Parliament and possibly for Canadian democracy itself will decline. Changes to end this and a host of other practices inherent in "executive democracy," under which Westerners and others have chafed needlessly for decades, must occur with considerable speed.

The discipline applied by all three parties represented in the House of Commons is similar to that which existed in tiny Britain three centuries ago, when only a small portion of the population was represented in Parliament. One inevitable consequence of this discipline – combined with prevailing notions of cabinet and caucus solidarity – is that MPs from all parts of "Outer Canada" frequently end up defending cabinet or caucus decisions which virtually always favour Ontario and Quebec. In the case of the CF-18 contract, we had the bizarre spectacle of western MPs from all three political parties defending Montreal as the best location for the work.

One means of reducing party discipline in the interest of greater fairness for every province would be to write into our constitution, as the West Germans have done in their Basic Law, that MPs and senators shall "not [be] bound by orders and instructions and shall be subject only to their conscience." Party discipline has certainly diluted this principle in West Germany, but when combined with another feature of their constitution – that no chancellor can be defeated in their equivalent of our House of Commons unless a majority of the members simultaneously agree on a new person to become chancellor — there appears to be a more independent role for members of West Germany's Bundestag than for our Members of Parliament. An amendment to the Standing Orders of the House of Commons might remedy this but, given the major change this would entail for our parliamentary institutions, an amendment to the House of Commons Act would seem preferable.

Reforming the practices of our national political institutions could enhance the political equality of the ten million of us who live outside Ontario and Quebec. The key issue here is the confidence vote in the House of Commons because federal cabinets can still declare, following any lost vote, that they regard it as a confidence measure. Most observers agree that a government which loses a vote on an amendment to its Throne Speech, its budget, or any motion which specifically mentions nonconfidence, has no real choice. In practice, however, a cabinet can still deem any lost vote, on even such a frivolous opposition motion as adjourning the House for a day, to have been a confidence issue. The result is a climate in which government and opposition MPs alike vote with their party leaders like sheep, as they have done for decades. The three party leaders could in effect today cast proxy votes on behalf of all of their Commons members for virtually all matters arising in the House other than private members' bills.

Long overdue reform in this area would allow MPs to vote according to their constituents' interests on all but genuine confidence matters, knowing that a defeat would bring down only the measure and not the government. It would reduce the suffocating nature of present discipline in all parties. Apologists for the Canadian status quo will counter, of course, that tight party discipline is necessary if the fused legislative and executive branches of government in Canada are to function effectively. In fact, the most important reason for this vise-like habit is that it makes life easier for the leaders of opposition and government parties in Canada. If discipline on votes were relaxed all MPs from all political parties, including those from all parties in Western Canada, would have an opportunity to put their constituents' interests first in Commons votes.

Experts attest that Canada now has the most extreme party discipline among the world's 55 or 56 genuine democracies. What a distinction for a country with our size, diversity, and regional pride!

Our unloved Senate will either have to be reformed through the Meech Lake process or abolished altogether. It no longer meets the needs of all the regions in our federal parliament. In any self-respecting industrial democracy, 104 appointees-for-life cannot pretend to fulfil a legislative role jointly with an elected House of

Commons. Senators having no electors represent either them-selves alone, or more often in practice their political parties in Parliament. The argument that an elected Senate with equal representation from each province would give us two elected houses and thus be incompatible with the principle of responsible government is superficially persuasive. On balance, however, I prefer the view that only an elected Senate, with the political clout to dispute when necessary the decisions of a government supported by the House of Commons, can satisfy the original intent of the Fathers of Confederation: a second chamber must counterbalance the weight of the Commons by safeguarding the legitimate interests of Canadians in the less populous provinces.

I support the concept of a Triple-E Senate: an elected body with effective powers and equal representation from each province. If this proves unacceptable to the legislatures of Quebec and On-tario on the grounds that six senators from each province would give to each resident of Prince Edward Island the same weight as 51 Quebecers, or 72 Ontarians, a compromise suggested by the Ottawa philosopher Theodore Garrets seems reasonable. He pro-poses a Senate of 132 elected senators broken down as follows: Western Canada, Yukon and Northwest Territories – 44, Ontario and Quebec – 44, Atlantic Canada – 34, Native peoples – 10. Our western and eastern provinces would thus have more senators than representation proportional to population would provide, and the third "E" would mean "equitable" instead of "equal." Even such a senate would improve Canadian federal democracy significantly.

A NEW NATIONAL POLICY
Over the decades and around the world, Canadian government officials have given stirring speeches about justice in North-South relations, peace-keeping, human rights and a host of other issues. At the same time, the national policies of federal govern-ments in our own country since Sir John A. Macdonald have fostered anything but a regionally just community in Canada itself.

Consider the following illustrations which strike me as unacceptable practices of successive national governments, the bodies from which all Canadians should expect scrupulous regional fairness:

Regional Development

The 1986/87 figures for Ottawa's Industrial and Regional Development Program (IRDP) indicate that our four western provinces received only 77 of 850 projects across the entire country. This amounted to $18.8 million, which was 9.1 percent of the total spent on major programs. On both population and regional unemployment bases, this was outrageous. The figures for 1987/88 evidently show a considerable improvement for the West, but reform is long overdue for all the regions outside the Windsor to Quebec City corridor. The Western Diversification Strategy and Atlantic Development Corporation are steps in the right direction, partly because they are placing more economic decision-making in the hands of people in the two affected regions. Left to themselves, generations of Ottawa policy-makers have all but forgotten that some parts of "Outer Canada" exist.

Federal Procurement

The various federal departments spent approximately $8.1 billion during fiscal year 1986/87 on goods and services. The four western provinces, with about 30 percent of the national population, received only about 11.5 percent of these procurements by total dollar amount. Only about 12 percent of Canada Post Corporation's goods and services, for example, were purchased in Western Canada.

Atlantic Canada, with about 10 percent of the population, received only about 7 percent of all federal dollars spent on goods and services in 1986/87. Ontario and Quebec received fully 76 percent of the dollar totals of these procurements.

This state of affairs, which appears to have persisted for many years, was defended on the basis that Western and Atlantic Canadians just do not produce the right kind of goods and services. According to the best information I can obtain, between 45 and 55 % of federal procurements now consist of services. In

257

the case of Western Canada, a recent Organization for Economic Cooperation and Development (OECD) study indicated that well over 50 percent of us are employed in the service sector (B.C. 66%; Alberta — 54%; Saskatchewan — 59%; Manitoba — 66%). Westerners are thus entitled to a fairer share of federal procurements both in services and in products. Only the political will to make it happen is missing.

Again, the procurement situation has reportedly improved for the West from 11 to 13 percent in 1987/88, but there is much room for additional improvement. If the West received 30 percent of federal procurements of $8 billion instead of even 13 percent, another $1.4 billion annually would be spent in Western Canada. Basic fairness in this area would of course help get a lot of unemployed Western Canadians back to work.

Crown Corporations

As of 1986, there were 53 federal crown corporations thought important enough to be "scheduled." Only 16 of the 53 have their head offices outside the two central provinces. Why, for example, does the federal Farm Credit Corporation, which evidently does most of its business west of Ontario, continue to have an Ottawa head office? Why is a good deal of the Energy Department not located in Alberta? Or the Energy section of the Canadian International Development Agency? Why isn't the Asia-Pacific section of the Canadian International Development Agency located in B.C.? And why isn't part of our federal environmental department located in the environmentally vulnerable provinces of Prince Edward Island and British Columbia?

Telefilm, our so-called national film and television production agency, is located in Montreal. When I telephoned its head office in 1987, I was told that Telefilm had financed 22 films in the previous twelve months, 14 in English, 8 in French. How many of these were done outside Ontario and Quebec? One – in Halifax. It is possible that no-one else applied from outer Canada, but is that likely? The chairman of Telefilm indicated that the current administrative budget for the organization's western office was

$185,214, which was 1.6 percent of its national administration budget. Our larger federal crown corporations which spend an estimated $14 billion yearly on goods and services should show exemplary national fairness. In late 1987, I wrote to the chief executive officers of most of them inquiring what portion of their employees lived in Western Canada and what percentage of their goods and services purchases were made in the region. Some disturbing information came back from those who replied. Twenty-five percent of Air Canada's employees lived in Western Canada, compared to our roughly 30 percent share of the national population. During 1986, Air Canada bought only 12.7 percent of its goods and services in the region. Canadian National conceded that two-thirds of its freight business originated and/or terminated in the West, but only about 37 percent of its employees lived in the region, and that overall it made only 25 to 28 percent of its purchases in the West. It contends that railroading in Western Canada is somehow less labour-intensive than it is in the East. VIA Rail, while admitting that 17 of its 22 Canada tours now featured western and northern destinations, said that only 19 percent of its employees were Westerners. Only 23 percent of Ports Canada employees lived in the West, although 42 percent of its overall operating expenses and 46 percent of its capital expenditures originated in the region.

The Federal Business Development Bank founded to assist business in every part of Canada is clearly not fulfilling its regional mandate. Its 1987 annual report indicates that the prairie provinces received much less of the bank's money than their populations would warrant. Alberta received only 4.9% of $862 million disbursed by the FBDB, Saskatchewan 2.4% and Manitoba 2%, while Quebec received 35.7% and Ontario 23.3% of the money.

The Canada Mortgage and Housing Corporation is doing reasonably well in the West in employment (26 percent of total employees live here), but less impressively in procurement (only 13 percent of its furniture and equipment are purchased in this region). The National Research Council has a dismal record. Seven percent of its employees are living in the West and it made only 16 percent of its entire 1986/87 expenditures here. Defence Construction Canada locates 25 percent of both its employees and expenditures in the West. The Export Development Corporation has only 13 of its approximately 500 employees living in Western Canada, all 13 living in either Vancouver or Calgary.

The Canadian Commercial Corporation, on the other hand, is now making more of an effort to be national in perspective. Western suppliers of goods and services to foreign governments through the CCC amounted to only 8 percent of the total number of Canadian suppliers in 1983/84, but by 1986/87 were up to 19 percent. The dollar amounts of the purchases by region would, of course, be a more meaningful indicator. The agency admits that its recent improvement might be linked to adding a number of western suppliers to its source list since 1983.

Ottawa's Dollars

Fortunately, regional justice is a growing concern of academics who have come to realize that an unemployed British Columbian, Newfoundlander, or northern Ontarian must have more justice from Ottawa than has been the practice over the decades. Western and Atlantic Canadians paid for the old national policy in considerable measure and we believe it is now our turn to be its net beneficiary. More affirmative action is needed for all unfavoured regions.

Robert Mansell of the University of Calgary brings some disturbing statistics to public attention. In the period between 1961 and 1985, the difference between what different provincial residents gained or lost from Ottawa per capita can be expressed as follows:

Territories	+$6903
Alberta	-$1956
British Columbia	-$132
Saskatchewan	+$562
Manitoba	+$839
Ontario	-$126
Quebec	+$562

New Brunswick	+$2107
Nova Scotia	+$2626
Prince Edward Island	+$2780
Newfoundland	+$2054

As a result of all federal taxation and spending during the 1961-85 period, each Alberta resident, adults and children included, contributed $1,956 more to the wellbeing of fellow citizens in other provinces than that resident received. To be sure, prairie Canada was helped a great deal by other Canadian provinces during the Depression. Dollars and cents do not make a great country, nor should they, but we should not ignore them in seeking greater regional equality in the future.

What I, Mansell, and so many others seek is a new national policy which for once will recognize the problems of regions, problems that were peripheral to the old national policy which was so successful in strengthening and diversifying the central economies. As Mansell puts it, ''For over one hundred years, national policies have on balance served to strengthen the centre; it is now time for a fundamental shift to national policies aimed at strengthening the regions.'' I agree completely.

Our private sector, including the print and electronic media, is obviously much more difficult to deal with than government is in a free society, and one can hardly condemn its members when agencies of the national government can get away for so long with blatant regional discrimination. Two executives of a large Canadian company came to my office in early 1988 as part of a campaign to enlist the support of Western MPs for a defence contract on which they were tendering. The presentation included their excellent record in the West, and it was convincing in other respects as well, until I happened to ask how many of their 12,000 or so employees lived in the region. ''Six hundred,'' was the limp reply. If moral suasion, common sense and a sense of fairness will not produce change here, a new criterion for awarding large federal government contracts might be the bidder's record as a corporate citizen from a regional performance standpoint. Companies such as the one cited would then lose points until their regional acts were cleaned up.

A better remedy is obviously more goodwill by individual decision-makers of all national firms. A consequence of changing some public and private mind-sets here would be a better and fairer Canada in which Canadians everywhere felt their opportunities to be approximately equal, regardless of where they happen to have been born or chose to live. A stronger and more stable ''Outer Canada'' would be one which could buy more goods and services from Central Canadians. If Toronto were not the centre of so much of our public, private and voluntary sectors, its stratospheric living costs would cease to be a ''national crisis'' for corporations and institutions transferring employees there.

The western region's overall experience in Confederation to date can be described as buoyancy and confidence encountering continuous disappointment at the hands of outsiders. Full economic and political equality with Ontario and Quebec continues to elude the region even as the twentieth century rapidly disappears.

This book was written in order to provide a basis for an understanding of the West, and to give a clear picture of the causes underlying our regional discontent. The events and issues outlined here will give, I hope, a better focus to the West's perception of itself and of our place in Confederation. History shows that Westerners have attempted within the framework of existing institutions to make our voices heard in Ottawa, yet have failed to achieve political and economic equality with Central Canada. Western alienation is, alas, alive and well.

What is the remedy? Major institutional changes are clearly required, but the major obstacle is probably the ongoing indifference of government and private sector policy-makers in Central Canada. Westerners seek major changes on both the attitudinal and institutional fronts. We believe strongly that our region is vital to Canada. Our experience indicates that democratization of our national institutions is long overdue. We have developed a truly multicultural and confident society. We wish neither to dominate nor to be dominated as a region, and we ask nothing that we don not also seek for our fellow citizens in every part of the country.

How long can a large bloc of Canadians continue to feel alienated, frustrated and impotent? This question is not rhetorical; it demands answers now. The West wants changes and insists on being heard. Its voice is growing stronger; its discontent is becoming more visible and articulate. The time has come to address a long-standing injustice and bring the West into equal partnership with all other regions of the country. Political, economic and cultural equality is the means of ending western alienation.

Western Canadians from Kenora to Nanaimo are seeking only fair play for everyone from our national government and institutions. We want every Canadian to be treated as well as those in the Central Provinces, but we need full recognition of our region's contribution and potential. We expect to be full players. The old national policy created diversified, stable and strong communities in Central Canada; a new national policy must do the same thing for the rest of the country. Western Canadians have achieved much for Canada and we can, if given a fair chance, help make it a place where every young person from sea to sea will believe that opportunities in life are equal regardless of where one happens to be born. Could not this be a goal of Western Canadians generally for the final years of the 20th century?

Western and other reformers across Canada cannot afford to be short of either wind or goodwill. Indifference is the real enemy of those seeking regional justice. To quote Nobel Laureate Eli Wiesel's words in another context, indifference is "the worst disease that can contaminate a society; evil is not the worst; indifference is the worst...indifference is the end.'' Combatting this form of inertia in all of its manifestations is a cause worthy of the best efforts of Western Canadians. It is the purpose of this book.

Bibliography

Chapter One: My West
Angus Reid Poll September 4, 1986 *Edmonton Journal.*
Blake, Donald E. 1984. Western Alienation: A British Columbia Perspective. In *The Making of the Modern West: Western Canada since 1945*, edited by A.W. Rasporich. University of Calgary Press, Calgary.
Canada West Foundation November, 1980 *Report* No. 7.
Canada West Foundation October, 1983 *Report* No. 16.
Canada West Foundation *Opinion Update* Nos. 1,4,7,9,12,16.
Cook, Ramsay 1963. *The Politics of John W. Dafoe of the Free Press* University of Toronto Press, Toronto.
Gibbins, Roger 1980. *Prairie Politics and Society.* Butterworths, Toronto.
Globe-Environics Poll, December 31, 1986. *Globe and Mail.*
Innis, Harold A. 1923. *History of the Canadian Pacific Railway.* McClelland and Stewart, Toronto.
Mansell, Robert and Michael Percy 1988. *Strength in Adversity, A Study of the Alberta Economy.* The Western Centre for Economic Research, University of Alberta and the C.D. Howe Institute, Edmonton.
Morton, W.L. 1950. *The Progressive Party in Canada.* University of Toronto Press, Toronto.
Owram, Doug 1981. *Reluctant Hinterland in Western Separatism.* Edited by Larry Pratt and Garth Stevenson. Hurtig Publishers, Edmonton.

Chapter Two: Frederick Haultain
Beck, Murray J. 1968. *Pendulum of Power.* Prentice Hall of Canada, Scarborough.
Brennan, J.W. 1976. *A Political History of Saskatchewan, 1905-1929* PhD thesis. University of Alberta, Edmonton.
The Canadian Encyclopedia, Volume II. 1st ed. 1985. Hurtig Publishers, Edmonton.
Hall, David 1986. Review of *Frederick Haultain: Frontier Statesman of the Canadian Northwest*, by Grant MacEwan. *Canadian Historical Review*, March.
Lingard, C.C. 1946. *Territorial Government of Canada: The Autonomy Question in the old Northwest Territories.* University of Toronto, Toronto.
MacEwan, Grant 1985. *Frederick Haultain: Frontier Statesman of the Canadian Northwest.* Western Producer Prairie Books, Saskatoon.
MacLaren, Sherrill 1986. *Braehead.* McClelland and Stewart, Toronto.
McConnell, W.H. 1980. *Prairie Justice.* Burroughs and Company, Calgary.
Robson, H.A. 1944. Sir Frederick Haultain. *Canadian Bar Review* Vol. XXII
Stevens, Doris and Claud (editors). *The Haultain Story.* Fort MacLeod Historical Association.
Thomas, Lewis H. 1970. The Political and Private Life of F.W.G. Haultain. *Saskatchewan History* XXIII, No. 2.
Thomas, Lewis H. 1978. *The Struggle for Responsible Government in the North-West Territories 1870-97.* University of Toronto Press, Toronto.

Chapter Three: A History of Anguish
Beck, Murray J. 1968. *Pendulum of Power.* Prentice Hall of Canada, Scarborough.
Darling, Howard 1980. *The Politics of Freight Rates: The Railway Freight Rate Issue in Canada.* McClelland and Stewart, Toronto.
Easterbrook, W.T., and H.G.J. Aitken 1967. *Canadian Economic History.* Macmillan, Toronto.
Egglestone, Sam 1987. Oral presentation to Transport and Communications Committee. *Proceedings of the Standing Senate Committee*, Issue No. 18, July 15.
Fowke, V.C. 1946. *Canadian Agricultural Policy, The History Pattern.* University of Toronto Press, Toronto.
Fowke, V.C. 1952. The National Policy - Old and New. *The Canadian Journal of Economics and Political Science*, vol. XVIII, no. 3, August.
Friesen, Gerald 1984. *The Canadian Prairies: A History.* University of Toronto Press, Toronto.
Hutchison, Ina Elizabeth 1986. The Formation of North Western Ontario. MA thesis, Carleton University, Ottawa.

BIBLIOGRAPHY

MacEwan, Grant 1985. *Frederick Haultain: Frontier Statesman of the Canadian Northwest*, Western Producer Prairie Books, Saskatoon.

McKillop, A.B. (ed.) 1980. *Contexts of Canada's Past*. Macmillan of Canada, Toronto.

Morton, W.L. 1957. *Manitoba: A History*. University of Toronto Press, Toronto.

Owram, Doug 1981. *Reluctant Hinterland in Western Separatism*. Hurtig Publishers, Edmonton.

Whalley, John and Irene Trela 1986. *Federal-Provincial Policy Components within Confederation*. University of Toronto Press in cooperation with the Royal Commission on the Economic Union and Development Prospects for Canada and the Canadian Government Publishing Centre, Supply and Services, Canada.

Chapter Four: Emily Murphy

Cleverdon, Catherine Lyle 1950. *The Woman Suffrage Movement in Canada* University of Toronto Press, Toronto.

Mander, Christine 1985. *Emily Murphy: Rebel*. Simon and Pierre, Toronto.

Sanders, Byrne Hope 1945. *Emily Murphy: Crusader* MacMillan, Toronto.

Chapter Five: The Pattern Continues

Asper, I.H. Submission to the Special Joint Committee on 1987 Constitutional Accord, Manitoba.

Beck, Murray J. op. cit.

Bercuson, David Jay (ed.) 1977. *Canada and the Burden of Unity*. Macmillan of Canada, Toronto.

Byfield, Ted 1987. Address prepared for public meeting of the Western Assembly, May. Vancouver.

Calgary Herald, November 8, 1986.

Canada West Foundation. *Opinion Update*. No. 9, May, 1981.

Canada West Foundation. A Western Perspective on the Meech Lake Accord. The Constitutional Reform Committee submission to the Committee of the Senate and the House of Commons on the 1987 Constitutional Accord, July 30, 1987.

Canadian Association for Adult Education 1987. *Voices of Concern: The Future of Canadian Broadcasting*. Report on a series of 11 public forums on The Future of Canadian Broadcasting, Toronto.

Canadian Broadcasting Corporation 1986/87. *Annual Report*.

Canadian Radio-Television and Telecommunications Commission. March 14, 1977. *Report of the Committee of Inquiry into the National Broadcasting Service*.

Cooper, Barry. June, 1986. Bias on the CBC? *A Study of Network AM Radio*. The original version presented to the annual meeting of the Canadian Communications Association, Winnipeg.

Doran, Charles F. 1984. *Forgotten Partnership, U.S.-Canada Relations Today*. The Johns Hopkins University Press, Baltimore.

Economist August 7, 1982.

Executive August, 1979.

Financial Post November 10, 1986. *CF-18 Press Reaction*.

Forsey, Eugene 1987. Notes on the Meech Lake Accord.

Gibbins, Roger 1983. Constitutional Politics and The West. In *And No One Cheered: Federalism, Democracy and The Constitution Act*. Edited by Keith Banting and Richard Simeon. Methuen Publications, Toronto.

Globe and Mail December 31, 1986, November 6, December 1, 1987.

Graham, Ron 1986. *The One-Eyed Kings: Promises and Illusions in Canadian Politics*. Collins, Toronto.

Laxer, James 1984. Taking Stock. Report to the NDP Federal Caucus on NDP Economic Policy. January 1984.

Maclean's Magazine. February, 1974.

Morton, W.L. The Progressive Party in Canada. op. cit.

Morton, W.L. The Western Progressive Movement, 1919-1921. op. cit.

Sheppard, Robert and Michael Valpy 1982. *The National Deal, The Fight for a Canadian Constitution*. Fleet Books, Toronto.

Special Joint Committee of the Senate and the House of Commons. Report on the 1987 Constitutional Accord. *Minutes of Proceedings and Evidence* No. 17, September 9, 1987.

BIBLIOGRAPHY

Standing Committee on Communications and Culture May 26, 27 and 28, 1987. *Minutes of Proceedings and Evidence*, Nos. 43, 44 and 45. House of Commons, Canada.
Task Force on Broadcasting Policy. September 1986 Report. Minister of Supply and Services Canada.
Toronto Sun, December 2, 1987.
Western Report, November 17, 1986.

Chapter Six: Emily Carr
Carr, Emily 1966. *Growing Pains*. Clarke, Irwin and Co., Toronto.
Carr, Emily 1966. *Hundreds and Thousands*. Clarke, Irwin and Co., Toronto.
Dilworth, Ira 1941. Foreword to *Klee Wyck* by Emily Carr. Oxford University Press, Toronto.
Hembroff-Schleicher, Edythe 1978. *Emily Carr: The Untold Story*. Hancock House, Saanichton, B.C.
Tippett, Maria 1979. *Emily Carr: A Biography*. Oxford University Press, Toronto.

Chapter Seven: Civilizations Collide
Beal, Bob and Rod Macleod 1984 *Prairie Fire: The 1885 North-West Rebellion*. Hurtig, Edmonton.
Bruyère, Louis (Smokey) Letter to the Editor. *The Citizen*, November 24, 1987.
Bruyère, Louis (Smokey) Unpublished notes and comments on Louis Riel made available to the author. January, 1988.
Bruyère, Louis (Smokey) Oral presentation to the Joint Committee of the Senate and the House of Commons on the 1987 Constitutional Accord. *Minutes of Proceedings and Evidence*, No. 12, August 25, 1987.
Cardinal, Harold 1977. *The Rebirth of Canada's Indians*. Hurtig Publishers, Edmonton.
Cumming, Peter 1972. Our Land - Our People: Native Rights North of '60. In *Arctic Alternatives, A National Workshop on People, Resources and the Environment North of '60, at Carleton University, Ottawa, May 24-26, 1972*. Canadian Arctic Resources Committee, Ottawa.
Dacks, Gurston 1981. *A Choice of Futures, Politics in the Canadian North*. Methuen, Toronto.
Dempsey, James 1983. The Indians and World War One. *Alberta History*, Vol. 31, No. 3, Summer.
Department of the Interior. *1876 Annual Report*. Quoted in *Subjugation, Self-Management, and Self-Government of Aboriginal Lands and Resources in Canada* by Richard H. Bartlett. Institute of Intergovernmental Relations, Kingston.
Erasmus, Georges. Interview with the author, September, 1987.
Frideres, James S. 1974. *Canada's Indians, Comtemporary Conflicts*. Prentice-Hall, Scarborough.
Friesen, Gerald. op. cit.
Gaffen, Fred 1985. *Forgotten Soldiers*. Theytus Books, Penticton, B.C.
Globe and Mail, September 21, 1987.
McLean, Don 1987 *Home from the Hill: A History of the Métis in Western Canada*. Gabriel Dumont Institute, Regina.
Morton, W.L. 1964. *The Critical Years: The Union of British North America 1857 - 1873*. Toronto.
New York Times, September 20, 1987.
Penikett, Tony. October 1, 1987. Letter to the author.
Petrone, Penny (ed.) 1983. *First People, First Voices*. University of Toronto Press, Toronto.
Report of the Special Committee 1983. Indian Self-Government in Canada. *House of Commons*, No. 40.
Statistics Canada, 1987. *1986 Census of Canada*.
Waite, P.B. 1971 *Canada 1874 - 1896: Arduous Destiny*. McClelland and Stewart, Toronto.

Chapter Eight: Louis Riel
Beal, Bob and Rod Macleod. op. cit.
Bowsfield, Hartwell (ed.) 1969. *Louis Riel: Rebel of the Western Frontier or Victim of Politics and Prejudice*. Copp Clark, Toronto.
Bruyère, Louis (Smokey). Unpublished notes and comments on Louis Riel made available to the author. January, 1988.
Bumsted, J.M. 1987. Review of *The Collected Writings of Louis Riel/Les Ecrits complets de Louis Riel*, 5 vols., edited by G.F.C. Stanley, in *The Beaver*, August-September.
Flanagan, Thomas 1983. *Riel and the Rebellion: 1885 Reconsidered*. Western Producer Prairie

BIBLIOGRAPHY

Books, Saskatoon.

Howard, Joseph K. 1974. *Strange Empire*. James Lewis and Samuel, Toronto.

Innis, Harold A. 1921 . *History of the Canadian Pacific Railway*. University of Toronto, Toronto.

MacEwan, Grant 1982. *Fifty Mighty Men*. Western Producer Prairie Books, Saskatoon.

McLean, Don. op. cit.

McLean, Don 1985. *1885: Métis Rebellion or Government Conspiracy?* Pemmican Publications Inc., Winnipeg.

Morton, Desmond *The Queen v. Louis Riel*. University of Toronto Press, Toronto.

Morton, W.L. 1967. *Manitoba: A History*. University of Toronto Press, Toronto.

Parkin, George R. 1908. *Sir John A. Macdonald*. Morang & Co. Limited, Toronto.

Scott, D.C. and Pelham Edgar (eds.) 1903-1908. *The Makers of Canada*. 20 volume series.

Stanley, George F.G. 1936. *The Birth of Western Canada*. Longmans Green and Co., Toronto.

Stanley, George F.G. 1973. *Louis Riel: Patriot or Rebel*. Seventh printing. The Canadian Historial Association, Ottawa.

Stanley, George F.G. 1985. *Louis Riel* (Second Edition). McGraw-Hill Ryerson, Toronto.

Thomas, Lewis H. 1977. A Judicial Murder - The Trial of Louis Riel. In *The Settlement of the West* (H. Palmer, ed.). University of Calgary, Comprint Publishing Company, Calgary.

Chapter Nine: An International Community

Abu-Laban, Baha 1980. *An Olive Branch on the Family Tree: The Arabs in Canada*. McClelland and Stewart, Toronto, and the Multiculturalism Directorate, Department of the Secretary of State and the Canadian Government Publishing Centre.

David Bai. 1986. *Equality, Diversity and Community - Problems with the Charter*.

B'nai Brith Canada 1987. *The Review of Anti-Semitism in Canada*.

Broda, Ihor. Presentation to the Special Joint Committee on the 1987 Constitutional Accord of the Ukrainian Committee. August, 1987.

Bumsted, J.M. 1982. *The Scots in Canada*. Canadian Historical Association and The Multiculturalism Program, Booklet No. 1, Government of Canada, Ottawa.

The Canadian Encyclopedia, Volume II, 1st. ed. 1985. Hurtig Publishers, Edmonton.

Cartwright, Donald G. *Official Language Populations in Canada: Patterns and Contacts*. Institution for Research on Public Policy, Occasional Paper No. 16. July, 1980.

Dreisziger, N.F. 1982 The Years of Growth and Change, 1918-1929. In *Struggle and Hope: The Hungarian-Canadian Experience*, N.F. Dreisziger et al. McClelland and Stewart Ltd., Toronto, in association with the Multiculturalism Directorate, Department of the Secretary of State and the Canadian Government Publishing Centre, Toronto.

Friesen, John. op. cit.

Gibbon, John M. 1938 *Canadian Mosaic: The Making of a Northern Nation*. McClelland and Stewart, Toronto.

Gray, James H. 1966 *The Winter Years: The Depression on the Prairies*. MacMillan of Canada, Toronto.

Lopreato, Joseph. *Italian Americans*. Random House, New York.

Norris, John 1971. *Strangers Entertained: A History of the Ethnic Groups of British Columbia*. British Columbia Centennial '71 Committee, Vancouver.

Palmer, Howard and Tamara Palmer (eds.) 1985 *Peoples of Alberta*. Western Producer Prairie Books, Saskatoon.

Prairie Line, July-August, 1988.

Reitz, Jeffrey G. 1980. *The Survival of Ethnic Groups*. McGraw-Hill Ryerson Ltd., Toronto.

Roberts, Stanley C. 1981. Sense and Sensibility in the West. In *Language and Society*, No. 4, Winter.

Rosenberg, Stewart E. 1970. *The Jewish Community in Canada*, Vol. 1. McClelland and Stewart Ltd, Toronto.

Sowell, Thomas 1981. *Ethnic America*. Basic Books Inc., New York.

Sunahara, Ann Gomer 1981. *The Politics of Racism*. James Lorimer and Company, Toronto.

Tan, Jin and Patricia E. Roy 1985. *The Chinese*. Canadian Historical Association and Multiculturalism Program Booklet No. 9, Government of Canada, Ottawa.

Thompson, John H. 1978 *The Harvests of War: The Prairie West 1914-1918*. McClelland and Stewart, Toronto.

Ukrainian World Congress of Free Ukrainians 1988. *Newsletter*, Vol. IX, No. 1. Jan.-Feb.

Vigod, Bernard L. 1984. *The Jews in Canada*. Canadian Historical Association and Multiculturalism Program Booklet No. 7, Government of Canada, Ottawa.

BIBLIOGRAPHY

Chapter Ten: Grant MacEwan
Foran, Max (ed.) 1986. *Grant MacEwan's Journals*. Lone Pine Publishing, Edmonton.
Friesen, Gerald. op. cit.
Macdonald, R.H. (ed.) 1982. *The Best of Grant MacEwan*. Western Producer Prairie Books, Saskatoon.
Macdonald, R.H. 1979 *Grant MacEwan: No Ordinary Man*. Western Producer Prairie Books, Saskatoon.
MacEwan, Grant 1948 *Sodbusters*. Thomas Nelson and Sons, Toronto.

Chapter Eleven: Making a Western Living
Cameron, Norman E.; Dean, James M. and Walter S. Good *Western Transportation in Manufacturing: A Perspective from Two Sectors in Manitoba*, Canadian Public Policy, XI Supplement. July, 1985.
Cook, Ramsay, op. cit.
Duncan, Stuart A. *Evaluating the Fine Print.... The Free Trade Agreement and Western Canada*. Canada West Foundation, Calgary. May, 1988
Economic Council of Canada. 1984. *Western Transition*. Ottawa.
Fry, Earl H. 1986. The Economic Competitiveness of the Western States and Provinces: The International Dimension. In *American Review of Canadian Studies*, Volume XVI, No. 3, Autumn.
Gunton, Thomas and John Richards (eds.) 1987. *Resource Rents and Public Policy in Western Canada*. Institute for Research on Public Policy, Halifax.
Haley, David *The Forest Tenure System as Constraint on Efficient Timber Management: Problems and Solutions*. Canadian Public Policy, op. cit.
Kerr, William A. *The Changing Economics of the Western Livestock Industry*. Canadian Public Policy, op. cit.
Lewis, H.V. *Comments on the Council's View of the Forest Industry*, Canadian Public Policy, op. cit.
North, Douglas 1985. Location Theory and Regional Economic Growth. In *Journal of Political Economy*, 63, June.
Norrie Kenneth H. and Michael B. Percy 1981. Westward Shift and Interregional Adjustment: A Preliminary Assessment. Economic Council of Canada, Discussion Paper No. 201. May.
Owram, Doug 1982. The Economic Development of Western Canada, An Historic Overview. Economic Council of Canada, Discussion Paper No. 219. November.
Postner, Harry and Leslie M. Wesa 1985. *Employment Instability in Western Canada: A Diversification Analysis of the Manufacturing and Other Sectors*. Economic Council of Canada, Ottawa.
Seifried, Neil 1986. The Westward Shift of Manufacturing on the Prairies. *Prairie Forum* Vol. 11, No. 1. Spring.
Velman, Terrence S. and Michele M. *Western Canadian Agriculture: Prospects, Problems and Policy*. Canadian Public Policy, op.cit.

Chapter Twelve: Whither Reform
All figures quoted here come from official government reports or from author's correspondence with the respective agencies.
Mansell, Robert 1987. Unpublished study.

Index

INDEX

270